RETHINKING ECONOMICS

RUDOLF STEINER (1923)

RETHINKING ECONOMICS

Lectures and Seminars on World Economics

Fourteen Lectures Held in Dornach, Switzerland
July 24 – August 6, 1922
TRANSLATED BY A. O. BARFIELD & T. GORDON-JONES

Six Seminars Held in Dornach, Switzerland
July 31 – August 5, 1922
TRANSLATED BY PETER CLEMM

RUDOLF STEINER

SteinerBooks

CW 340/341

SteinerBooks
Anthroposophic Press

610 Main Street
Great Barrington, Massachusetts 01230
www.steinerbooks.org

Lectures are revised from the translation from the German by A. O. Barfield and
T. Gordon-Jones. Seminars are translated from the German by Peter Clemm.

The Collected Works of Rudolf Steiner 340/341

This book comprises volumes 340 and 341 in the Collected Works (CW) of Rudolf
Steiner, published by SteinerBooks, 2013. The original German texts, from shorthand
reports unrevised by the lecturer, are published in German as *National-ökonomischer
Kurs* (GA 340) and *Nationalökonomischer Seminar* (GA 341) by Rudolf Steiner Verlag,
Dornach, Switzerland, 1961 and 1979. The first fourteen lectures were originally
published in English as *World-Economy: The Formation of a Science of World-Economics* by
Rudolf Steiner Press, London 1936/37.

Library of Congress Cataloging-in-Publication Data is available on request.

ISBN: 978-1-62148-049-5
eBook ISBN: 978-1-62148-050-1

CONTENTS

PART I : LECTURES

I.

The Transition from Industrial, National Economies to a World Economy

DORNACH, JULY 24, 1922

Economy as it is spoken of today arose when modern economic life was already quite complicated. In first third of nineteenth century, instinctive trade relationships in England; in second third, consciously formed industrial economics in Germany; in the final third, the era of the state. Contrast between England and Germany in the 19th century. The threefold social order. Method of economy: ponderable and imponderable concepts. Economic theories must contain living ideas. Economic life between nature and capital. Intervention of state boundaries in economic life. The world as a whole economic organism, or social organism.

2.

The Fluid Nature of Economic Processes

DORNACH JULY 25, 1922

The building up of price out of buying and selling cannot be grasped with tightly bounded concepts. The three production factors: nature, labor, and capital. The basic qualities of labor in the economic sense. Nature modified by labor is one aspect of value formation. Labor modified by Spirit (human intelligence or mind) is another aspect of value formation. The constant behind fluctuating values. The polarity of nature and capital.

3.
Economics and Egotism
DORNACH, JULY 26, 1922

Economics is both a theoretical and practical science. Integration of work in the social life. The emancipation of rights and labor. Striving for democracy and the division of labor. Anti-egotistical and cost-lowering function of the division of labor. Example of a tailor. Objective altruism required in the economic division of labor. Question: how does one bring out of the economic process labor as earnings? The wage earner as self-supplier. Price-increasing tendency of labor on nature and price-decreasing tendency through working with capital. Mean price through the intermediary or wholesale agent. The capitalist as merchant.

4.
Labor and Value
DORNACH, JULY 27, 1922

Example of tailor again. Origin of capital through the division of labor. Example of a wagon or cart. Capital 1: stage attained through emancipation from nature; capital 2: stage attained through emancipation from labor. Money-economics and money-capital. Money as realized Spirit. Loan capital as the second stage of the capital process. Division of labor, a relationship of commodities and the value of money. The value of nature is divided by the labor taken hold of by Spirit. Need to think the way into economic processes inwardly.

5.
Production and Consumption
DORNACH, JULY 28, 1922

The economic process as an organic circulatory process. Building up of value and devaluation. Devaluation and value-building tensions through consumption. Personal credit and "real credit": the first makes things cheaper; the latter, more expensive. Damming up or congestion of capital in the land; through this arises artificial value. Necessity to use up capital completely as seed. Associations must regulate the economic process through a proper distribution of workers. Price depends on the number of workers per a specific area.

6.

Price, Cultural Activity, and Gift

DORNACH, JULY 29, 1922

The formula or conception of the correct price. Low rates of interest make commodities less expensive, and land value higher. Spiritual-cultural work is, in relation to the past, unproductive and consuming; in relation to the future, it is productive. Payment, loan, and gift as necessary concepts for a healthy economy. Free and half-free spiritual-cultural life—spiritual-cultural life and economic life. Associations for the regulation of gifting.

pages 67 – 78

7.

Price Formation

DORNACH, JULY 30, 1922

Three motivating factors in economic movement: Purchase or sale, loan, and gift. The three factors of rent: labor, land, and capital. Value arises in the economy only in exchange of products. Loan relationship as a sale-purchase relationship. The price of land is brought about through power relationships, thereby a differential of fall in price from land products to industry. Tendency for rent of land. Tendency of the business person to devalue capital. Social tensions arising through the tendency for prices of farm products to increase and prices of products created by independent human will to decrease. The opposite movement in the economic circulation: of means of production to business capital and, on the other side, to commodities. Associations needed in order to balance out disturbances in the economic process.

pages 79 – 90

8.

Supply and Demand

DORNACH, JULY 31, 1922

Correction of several economic concepts. Supply and demand. Three price equations. In the market, money becomes a rights factor. Impossibilities today: exchange between rights and commodities; between abilities and rights. Surplus value is a moral concept, not an economic one. Real judgments about the economic process not theoretical, but only possible through associations. Money cannot be understood by means of exchange. Exchange or barter economy—money economy—economy based on human faculties.

pages 91 – 103

9.

Trade, Loan, and Industrial Capital

DORNACH, AUGUST 1, 1922

Indirect values in the economic relationships. Shoemaker's products, price of rye, and services of the physician. Internal economy. Threefold productivity of redistributing capital through sale and purchase, loan, and gift—the last being the most productive. Trade capital in England—loan capital in France—industrial capital in Germany, and the human faculties behind them all. The nature of banking; a non-personal money circulation and objectless imperialism.

pages 104 – 116

10.

Associations

DORNACH, AUGUST 2, 1922

Economic profit. In the act of exchange both sides profit. Origin of money from commodities. Push and suction in the economic process. Mutuality in the economic process. Interest: arises through forfeiting mutuality in a loan, which is repaid or made up by lending again. Method: think the economic process in pictures. Self-active reason and objective community spirit in associations stands above personal interests. Objective selflessness instead of subjective morality. Economic life between the rights life and the spiritual-cultural life.

pages 117 – 129

11.

World Economy

DORNACH, AUGUST 3, 1922

The development of the economic life from rural, personal economy to world economy. Hindrance through the state economy. England as the leading economic power. Economic thinking did not progress. World economic thinking. Closed economy is the cardinal problem of world economy. The significance of the length of the life of economic products. Money does not become used up as compared to commodities. The relationship of those who are seeking food to those who offer food. Necessity of gifts in the closed economic domain. The relationship of food production – free gifts – cultural life.

pages 130 – 143

12.
Money
DORNACH, AUGUST 4, 1922

What works behind price formation: the objective in the subjective. Money and its conventional characteristics. Money as a medium of exchange. It arises out of commodities, but is an unreal competitor of commodities. As loan money, it receives its value through the human Spirit. As gift money, it is given for education or as a grant and is protected from being capitalized in the land. Transition of loan money into gift money. Metamorphoses of money in the economic process. Aging and dying of money. Old money as gift money. Balance among purchase money, loan money, and gift money. Rejuvenation and management of money is mediated through an association.

13.
Spiritual-Cultural Needs
DORNACH, AUGUST 5, 1922

The economic value of spiritual-cultural accomplishments. The starting point for all economics: working on the land. Example of the closed village economy. Valuation of spiritual-cultural accomplishment according to the labor it saved. Valuation of manual labor in relation to the spiritual-cultural. The relation of land production to spiritual-cultural production.

14.
World Economy: Living Concepts
DORNACH, AUGUST 6, 1922

Living pictures, not dogmatic concepts, in the examination and analysis of money and price. Money as world bookkeeping. Token value and real value. Money is principally means of exchange. Falsifications through intermediate or wholesale trade with money. Money as indicator. Work applied to nature as the builder of economic value. Amount of money as expression of the sum-total of the usable means of production. Nature currency. Concept of means of production. The final basis of price: the ratio of the number of people to the amount of usable land in a specific area. The empty phrase, convention, and routine hold sway today.

Part II : Seminars

First Seminar

DORNACH, JULY 31, 1922

Thinking about economics is no longer creative, merely observational. The method of economic thinking in accord with reality is the formation of concepts that characterize, not concepts that relate to the law. A method that is neither deductive, inductive, nor derived from theory, but that only describes the facts. Economic inspiration and symptomatic observation. The accordance with reality of "The Social Question." The conditional validity of the ironclad wage law of Lassalle. The recurrent method: leads to causes from the quality of the effects. The revenue creating effect of inflation on the state.

pages 185 – 200

Second Seminar

DORNACH, AUGUST 1, 1922

Economics and physical processes. "Acknowledgment" not a category in economics. Biological thinking in economics: building up, tearing down; creating value, destroying value. Value is a function of work having a natural objective. Work of head and work of hands are not really opposites. The antithesis of work in the physical sense and in the economic sense. Valuation of overtime work.

pages 202 – 213

Third Seminar

DORNACH, AUGUST 2, 1922

The character of politics. What is "real" politics? Example of the tailor illustrates the division of work between producers and dealers. Division of work means to fructify it. The relationship between consumers and producers can be made apparent only through an organization of members. The cost relationship between agriculture and industry. The division of work and its limitations. The necessary number of dealers—what is too many or two few. Threefolding of city constitutions.

pages 214 – 224

Fourth Seminar

Fifth Seminar

Sixth Seminar

FOREWORD

Exactly ninety years ago Rudolf Steiner delivered his course on economics in Dornach, Switzerland. He gave fourteen lectures over a period of two weeks, and used the remaining time for seminar discussions in a question and answer format to deepen certain topics brought up by the participants. Reading Steiner's largely ignored economic lectures in 2012, one becomes aware that most of his concepts are still as fresh and counter to the mainstream as they were in 1922.

As we are entering an age of social, economic, and ecological disruption at this early stage of the twenty-first century, many people are beginning to realize that perhaps the most important root causes for this crisis originate in an economic thinking that is increasingly out of touch with the social, ecological, and spiritual realities of our time.

How, then, can we rethink and redefine the fundamental economic concepts that frame our discussions and shape our key institutions in society today?

This is the big question on the table today.

Rudolf Steiner's lectures on economics may not seem like the most accessible reading. Yet, they offer a largely unused goldmine of fresh economic ideas that could not be more timely and relevant.

Here is a little ten-point guide that outlines some key ideas that he develops throughout these lectures. All ten ideas seem to me to be more pertinent and necessary today than they already were ninety years ago.

1. **Economics today has to be based on a world economy, not a national economy.** While many economists today would agree with this proposition, mainstream economic thought in our public conversation and in business schools is still organized around frameworks and mindsets that gravitate around the wealth

of nations, rather than the well-being of all in our global economy today.

2. **Economic realities today require us to shift our ego-centric frame of thought to an eco-centric mindset.** Think about the current Euro crisis. Think about the Wall Street crisis in 2008. Think about the climate crisis ahead of us. What do they all boil down to? The same thing. That none of them can be solved within an economic framework that revolves around ego-system awareness. They all require an economic thought that revolves around eco-system awareness, or, in the words of Steiner, "altruism."[1]

3. **All economic value creation begins with nature and agriculture.** Today many leading thinkers of the emerging new economy have started to make nature and agriculture a more central variable in economic thought.[2] Steiner's economic thinking starts with nature, that is, work applied to nature, and continues with capital (organization and leadership) applied to work, that is, the division of labor. Organic agricultures—such as biodynamic agriculture, which happens to be one of the seedbeds of the emerging local living economy in the US today[3]—are, in Steiner's view, microcosms of a closed loop economy.

4. **Wages are not the price for labor, but the price for goods or services.** Steiner proposes that work or labor is not a commodity. Hence it cannot have a price. What has a price are the fruits, the results of what we create. In a world in which we have 1.2 billion young people joining the job market during this decade and only 300 million jobs available for them, we face a shortage

---

1. For more detail on ego-system vs. eco-system awareness, see my forthcoming book, co-authored with Katrin Kaufer, *Society 4.0: From Ego-system to Eco-system Economies*, to be published by Berrett-Koehler in Spring/Summer 2013.
2. http://neweconomicsinstitute.org/
3. http://www.livingeconomies.org/

of about almost a billion jobs. Steiner's framing of work as not a commodity, but more as a human right, points to a different way of searching for a solution that focuses on awakening and empowering the deeper entrepreneurial capacities of the human being.

5. **Capital is not money but spirit-in-action.** The essence of capital and money is that they are realized spirit—the realization of deep human creativity applied to economic value creation. This is certainly one of the most interesting propositions that stems from Steiner's economic thinking, which leads to a number of interesting frameworks and suggestions.

6. **The problem of our economy is a lack of balance between three types of money, resulting in capital congestion related speculative bubbles.** Steiner suggests that there are three types of money, which differ in terms of their use: purchase money, lending money, and gift money. Purchase money is used for consumption expenses. Lending money is used for building up new enterprises and usually is more productive than money used just for consumption. The highest long-term productivity, however, comes with gift money, such as expenses for education, parenting, or cultivating the global environmental commons. While we have an oversupply of profit-seeking capital today (about 200 trillion dollars), we have a vast undersupply of gift money, which would be available for social entrepreneurs, schools, and other initiatives that try to cultivate our environmental, social, and cultural commons. Steiner's framework here suggests that the financial meltdowns of our time are the result of not properly balancing the three main domains of money.

7. **Aging of Money as a point of leverage?** Today we know that the decoupling of the financial and the real economies is one of the biggest challenges of our time. Already, in 1922, Steiner suggested a possible structural solution for this: That money should, just like goods, "wear out" a little. Because, if it does not, it will create an unfair advantage for money relative to goods,

which always tend to wear out. Thus, for the financial and the real economies to have an equal playing field, we need money that would "wear out"—that is, that incentivizes the user to use it as gift money before the end of its life cycle. Otherwise money and the real economy would be "unfair" competitors, which is kind of what we have today.

8. **Awareness based self-regulation of the economic process.** Steiner also proposes an evolution in our view of how markets work. He suggests a new way to think about coordination mechanisms by closing the feedback loop of economic actors, their collective action, and their awareness. The leverage point to improve the economic process is that the "process" is being observed at each stage and that the observers can instantly respond to what they see through their individual and collective actions and decision-making. Thus, Steiner's view of evolving the market economy is to build in a higher level of whole systems awareness and self-regulation.

9. **Imagine every human being would get an average amount of agricultural land.** Another idea that sounded totally crazy in 1922 but has now already entered the discussion in 2012 is the concept that every human being would receive a certain amount of agricultural land in order to take care of it. All approaches to climate change and climate security based on human rights build on a very similar type of idea: that we all, all current (and future) human beings, share the same planet. Thus, we all should be given equal rights of use of global commons-based resources. But, as the Happy Planet Index (HPI) of the New Economics Foundation points out, the developed countries use way more of these resources than their fair share, while the opposite is true for the developing countries.[4] As this concept enters more and more into the global conversation, it will be used as a rationale

---

4. http://www.happyplanetindex.org/

for transferring capital and technology from places where there is too much (Global North) to places where there is too little (Global South and/or developing countries). Eventually, all economic thinking must be grounded in our one-planet reality.

10. **We need concepts that are more flexible, fluid, and in synch.** Steiner calls not only for a new economics, a new kind of economy, but for a new kind of economic thinking that coevolves with the changing reality in the field. Economic theory has to be different from the natural sciences that look at reality from outside. Research on the economy means being a participant in the reality that you are trying to describe. This type of participatory action research calls for different methods and concepts that are more flexible, fluid and dynamic, and that can coevolve with the reality that they mirror and are part of.

These are ten golden nuggets out of a much larger number of fresh and new ideas. I have just mentioned a few that stood out to me and that have inspired me in coauthoring my forthcoming book *Society 4.0*. Take your own journey through this wonderful material—let your own interest and questions be the guide.

The Ten Points above are meant only as a first spark to ignite that journey. Enjoy!

OTTO SCHARMER
MIT, Cambridge
August 2012

PREFACE

These lectures by Rudolf Steiner have been guideposts for all of my work. They were critical in the shaping of RSF Social Finance, and were helpful to me both as Managing Partner of TBL Capital and as Chairman of the New Resource Bank in San Francisco. Wrestling with the key ideas contained in these lectures gave me the strength to apply all of my endeavors to making a deep social impact appropriate for our time.

Some thoughts can be visited again and again. Nowhere else are the three fundamental monetary transactions described so accurately. Understood as Steiner describes them, they contain all the transformative forces needed in today's economic environment. The discussions around the forming of capital, the social effects of interest, and the historical development of the monetary system place many of today's problems within a useful perspective.

We are living beings that think, feel and, act—and each of these activities corresponds to the outer conditions of society at large. With these three capacities we can understand the rightful role in society of our culture (our freed thinking), human rights (our democratic process) and economics (providing the goods and services that support us.)

So much of current economic thinking is derived from a mechanistic worldview. These lectures present an alternative view, providing a foundational road map for anyone who is interested in understanding what lies behind every financial transaction, enabling us to become co-creators in developing new methods and approaches to finance.

The lectures help us to understand what is possible when we bring our full humanity into the community-building we need for the future. Many practical initiatives have arisen from people coming together and studying these lectures, and others, by Rudolf Steiner. Today there are, for instance, socially motivated banks, people-centered clinics, therapeutic communities, holistic farms, and independent whole-person centered Waldorf schools (from K-12th grade) and centers for higher education, all deriving their inspiration from the far-reaching ideas of Rudolf Steiner.

Never before has it been so urgent to reconcile our differences, recognize our common future, and collaborate in our diverse actions.

I urge the reader to take time with the thoughts in these lectures, allowing them to grow and develop, and not too quickly come to accepting or rejecting an idea. If you can do this, you too will find inspiration here for your own work.

MARK A. FINSER
Chairman at New Resource Bank
Board Chair at RSF Social Finance

August 2012

INTRODUCTION

CHRISTOPHER BAMFORD

Right action comes from right thinking;
wrong action from wrong thinking...

— Rudolf Steiner

Previously published as *World Economy*, and presented here under the title *Rethinking Economics*, this complex sequence of subtle, dense, multileveled lectures and seminars, given to economics students in the summer of 1922, reflects a lifetime of thinking on the subject and marks the conclusion of Rudolf Steiner's intense five-year period of activism in the service of social, political, and economic issues. During this period, which began as the First World War was ending in 1917, he worked tirelessly to promote the cause of what he called "threefolding" (*Dreigliederung*), by which he meant rethinking the social order on the basis of the clear separation and independence of the three fundamental spheres of activity that make up society. In place of our present centralized, unified, nation-state with its virtually impenetrable complex of competing interests and power bases, he proposed three independent systems: namely, an autonomous rights sphere (limited to judicial and political matters); an autonomous economic sphere (cooperative or associative by nature); and an autonomous, independent spiritual-cultural sphere. The autonomy of these three spheres, he believed, would make possible a spiritually healthy, productive society and open the possibility of a lasting peace.

To describe and explain the background, theory, and practical ramifications of such "threefolding," Steiner promoted the idea in books, pamphlets, and countless articles; he spoke frequently at public events, delivered sixteen courses of lectures, and conducted seminars with both business leaders and workers. The fact that this "threefold" aspect of his life's work occupies more than four thousand pages in his Collected Works gives some idea of the importance Steiner accorded both these ideas and the historical crisis of 1919-1922, which seemed, for a fleeting moment, to make their practical implementation possible.

Simply put: after many years of research and reflection, Steiner had concluded that "threefoldness" was a near-universal prerequisite for the healthy functioning of any organic phenomenon, including modern societies in a global era. In this case, it was clear to him that the healthy *interdependent* functioning of the legal, the cultural, and the economic spheres depended upon each being *independent* of the others. A lifetime of experience had taught him that societies become unhealthy, spawning "evils" of all kinds, when any one sphere—for instance, corporate capitalism, the financial sector, the judiciary, or the state—trespasses upon and comes to dominate the others. With clarity and prescience, he foresaw what would happen if things did not change. And, although he recognized the radical, quasi-utopian nature of what he was proposing, he also understood that the First World War and its aftermath had not only revealed the inherent instability—even bankruptcy—of the existing egotistic paradigms, but had also created a rare opportunity to actually turn the course of civilization toward a new conception of freedom, justice, and human community. In other words, a truly new "third way" existed, different from both Anglo-American capitalism and the Marxist communism/socialism, following the Bolshevik Revolution of 1917, that seemed so promising to many at the time.

Hence, for as long as its realization seemed to him possible, Steiner dedicated himself wholeheartedly to this task. It was an immense labor, and he devoted his entire being to it. He felt nothing was more important. The moment was right. And, indeed, for about a year or so, it seemed that something might be accomplished. A radical Central European alternative to both Western, Anglo-Saxon/American capitalist democracy and Bolshevik-style Marxist socialism seemed possible. But then, however, the situation changed. It became clear that Germany was not ready; the situation was too chaotic, too filled with fear. Ever the pragmatic realist, Steiner therefore began to wind down his activity, to focus on applying the threefold idea in more limited, local situations, simply doing what he could to influence the discussion. For a while, he was able to do so. Not just in Germany, but also in England, "threefold" ideas were taken seriously and widely discussed. His book *Towards Social Renewal* was a best-seller, first in Central Europe, where eighty thousand copies were sold in the first year, and later in England. But the window of opportunity quickly and tragically closed. What might have been possible—a global "threefold" reorganization of society, including the rethinking of economics and the establishment of peace—no longer was so. Other directions were taken; other choices were made. Perhaps people had not been sufficiently awake. Forces with which humanity would have to live—and still lives with—proved too strong.

At this point, in the summer of 1922, when the possibility of realizing the threefold idea was already lost and Steiner had done all he could, a small group of economics students (part of the movement of young people, college students, and academics who had turned to Anthroposophy after the war, seeking cultural, spiritual, and existential renewal) came to him and asked him for a course of lectures on economics. The circumstances are hazy. We do not know who asked him or who attended, except that it was a small group, and that Steiner was, as usual, in the midst of many other projects. This did not deter him; daily, for two weeks, he gave the surprisingly radical lectures that compose this volume. He was still convinced that reimagining economics (that is, transforming how we think about labor, land (nature), and capital—and consequently also monetary policy, production, price, exchange, and so on) provided a key to transforming our understanding of the whole social-earthly organism—that is, the human future. He must have hoped that, if read in the right way, these lectures would function as kind of Rosetta Stone for any future understanding of the principles underlying "threefolding." Having made his last, best statement, he turned to other tasks.

*

Generally speaking, Steiner's social teaching is unfortunately the least studied part of his works, notwithstanding the enormous effort he put into it. This might be changing. A small group of Anthroposophists has always worked with and tried to implement the basic ideas (through the Waldorf schools, the Camphill and biodynamic movements, and other anthroposophical initiatives, which both internally and, to the extent that they can, externally try to move toward "threefolding"). This group is now growing and attracting the interest of young people. At the same time, scholars, academics, and intellectually inclined political and social activists are also beginning to take Steiner more seriously as a social and economic thinker. Moreover, the whole field of and impetus for an alternative economics is growing. Grass roots initiatives—such as the Community Supported Agriculture (CSA) movement and alternative currency movements—are experimenting with new forms of community and association. Non-governmental organizations are growing in number, and the notion of "civil society" is gaining traction. New models are being created within the system (for instance, at the Massachussetts Institute of Technology) that seek to move thinking—and the global economic paradigm—from an "ego-systemic" to a "eco-systemic" model, similar to what Steiner proposed. On the basis of anthropological data on indigenous economies and forms of community, "anarchism" as an economic, social, and cultural form is also receiving new and serious attention. The time is ripe, therefore, for a revisiting of these lectures.

The lectures themselves represent the purest kind of descriptive thinking of economic phenomena from the ground up, from within, according to their own logic. Habitual thinking must be laid aside. To understand them one must therefore think along with and through Steiner's thinking, which is simultaneously practical, grounded in economic experience, and ethical. This is not easy. It requires, as we shall see, a new kind of thinking. At the same time, much that might place the lectures in their deeper, spiritual context remains unstated—bracketed out in favor of pure thinking itself—which further contributes to their difficulty. Some background or context, therefore, is necessary to prepare one for the hard work of thinking with and through these lectures.

*

The immediate, initiating circumstances for Steiner's turn to social action lay not only in the First World War but also, and above all, in its causes and consequences. Although a devastating and brutal experience, affecting the whole of Europe and leaving Germany and the remnants of the Austro-Hungarian Empire on their knees, the war itself was more a symptom of an underlying systemic flaw than the cause of the chaos and confusion confronting Central Europe in the years following it. For those like Steiner with eyes to see, therefore, the war represented a call for deep change and not just "band-aid" half-measures that would reinstate "business-as-before." Indeed, quite apart from the war, Steiner had long foreseen the need for the kind of change he would advocate; and on the basis of his studies in history, the evolution of consciousness, and the nature of what it is to be human, he understood that the changes required were demanded by the spiritual necessities of the time. It was these that, for him, made the tragic crisis precipitated by the war and its deceitful termination through the Treaty of Versailles the occasion of both a personal and a philosophical call to action.

Of what, then, was the war a symptom? Steiner began his lectures by pointing out that "the subject of economics, as we speak of it today, is in reality a very recent creation." Moreover, economics as we understand it—that is, free market capitalism—began in England, Germany's "opponent." Great Britain, after all, was where the Industrial Revolution had begun. In fact, whatever theory one espouses—that capitalism as we know it began with the Industrial Revolution; or in the seventeenth century with the colonization of the New World; or with the Puritan Revolution; or the Protestant-Calvinist work ethic; or with the Royal Society's incipient marriage of science and technology; or in the eighteenth century with the founding of the East India Company; or in fact much earlier with the agrarian revolution of the fourteenth and fifteenth centuries when, following the Black Death, landowners shifted from a feudal economy to one based on wage-earning tenant farmers—Britain is where modern economics as we know it developed.

In other words, with the political economists Adam Smith and David Ricardo on one hand, and utopian social reformer Robert Owen on the other, "the great social questions that arise out of economic questions in modern times were being asked in England as early as the first half of the nineteenth century." This is because large-scale trade and commerce had already arisen, accustoming the population to a faster-moving life than ever before. "Progress" was institutionalized. As for its engine, thanks to imperial expansion through her colonies—first in America, and then in India—Britain's trade capital was already in place. Thus, as Steiner said in these lectures, the transition to "industrial life" took place almost "instinctively. . . like a natural event."

Germany, on the other hand, was still largely agrarian until the middle of the nineteenth century. Although it was spiritually and culturally in the vanguard (witness the great philosophers, poets, scientists, composers, and painters of the "Romantic" era), Germany was socially and politically conservative. It did not begin the transition to an industrial economy until the second third of the nineteenth century. When it did, it did so consciously. At first, the move was experienced as a great liberation. True liberalism, democracy, the freedom of the individual in economic life seemed to be on the horizon. Under the conservative statesman Bismarck and the disciplined, martial core of the kingdom of Prussia, however, this rosy scenario soon gave way to the dominance of the idea of "the state." As Steiner said: "the state was consolidated, and moreover by sheer force or power."

As a result, the state—the Second German Empire or Reich— became extraordinarily powerful, and entered the new global economy (originally made possible by England's imperial possessions) on its own and very different footing. Intense competition arose. Marrying Prussian discipline with the best thinking available (in science, philosophy, music, historiography, and so on), Germany became formidable. Before Bismarck, Germany had acted simply as a supplier of foodstuffs and a recipient of manufactures; but now, because German industrialism was younger, it could adapt and perfect existing technologies to sell things more cheaply. As a result, its wealth and industrial power increased exponentially, and soon, discovering its own "imperial longings," it became a "threat"—developing its fleet and seeking new markets through colonial ventures in Africa, the Pacific, and the Far East. Worried by the competition for its imperial dominance, Britain began sweeping and successful maneuvers against Germany to hem it in. Soon, following the strategic alliance (the Entente Cordiale, 1904) between Britain and France, and another between Britain, France and Russia (the Triple Entente, 1907), Germany's access to the Eurasian "heartland" was closed off.

Economically, as Steiner pointed out, "through all these developments a radical contrast, an antagonism of *principle*, was created, not only in thought but also in the whole conduct of economic life itself between the English and the Central European economy." The contrast (or antagonism) was between an economics that had developed as part of a quasi-natural evolutionary process, and in this way had become pervasive, for better or worse, in the culture and one *that was subject to the idea of the state*—an idea that, though partly conscious, was nevertheless in another sense, as Steiner said, "quite unconscious." At the same time, economic life as a whole was changing. It was becoming much more international, proto-global. That is, it no longer depended on what one experienced locally, in one's own country, but on "great reciprocal relations in the world at large." What was happening was, as Steiner put it, that "the world as a whole was entering the state of a world economy—and could not enter!"

It could not enter, as Steiner saw it, because of the competitive confusion regarding proper activities and responsibilities of the three parts of the social body—that is, the government or state, the economy, and the sphere of scientific, artistic, and cultural creation—and the struggle for power among them. Perhaps the same is still true today.

*

The narrative of Steiner's contribution to these questions usually begins with his *Memoranda*, prepared in May-June 1917. This constituted his first exposition of the "Threefold Commonwealth," which itself followed the conceptual breakthrough that had allowed him (after more than thirty years of research) to articulate the way in which the soul—in its threefold form of thinking, feeling, and will-ing—inhabited the body. But, in a way, it began long before that. In fact, Steiner had been a social thinker almost from the start, although not always explicitly. His concern with social questions was not something he picked up suddenly in 1917. An impoverished childhood, lived in the interstices of the ethnic jigsaw puzzle at the margins of the Hapsburg Empire, coupled with his realistic, practical bent and his profound sense of human life as service to something greater than oneself—in the first place, humanity (as a single being) and human evolution as a whole—meant that the human social realities and responsibilities of whatever he was doing were always inwardly present in his consciousness and guiding it. In other words, though this is not always recognized, whatever the context, ethics was always primary for Steiner.

This was true throughout his life. Ethical realities, consequences, and principles were always present in his thinking and research—and were, at a certain level, paramount—whether he was work-ing outwardly with epistemology, science, culture, spirituality, Theosophy, or Anthroposophy. This was true even when he felt that his auditors were not ready to receive what he had to say from that perspective. Thus certain fundamental principles or convictions that he had come to early in his life, which he believed to be active in the world as human-cosmic realities, and which he continued to develop as his thinking and teaching matured, are clearly present and indeed foundational in his exposition both of "social threefolding" and his economics. In a sense, his thoughts on social threefolding and economics cannot be understood outside the context of these principles.

It might be asked, was Steiner an "economist"? He was not an economist in the modern academic sense of the term: his degree was not in economics. But then neither was Adam Smith's (he was a moral philosopher); Thomas Malthus was an Anglican clergyman and scholar. David Ricardo was a stockbroker and politician; Karl Marx was a philosopher; and John Maynard Keynes was a mathematician and philosopher. In this sense, Steiner's academic qualification was similar — a PhD in philosophy, followed by the writing of philosophical works. Of course, to some extent, his later life as a spiritual researcher, Theosophist, and Anthroposophist makes him different; but no more different perhaps than F.H. Hayek is from Friedrich Engels. Steiner's economics is different, radically different, but he is still engaged with "economics"; in fact, with rethinking economics from the ground up. In this sense, we might think of Steiner as paralleling—at a higher turn of the historical spiral, at a moment when the financial/monetary aspect of economic life was experiencing great stress and crisis—Aristotle's accomplishment in his economic writings at the very beginning of a monetary, market economy. Brief though Aristotle's remarks are (a few pages in *Nichomachean Ethics* and *Politics*), they served as the foundation of economic thinking up into the Middle Ages, where they formed the basis of Thomas Aquinas's thought. Just as Aristotle framed the debate up to the rise of capitalism, Steiner hoped to reframe that debate for a post-capitalist—we might even say post-monetary—global economy. What makes Steiner's economics seem so radical is that just as for Aristotle and Aquinas, so also for Steiner, ethics was inseparable from economics. Indeed, this fusion of ethics and economics is one of the difficulties present-day readers have in understanding Steiner's economics. If economics today has any ethical basis, it is only a vestige of Jeremy Bentham's and John Stuart Mill's nineteenth-century utilitarianism. Steiner's economics, however, has a quite different source, as we shall see. To understand all this, it will perhaps be helpful to view Rudolf Steiner's life from a somewhat different perspective than usual.

*

With the exception of ten years as an adolescent in Neudorfl (near Vienna) and seven in Weimar (at the Goethe Archive), Steiner's life was nomadic. According to his biographer, Christoph Lindenberg: "Homelessness—the core experience of modern humanity—sculpted his destiny." Steiner never owned a home. This lack of attachment to the bourgeois comforts of life undoubtedly gave him his objectivity and radical clarity with regard to social conditions, but there is more to it than that.

Born of Lower Austrian peasant stock in one of the constantly-shifting liminal cultural and linguistic zones of the Hapsburg Empire, the young Steiner was from the start an outsider. As he put it in his *Autobiography:* "a stranger in the village" and "a stranger in my home." A German speaker without a gift for languages (though he could read and translate), he grew up surrounded by speakers of other languages (Hungarian, Croatian, and so on). Meanwhile, his home life was (to us today) unimaginably simple, and poor, without family friends or relatives nearby. In other words, Steiner knew poverty intimately, and for much of his life—essentially his whole life—he had to improvise ways of overcoming it, of making his way and following his chosen path despite it. Nor did he ever forget where he came from. As he said, speaking to workers in 1919:

> I come from proletarian circles myself. I can still remember looking out the window as a child and seeing the first Austrian Social Democrats passing by in their big hats, on their way to their first Austrian assembly in the nearby woods. Most of them were miners. From then on, I was actually able to witness everything that played out in the socialist movement…as it appeared to someone destined to think not only *about* the proletariat but *with* the proletariat, while at the same time preserving an independent view of life and all its various facets. Perhaps it was my testimony when, in 1892, I wrote my *Philosophy of Freedom*, which truly advocated for the social structures I now see as necessary for developing human talents. (CW 330/331; untranslated)

As a child, he was surrounded by nature, and he spent much time in it. At the same time, around the railroad station where he lived he witnessed the signs of growing industrialization (endless freight trains) and technology (the telegraph). His father, a rural stationmaster, was a freethinking liberal skeptic. Around the family table there was much talk of politics and social issues, but not religion. Individuality, however, was valued. The young Rudolf was encouraged to walk his own path, and did so with an innate sense of his own dignity and independence and with scant regard for convention. He refused, for instance, to greet railroad dignitaries who happened to be passing through, just because they were dignitaries. Similarly, in his relentless passion to know, he was extraordinarily self-reliant. Self-taught, he followed his perplexity, wonder, and questioning—as well as his natural gifts and capacities— wherever they led him.

In this way, on his own, he explored geometry and mathematics, physics, history, and the philosophy of Immanuel Kant. Scholarships, hard work, and his native intelligence carried him forward. He taught himself stenography to record lectures that interested him and book-binding so that he could resell his textbooks in order to buy those that really interested him. In a multi-ethnic, pluralistic culture, he lived its problems firsthand. Once, living in Neudorfl and traveling to school in Vienna during the period of "Hungarianization," he got off the train at Sauerbrunnen, newly renamed Savanykut, but refused to hand over his ticket because no sign said "Sauerbrunnen." Such was the young man who arrived in Vienna in July or August 1879 to attend the Technical University, and whose first stop was to visit the used bookstores. His goal: to sell the textbooks he had meticulously rebound, so that with the proceeds he might buy philosophy books in which to immerse himself until college courses began in October.

He was eighteen. Vienna was in the midst of a political storm. Following the Revolution of 1848 and the revolutionary overthrow of Klemens von Metternich's conservatism by those demanding civil liberty and a written constitution, liberalism had slowly taken hold. Beginning in 1861, liberals tried to push Austria toward political modernization. However, after the Austrian defeat by Prussia in 1866 at Königsgrätz in the Seven Weeks War (demonstrating that Austria was no longer a major power) and the collapse of the Austrian stock market in 1873 due to speculation (leading to a twenty-year world-wide recession), the liberals gradually lost support. In fact, just as Steiner arrived in 1879, they were badly defeated. The result was a return to nationalistic, anticapitalist, pan-German conservatism.

Like other young people of the time, Steiner thought that nothing much could come from liberalism, which seemed weak and to have passed its moment. For a while, he sided with the German Nationals, a diffuse, idealistic student and petit-bourgeois movement that no longer felt at home in a monolithic Austrian state. As he wrote:

> The leaders of this movement did not concern themselves with what used to be called the "idea of the Austrian state." They viewed this as abstract and inimical to the reality. An Austrian state that took no interest in the multitude of ethnic cultures of which it was comprised, but merely strove to maintain a sort of creeping progress with a compromise democracy that bowed to all possible inherited prejudices and rights, seemed ... an impossibility. Young German students believed that they could view the future with greater hope, if they were able to emphasize their own ethnicity, to immerse themselves in their national culture, and to nurture a connection to the development of spiritual life in Germany. It was with such ideals that young German students lived in the 80s. (CW 31; untranslated)

Steiner followed these events closely. The issues they raised were of more than intellectual interest. Indeed, as a matter of conscience, they spoke to him of a fundamental ethical and spiritual concern. He became a member of The German Reading Room, a political student association. Soon he was elected its librarian and later, for one semester, chairman, after which his radical independence of thought became evident. "After I had been Chairman for six months, everyone voted against me. By then they had discovered I did not agree as fully with one party as its members wished." He wrote in his *Autobiography:*

> Current political and cultural issues were discussed in both large and smaller gatherings. All the views, possible and impossible, of young people were aired. Much that took place among these young people was stimulating, but also agitating. This was a time when national parties were becoming even more sharply divided. In Austria at that time one could experience the beginning of what eventually led to the breakdown of the empire and all the consequences that appeared after the World War.

Steiner's interest in politics led to his observing political life from the galleries of the Austrian Houses of Parliament. He followed the debates in both the Chamber of Deputies and the Upper House, finding the different personalities, styles, and manifestations of political rhetoric fascinating. On the other hand, the whole situation seemed too confused to be instructive or conducive to inner clarity. As he wrote: "I had no insight into the public affairs of Austria that stirred me inwardly. I merely *observed* the extremely complicated situation."

However, by 1884, at the age of only twenty-three, he had already begun to formulate his priorities. In an article entitled "A Free Glance at the Present," he wrote of the striving of European peoples *"to find a form of government in which the moral dignity and freedom of each individual can come to expression."* The state, he wrote, could not make people free; it could only seek to ensure the possibility that each person could discover freedom individually, and to provide the context in which one could exercise it if one did.

> Government has to ensure that individual happiness is not solely dependent on coincidence or willfulness. Within the rationally constructed whole, it must be able to guarantee the well-being of the individual to such an extent that the individual is able to develop in freedom, both physically and spiritually. Government cannot make people free; only education can achieve this. Government does, however, have to ensure that each individual can find the soil in which his freedom can grow and blossom." (CW/30; untranslated)

As Lindenberg comments:

> This basic idea, which sees individual freedom as playing a central role in any theory of government, is one to which Rudolf Steiner always remained true. The state cannot make people free, but public life should strive to overcome coincidence and willfulness. His later work on the threefold social order would show the ways in which reason can come to practical expression and create the foundation upon which productive freedom can flourish.

Another fragmentary yet prescient passage from the same period deals with the Austrian situation:

For Germans in Austria there are only two possible parties. Either one is in the minority and must unfold the flag of national culture to impress the Slavs and Magyars. Or, one is in the majority with one's hand on the rudder. Then, in true democratic spirit, one must raise the flag of autonomy and self-determination of the various peoples and work toward the sort of future state that is most conducive to culture: the closed trading state, free of both money and stock markets. (CW 38; untranslated)

Again Lindenberg comments:

This passage is extremely interesting not only in that it gives insight into Steiner's political thinking, but, more importantly, because it alludes to ideas about the formation of the social organism. Steiner recognized that the fundamental problem in the social structure lay with the uncontrolled dominance of wealth that was not in the service of production or trade but able willfully to steer the national economy in a one-sided manner. He viewed the speculative interests of the stock market as an obstacle to the sound regulation of economic forces. Such interests focused economic development on increasing profits rather than meeting the needs and rights of human beings.

Later, of course, Steiner would reject the Fichtean idea of a "closed trading state," convinced that economy was now unquestionably global: a world economy. But the idea of the primacy of individual freedom and social justice would remain with him, as would the need to transform monetary policy in such a way as to limit the concentration of wealth. He had witnessed firsthand—and the experience went deep—how the social injustice of the "money and market" years, beginning in 1883, had led to the violent ascendancy of the anti-Semitism that gradually became the dominant political power in Vienna. This again was a warning sign. At the same time, as another side of the "money and market" phenomenon, he knew that 1884 also marked the emergence of conscious imperialism in Germany. Thus, adding to the complexity, he witnessed how *Machtpolitik* [power politics], *realpolitik*, and social Darwinism—the struggle for survival in society and among nations—became the ominous new paradigm.

All this demonstrates that although it was rarely the explicit focus of Steiner's work, he nevertheless had from the beginning a passionate and committed ethical interest in social, political, and economic problems. Always in the world (and in the largest sense dedicated to the service of it), fully incarnated, realistic, and compassionate, he could not separate his chosen spiritual path and the realization of it from its consequences for social renewal as a fundamental aspect of the evolution of human consciousness. Doing so was an ongoing and constant concern. Steiner, in other words, was no ivory tower mystic and philosopher. His own soul path led him to embrace and make his own *all* contemporary manifestations of humanity's spiritual and cultural longings. Thus, at the same time he was forging his own meditative way through Kant, Fichte, and Schelling; participating in various literary and philosophical circles; beginning to explore Goethe's epistemology and worldview; and entering the worlds of esotericism, hermeticism, and Theosophy; he was also beginning his readings of Marx, Engels, and other socioeconomists.

With regard to the latter, for instance, on January 1, 1888, he became editor of *The German Weekly*, a "voice for the national interests of the German people." His tenure lasted six months, during which he wrote eight articles. It is most important that the job forced him to pay close attention to political developments. As he himself confirmed later in various lectures, the insights that he gained from these days of political observation and discussion would later come to practical expression in the concept of the threefold nature of the social organism. Certainly, the thirty-year gestation period (1888–1918) allowed for further thinking and maturation. Equally important, as part of the same learning process, his editorial duties also brought him in touch with many people he might not otherwise have met. In this way, he met Viktor Adler, the then-controversial leader of the social democrats; and Egelbert Pernerstorfer, editor of the

German Word, in which Steiner would publish several articles. It was Pernerstorfer who first introduced him to Marx and Engels—a study that he would deepen immeasurably when he came to teach at the Workers' College in Berlin. Naturally, at this stage Steiner was still a very young man, without the experience to grasp the full complexity of what he was dealing with. Nevertheless, he was learning. He had already learned that, for him, everything had to be approached from the point of view of the individual.

Indeed, whatever the subject at hand, Steiner always approached it from the point of view of the individual. From this perspective, on which he was unwavering, the task of the community of nations was to assure that every individual was able contribute the full measure of his or her capacities to the whole. As he wrote in *Goethe's Theory of Knowledge* (1886) (CW 2):

> What is important is that an individual's position within a people is such that the person can bring the full force of his or her individuality to bear. This is possible only if the political organism is such that each person can find the spot upon which to apply leverage. Whether or not the person finds this spot must not be left to coincidence.

*

Philosophically, this first period of his life culminated in 1894 with *The Philosophy of Freedom*, which Steiner considered his most important work, the one that he thought would remain after all his others had disappeared and which, for him, contained in seminal form the entirety of his work. Difficult to categorize, it is most often described as epistemological; that is, concerned with how we know. This is true. And yet the second half of the book—to which the first part leads—has to do with how we act; that is, with ethics. Obviously so, since as human beings our knowing/thinking must result in acting or doing—"doing the truth," as the Gospels put it—or else remain mere idle fancy. At the same time, and quite consistently, the very heartbeat of the book is a search for the meaning and experience of *freedom*—of whether and when (and how) we have free will—which, in turn, implies the discovery of the free "I" or individuality (self). Complicating matters further, the book is not written so much as a logical exposition of these ideas but as an account of one person's path toward and realization of them. Such a path is never easy. It involves trials and inner struggles, and although intuitive realization may be instantaneous, the fulfilled embodiment of what has been realized may take much longer and involve its own and different trials.

Steiner's inner struggle, of which *The Philosophy of Freedom* is the immediate resolution, was twofold. He sought both to unite spiritual and sensory reality cognitively—to open a cognitive path from the sensory world to the spiritual world—and to demonstrate that in the activity of creating and knowing *meaning*, the true human "I" is *free*. This focus never changed. Indeed, one may say that in all Steiner's thinking—from the most esoteric aspects of his spiritual teachings to his educational, social, and political philosophy—the freedom of the true human "I" was his principal concern.

In fact, the earliest document we have from Steiner's hand is a letter, written to his friend Joseph Köck on January 13, 1881.

It was the night from January tenth to the eleventh. I didn't sleep a wink. I was busy with philosophical problems until about 12:30 a.m., when, finally, I threw myself onto my couch. I had striven the previous year to research whether what Schelling said was true or not: "Within all of us a secret, marvelous capacity dwells whereby we can withdraw from the mutability of time— out of the self clothed in all that comes to us from outside—into our innermost being and there, in the immutable form of the unchanging, behold the eternal in ourselves." I believed then and still believe now that I discovered that inner capacity within myself. I had long had an inkling of it. Now the whole of idealistic philosophy stands before me transformed in its essence. What's a sleepless night compared to that! (CW 38; untranslated)

How did he come to this? In addition to the spiritual search imposed upon him by his intuitive capacities, which made the existence of "spiritual worlds" irrefutable for him, Steiner had studied Kant since he was sixteen. He was widely, deeply, and meditatively versed in German idealism (above all, Fichte, Hegel, and Schelling), as well as in the contemporary, mostly neo-Kantian philosophical literature of his time. As a person of his time, he lived in the wake of Kant's "Copernican revolution," which had reduced the human capacity to know to knowledge of the reasoning mind. This, for Kant, was the sole source of knowledge. "Reality"— the "thing in itself"—was unknowable. One could know only one's own forms of knowing. One could not truly know reality, or the world as it is in itself. Consciousness was therefore not universal: it was not the stuff of reality as Steiner experienced it. On the contrary, it was an impermeable barrier shutting off the world, which, in its own reality, was condemned to remain unknown. The phenomena of nature—"things in themselves"—and all realities that were not those of reason were intrinsically unknowable. At the same time, and by the same token, human freedom was limited, even illusory.

Because he knew from his own experience that the reality was otherwise, Steiner from the beginning sought a different path: a nonreductive, nondualistic epistemology, founded in the universality and unity of consciousness, and the wholeness of spirit and of the human person. Without such a "monistic" epistemology, science in the sense of true knowledge of the world was impossible, or at least remained a merely abstract construct. However, it was not truly abstract, like mathematics, which had its own reality, but rather it was a kind of abstract figment—not really true either to the physical or the spiritual world. The same, he believed, was true of ethics—understood as selfless action for the benefit of the whole.

Fichte's philosophical work gave him a clue about to where to start. The clue would lead to the primacy of the "I"—that is, of freedom— as the source of any truly inclusive epistemology or ethics. While initiating his epistemological revolution, Kant had left open the starting point or foundation. Fichte's contribution was to discover this foundation, "the ground of all experience," in the "I." Through experiential, phenomenological observation, Fichte had discovered that conscious awareness depended on three movements: identity, contradiction, and synthesis. He experienced that the principle of identity ($A = A$) was presupposed in every moment of consciousness. Identity was thus a logical "fact." To become an *"act"* of consciousness, however, something must *posit* it. The "I" must be "posited." In this way, Fichte came to the self-positing "I" ($I = I$). But in doing so, he experienced a contradiction; for, in positing itself, the "I" also posits an "object," an "other," by definition a "Not-I." At the same time, in the act of self-consciousness, he realized that we experience ourselves as identical with ourselves, thereby achieving a synthesis. Such, for Fichte, was the process of knowing. It rests on the fundamental proposition that "the 'I' posits itself purely and simply."

As Steiner wrestled with the many intractable problems presented by this view, he found himself returning again and again to the unitive character of consciousness. The work of the poet, philosopher, and dramatist Schiller came to the resue by focusing attention on the reality that human consciousness, in its relationship with the world, oscillates among different states. For Schiller, the most important state is the in-between state, between the one in which we are surrendered to the senses, and the one in which we withdraw from sensory reality into the world of thought, logic, and reason. He called this intermediate state "aesthetic." Through this state, we experience beauty, which lives through the senses but brings something more to them, in that it unites sense perception with a kind of thinking. In other words, in the experience of beauty we enter a state in which we are united with the world in such a way that allows it to reveal its suprasensory nature.

Focusing his attention on this state, Steiner began to understand that what unites us with the world in the experience of beauty can be experienced in itself. Experiencing the cognitive reality of beauty, he realized that thinking itself is quite different from having thoughts. Penetrating this experience more deeply, he began to sense how a different kind of thinking—living thinking—can provide a kind of entry point into a single reality, which ordinary consciousness bifurcates into the subjective and objective worlds. He realized that there is, in fact, an extrasensory, intuitively attainable reality within the sensory world, and that to be free means living from that reality, which is available in principle to all.

Therefore, when he came to write *The Philosophy of Freedom*, he titled the first, epistemological part "Theory: The Knowledge of Freedom"and the second part "Practice: The Reality of Freedom," by which he meant the embodied practice of freedom in true ethical action—that is, action based not upon any inner or outer "moral authority" but upon intuitively grasped ethical insight into any given situation.

In other words, having established in the first part of his book the epistemological path leading to the experience of freedom and the "I"—that is, the capacity to live without mediation out of pure, living thinking as an autonomous reality—Steiner turned to the embodiment of this capacity in the physical-sensory world. He focused on the creative, intuitive, true I-being's ability to exercise this capacity in the service of the welfare of humanity and human evolution (that is, the future)—the sacrificial principle of service, drawing the "I" (as if from the future) into harmonious concert with the free intuition of the "I" and its love of humanity. At this level of morality, he wrote,

> We consider the needs of a moral life and allow our actions to be determined by them. Such needs are (1) the greatest possible welfare for all humanity, purely for the sake of that welfare; (2) the progress of civilization or the moral evolution of humanity to ever greater perfection; and (3) the realization of individual moral goals that have been grasped purely intuitively.

He added:

> Allowing intuitive content to live itself out fully is the highest driving force of morality. At the same time it is the highest motive of those who realize that, in the end, all other moral principles unite with it. We can call this standpoint *ethical individualism*.

But that is only the beginning. For ethical action—ethical individualism—to become a reality, what is needed in addition is what Steiner called *"moral imagination."* He wrote: "Free spirits need *moral imagination* to realize their ideas and make them effective. Moral imagination is the source of a free spirit's actions. Therefore, only people with moral imagination are really morally productive." Moral imagination is what gives us the capacity to meld intuition with any given sensory reality or situation, to produce a "mental picture" out of which to act freely—that is, without any kind of inner or outer compulsion—which is to say, ethically. As Steiner put it:

> To be free means: to be able—on my own, through moral imagination—to determine the mental pictures (motives) underlying an action. Freedom is impossible if something outside myself (whether a mechanical process or a merely inferred, otherworldly God) determines my mental pictures. Therefore, I am free only when I produce these mental pictures myself, not merely when I carry out motives that another has placed within me. Free beings are those who can will what they themselves hold to be right.

As he stated in his final addendum of 1918: *"Freedom is to be found in the reality of human action... in actions that realize conceptual intuitions."*

For this to occur, however, the individual must first have realized his or her true self, or individuality, which the first part of *The Philosophy of Freedom* had shown to lie in "an inner spiritual activity of the human being that is actually experienced," an experience "equivalent to knowing the freedom of intuitive thinking." This, Steiner held (and had shown), was the self-sustaining action of a self-sustaining being. Such convictions—arrived at by intense inner work—together with observations of the social, economic, and political realities surrounding him, and supplemented by continued reading in the field, shaped his ever-deepening understanding of the evolutionary need for radical change.

*

When it was published, *The Philosophy of Freedom* had little impact. Few reviews appeared, and sales were low, in part due to the personal nature of the work, and in part perhaps to its radical nature. Some interest was shown by the theoretical anarchists around John Henry

Mackay, the publisher and biographer of Max Stirner, the author of *The Ego and its Own* (1845). Steiner later became a friend of Mackay's. His was a friendship Steiner reciprocated; he was the witness at Steiner's first marriage (to Anna Eunike). Writing a letter in 1898 in response to a request to disassociate the "tactics of violence" and "the propaganda of the deed" (being used by "revolutionary communists" posing as anarchists) from true anarchism, he said:

Dear Herr Mackay!

Four years ago, after the appearance of my *Philosophy of Freedom*, you expressed to me your agreement with my direction of ideas. I openly admit that this gave me deeply felt joy. For I have the conviction that we agree, with respect to our views, every bit as far as two natures fully independent of one another can agree. We have the same goals, even though we have worked our way through to our world of thought on quite different paths. You too feel this. A proof of this is the fact that you chose me to address the above letter to. I value being addressed by you as like-minded.

Hitherto I have always avoided using even the term "individualist anarchism" or "theoretical anarchism" for my worldview. For I put very little stock in such designations. If one speaks one's views clearly and positively in one's writings, what is the need of also designating these views with a convenient word? After all, everyone connects quite definite traditional notions with such a word, which reproduces only imprecisely what the particular personality has to say. I utter my thoughts; I characterize my goals. I myself have no need to name my way of thinking with a customary word.

If, however, I were to say, in the sense in which such things can be decided, whether the term "individualist anarchist" is applicable to me, I would have to answer with an unconditional "Yes." And because I lay claim to this designation for myself, I too would like to say, just at this moment, with a few words, exactly what distinguishes "us," the "individualist anarchists," from the devotees of the so-called "propaganda of the deed."

...The "individualist anarchist" wants no person to be hindered by anything in being able to bring to unfolding the abilities and forces that lie in him. Individuals should assert themselves in a fully free battle of competition. The present state has no sense for this battle of competition. It hinders the individual at every step in the unfolding of his abilities. It hates the individual. It says: I can use only a person who behaves thus and thus. Whoever is different, I shall force him to become the way I want. Now the state believes people can get along only if one tells them: you must be like this. And if you are not like that, then you'll just have to—be like that anyway. The individualist anarchist, on the other hand, holds that the best situation would result if one would give people free way. He has the trust that they would find their direction themselves. Naturally he does not believe that the day after tomorrow there would be no more pickpockets if one would abolish the state tomorrow. But he knows that one cannot by authority and force educate people to freeness. He knows this one thing: one clears the way for the most independent people by doing away with all force and authority.

But it is upon force and authority that the present states are founded. The individualist anarchist stands in enmity toward them, because they suppress liberty. He wants nothing but the free, unhindered unfolding of powers. He wants to eliminate force, which oppresses the free unfolding. He knows that at the final moment, when social democracy draws its consequences, the state will have its cannons work. The individualist anarchist knows that the representatives of authority will always reach for measures of force in the end. But he is of the conviction that everything of force suppresses liberty. That is why he battles against the state, which rests upon force—and that is why he battles just as energetically against the "propaganda of the deed," which no less rests upon measures of force. When a state has a person beheaded or locked up—one can call it what one will—on account of his opinion, that appears abominable to the individualist anarchist. It naturally appears no less abominable to him when a [Luigi] Luccheni stabs a woman to death who happens to be the Empress of Austria. It belongs to the very first principles of individualist anarchism to battle against things of that kind.... He battles against force, which suppresses liberty, and he battles against it just the same when the state does violence to an idealist of the idea of freedom, as when a stupid vain youngster treacherously murders the likeable romantic on the imperial throne of Austria.

To our opponents it cannot be said distinctly enough that the "individualist anarchists" energetically battle against the so-called "propaganda of the deed." There is, apart from the measures of force used by states, perhaps nothing as disgusting to these individualist anarchists as figures like [Sante Geronimo] Caserio and Luccheni.... (CW 31; untranslated)

Quite possibly—and indeed, most likely—the reception of *The Philosophy of Freedom* in anarchist circles, even though those circles were very small, frightened away other readers. Anarchist readers, however, did not wholly misread the book. They understood that there was no phenomenal *"arche"* (authority or principle) external to the individual; that the book was anarchist in that sense. What they missed was that the self was not an end in itself: the end was service, selfless dedication to the welfare and evolution of the whole; in other words, that, in some sense, Rudolf Steiner's "anarchism" was closer to Fyodor Dostoevsky's Christ-centered Russian ideal, as this was articulated in *Winter Notes on Summer Impressions* (1863):

To attain the full power of consciousness and development, to be fully aware of one's self—and to give up all of this voluntarily for everyone....

There is something higher than the belly god of the socialists. It is to be the ruler and master even of yourself, of your own self, and to sacrifice this self, to give it up—for everyone... In this idea there is something irresistibly beautiful, sweet, inescapable, and even inexplicable.

Notwithstanding the act of friendship the letter to Mackay represents, the places where Steiner condemned both anarchist and socialist/Social Democrat positions equally, outnumber by far any positive mention. That is, outside the framework of friendship, which was to him an important value, Steiner would never describe himself as "anarchist." In retrospect, in fact, Steiner would refer to *The Philosophy of Freedom* as a "Pauline" theory of knowledge, because it unveiled in contemporary terms the meaning of the great Pauline maxim, "Not I but the Christ in me."

Much work, however, remained to be done before he could fully realize this dimension of *The Philosophy of Freedom*. Nevertheless, for the rest of his life *The Philosophy of Freedom* remained the philosophical, epistemological, ethical, and existential foundation that would orient all his future activities—from spiritual teacher and spiritual researcher to social and political thinker.

*

Before Steiner could fully come into his own—as he would following the turn of the century and his entry into public life as a spiritual teacher and the General Secretary of the German Section of the Theosophical Society—further initiatory experiences or "trials" would continue to shape, test, and transform him. This would be a dialectical process. It would begin with passage through the thought-worlds of Nietzsche and Max Stirner, which would then be called into question, first by a transformation of the understanding of the sensory-physical world. Finally and determinatively it would then be sublated—even "redeemed"—by what we might call his "Christ experience," which occurred at the end of this period of testing (around 1898-1900).

*

Nietzsche was and still is a complex, confusing, and ambiguous thinker. Steiner first read *Beyond Good and Evil* (1886) around 1889. Before that, he claimed in his *Autobiography*, he had not read "a single line" of Nietzsche's work. He rejects any suggestion of Nietzschean influence on *The Philosophy of Freedom*, in which Nietzsche is not mentioned, yet he confesses to "being drawn to his style because of his relationship to life" and to appreciating how Nietzsche "was compelled by disposition and education to live intensely with the cultural and spiritual life round him." At the same time, he recognized that Nietzsche found that life so "repugnant" that it made him ill. His experiences impelled him to seek a different reality, a "true reality"; but he could not realize his desire, and fell to earth a broken man. Despite this, however, Steiner "was fascinated by the free-sailing levity of Nietzsche's ideas." As Steiner described it: "I found that his free-floating caused many ideas to develop in him that were like those I experienced, though attained along a very different path."

Thus we may say that Steiner was both greatly impressed by what he read and also deeply disturbed. Nietzsche simultaneously attracted and repelled him. Nietzsche's style, honesty, and courage captivated him, but his whole way of approaching ideas seemed pathological. Three years after encountering Nietzsche's work (1892), Steiner wrote in a review that following Nietzsche's thinking made him feel "that my brain had broken loose of its moorings." It was, he described, as if Nietzsche wrote with his nerves, becoming, as he did so, "increasingly an electrical nerve apparatus," bumping against things, throwing off sparks, bouncing back, hitting another hard corner, and so on, "until he went crazy." After following Nietzsche's thought, Steiner wrote, readers would need "weeks of healthy Alpine air and lots of cold baths, and not theoretical refutations" to get themselves back into shape.

And yet, the problems in which Nietzsche "totally senselessly" buried himself continued to "devour" him. Then, in 1894, Nietzsche's sister, Elisabeth Förster-Nietzsche, hoping to establish a Nietzsche archive, visited the Goethe Archive in Weimar, where Steiner was working, and invited him to visit her at Naumburg. Hoping for a job (which, in fact, he did not get), Steiner accepted the invitation immediately. While he was there, he heard Nietzsche's *Antichrist* (1895) read aloud and was deeply moved. He also witnessed the now-absent philosopher in his agony. In inner perception, as he noted in his *Autobiography*, he saw:

> Nietzsche's soul hovering above his head. It was infinitely beauti-
> ful in its spiritual light, freely surrendering to the spirit worlds it
> had longed for so much but had been unable to find before illness
> clouded his mind. The soul was fettered to that body, which
> had known the soul only when filled with yearning. Nietzsche's
> soul was still there, but it held the body together only from the
> outside—the body in which it had met such strong resistance in
> developing its spiritual powers.

Thus moved, in 1895 Steiner wrote his short book *Friedrich Nietzsche, Fighter for Freedom*. Perhaps he was still hoping for a job at the Nietzsche Archive, for the editor originally chosen had resigned. We do not know. Seeking to assert an affinity between his own thought and Nietzsche's, he wrote: "I am among those readers of Nietzsche who, once they read a page, know absolutely that they will read every page and listen to every word he has ever spoken…. I understood him as though he had written in place of me, to express me." And he added: "As early as 1886, in my book *Goethe's Theory of Knowledge*, the reader will find that I express the same sort of convic-tions as those expressed by Nietzsche in some of his works."

In other words, Steiner appeared to put himself into Nietzsche's lineage. Perhaps he wished simply to give honor where honor was due; to recognize Nietzsche's struggle with the retarding tendencies of his time and his celebration of the autonomy of the sovereign individual, the "Superman"—some of whose lineaments seemed in certain more superficial respects (though not in any deeper sense) in harmony with his own claims for the self-determination and realization of the "I."

At the same time, he linked Nietzsche to Max Stirner, the author of *The Ego and its Own*, writing:

> One cannot speak of Nietzsche's development without being
> reminded of the freest thinker produced by humanity in recent
> times, namely Max Stirner. It is a sad truth that this thinker,

who fulfills in the most complete sense what Nietzsche requires of the superman, is known and respected by only a few. Already in the eighteen-forties, Stirner expressed Nietzsche's worldview. Of course he did not do so in as saturated, heartful tones as Nietzsche, but nevertheless he did so in crystal clear thoughts, beside which Nietzsche's aphorisms often seem like mere stammering. What path might Nietzsche not have taken, if, instead of [Arthur] Schopenhauer, his teacher had been Max Stirner. (*Friedrich Nietzsche, Fighter for Freedom*)

For a period, then, Steiner interpreted Nietzsche in the light of Stirner's philosophy of Egotism, reading both in the light of his own work, *The Philosophy of Freedom*. Ignoring Nietzsche's nihilism, positivism, and his whole-cloth acceptance of the results of natural science, Steiner focused on their apparent agreement on the sovereignty of the "I," while nevertheless admitting that Nietzsche's view lacked any understanding of "moral imagination," without which the "I" becomes synonymous with egotism. Despite this fundamental difference, as the friend of such well-intentioned figures as the anarchists John Henry Mackay and Benjamin Tucker, Steiner seemed tempted to pursue the "Nietzschean" aspect of "individualism" to a kind of extreme of near solipsism and egotism. We witness this, for instance, in his extraordinary essay "Individualism in Philosophy," written in 1899 for Mackay for inclusion in a Max Stirner commemorative volume. Although Steiner moderated his view toward the end of the essay, referring to his own position in *Truth and Science* and *The Philosophy of Freedom*—that within our individuality "picture-like ideas becomes manifest, revealing the inner nature of things," which, if consciously experienced, may enable a person "to cross into the spiritual world"—his general affirmation of Stirner's and Nietzsche's essential egotism and opposition to the spirit (and Christianity) appears to be unconditional. For example, he wrote:

What is religion? The content of religion springs from the human mind or spirit [*Geist*]. But our mind does not want to accept responsibility for being this source. As humans we submit to our own laws, but then we regard these laws as foreign to us... The essence of religion consists precisely in the fact that it is unconscious of this. It looks upon what it reveals as if it were a revelation from without.

...[Christianity] goes so far as to present the highest being in a single historical person. The philosophical spirit of Greece could not work with such a crude idea... For centuries this childish form of human self-alienation had an inconceivably great influence on the development of philosophical thought. Christian teachings have hung like a fog over the light from which the knowledge of our own being should have gone forth. (*Individualism in Philosophy*)

As Steiner himself later recognized, such statements seem to stand in direct contradiction to his later, more mature position, but they may also be seen as marking the path toward it. Steiner was extremely practical and empirical. He would test his experiences (which are also interpretations) by pushing them to their logical conclusions: he would pass through the fire. He did this with his understanding of the "I"; he submitted it to the most radical Stirnerian-Nietzschean perspective. He did not say so, but one imagines the result shocked and purified him, while at the same time he actively worked through what would give him the ultimate corrective. Later, he spoke of these experiences as indicating profound "trials of the soul," and in his *Autobiography* he described this moment of his life as a descent into the "abyss."

Destiny now turned my experience with Mackay and Stirner in such a way that I had to delve into a world of thought that became a spiritual test for me. My ethical individualism was a pure inner experience of the human being. To make it the basis of a political view could not be further from my intention when I elaborated the concept. But at the time my soul...was dragged down into a kind of abyss. From being a purely human inner experience, it was made external. The esoteric was diverted into the exoteric.

*

Steiner also described this key period of his life (1897-1899), which began with the end of his time in Weimar and extended into the beginning of his time in Berlin, as "standing at the threshold of the spiritual world"—the threshold that would unite the "spiritual" and "sensory-physical" worlds, making possible the realization of their co-participation and intertwining. As he put it, "a new attentiveness for sensory-physical phenomena" awoke within him, giving him "a new precision and thorough penetration" of the sensory-physical, and opening "a door to an entirely new world."

He wrote that he began to experience life as the continuous overcoming and recreating of the relationship between the two worlds. He also began to understand that if life is a mystery, humanity is the stage on which (or the vessel in which) the mystery is resolved. Cognition, knowing, consciousness thus became a process within this dual reality, demonstrating to him the nature and function of meditation in a new way. At the same time, experiencing the human being as "in between," he also—experientially, existentially—became aware of and passed through the two "trials" that face humanity and human consciousness: the one, which he would later call "Luciferic," drew consciousness one-sidedly toward spirit; the other, the "Ahrimanic," sought knowledge only of nature as a "machine," divorced from spirit, its source.

At the same time, with irrevocable consequences, the missing "third"—the center—was also dawning:

> This period, when the contents of my statements about Christianity seem so contradictory to my later claims, was also that during which the true content of Christianity like a bud began to unfold cognitively before my soul in an inner manifestation. Around the turn of the century, this bud continued to open more and more. The soul trial I described previously occurred before the turn of the century. My soul's evolution arrived then at the point that *I stood spiritually before the Mystery of Golgotha in a most inward and most solemn festival of insight.*

Out of this profound experience of Christ, here simply stated and never further elucidated, Steiner unfolded in innumerable ways and from multiple aspects his radical understanding of what he would always call "The Mystery of Golgotha." For our purposes, all we need to realize is that it confirmed what he had already intuited but perhaps not fully grasped in *The Philosophy of Freedom*—that the "I" is realized through the other, in relationship. Speaking in 1907 of "The Purification of the Blood from the Passion of Selfhood through the Mystery of Golgotha," he said, referring to the threat of egotism to human evolution:

> …Human feelings became increasingly egotistic. More and more self-seeking entered into the blood. This blood, which had grown egotistic, had to be overcome. This excess of human egotism in the blood was sacrificed. In a mystical yet real way, it actually flowed from the wounds of Christ Jesus on the Cross. Had this blood not flowed, the self-seeking element of human blood would have become greater and greater in the course of evolution. The Mystery of Golgotha purified blood from self-seeking… (*The Christian Mystery*)

With these experiences, Steiner's life changed.

*

As if all this were not enough, much else was happening in Steiner's life that would contribute to what would become his social philosophy. In 1897 he had moved to Berlin, the third largest city in Europe, with a population approaching two million, and had become the editor of the weekly *Review for Literature*, a position that engaged him actively in social, cultural, and political life. He met the leading lights of the day and wrote many articles as a kind of cultural journalist, focusing mostly on literary topics, but also writing passionately on social issues. For instance, he covered the first Zionist Conference, viewing it from an assimilationist point of view. He also wrote in support of Alfred Dreyfus, the French Jewish artillery officer falsely accused and convicted of treason for betraying military secrets. Presciently recognizing the critical nature of the Dreyfus Case, he penned a lengthy defense of Emil Zola's accusation that the military had framed the officer, who happened to be Jewish. At the same time, in a book review, he provided a profound treatment of the necessary interrelation of freedom and society—the first seeds of what he would come to call the "fundamental social law":

> At the beginning of human culture, humanity strove to form social associations. The interests of these associations then became sacrificed to the interests of the individual; further evolution led to the freeing of the individual from the association and to the free unfolding of his or her needs and powers.
>
> From these historical facts, one can draw the following conclusions. If all social development follows from an individualizing process, what is the only kind of state and social form that can become worth striving for? The answer cannot be too difficult. Those states and societies, which have themselves as their own goal, must strive for control over the individual, irrespective of how this control is exercised, whether in absolutist, constitutionalist, or republican ways. However, if the state no longer considers itself its own goal, but sees itself as a means, it will no longer emphasize its principle of control. It will direct itself so that each single individual achieves the greatest value. Its aim will be powerlessness. It will be a community that does nothing for itself, but everything for single individuals. (CW 331; untranslated)

During this period, the milieu Steiner moved in was bohemian. He enjoyed free-for-all open café discussions on Darwinism, women's suffrage, socialism and anarchy, as well as on experimental literature and drama. Always, however, his own concerns were quite different from those discussed in the places he frequented. As he later wrote to Anna Eunike, his first wife: "I have never been interested in anything but what has to do with the spirit. Even if it appeared otherwise in the years when I first moved to Berlin, it was not so."

It is somewhat paradoxical, therefore, that during this same period (December 1898), although he had recently written of "the social-democratic nonsense of Marx, Engels, and [Karl] Liebknecht," he was approached by the trustees of the Social Democratic Workers' College to teach history. Steiner accepted, with the stipulation that he would do so on his own (not Marxian) terms, to which the trustees agreed. Thus, for the next six years or so (until January 1905), he became a much-loved and very popular teacher, lecturing to the workers (who would come to the classes after a hard day's labor) on a wide range of topics. To do so, he had to develop a new way of speaking. It was an extraordinarily useful training. As he put it later, "The mental outlook of my students was my business. I had to find a completely different way of expressing myself... To make myself understood to some degree, I had to find my way into their form of concepts and judgments."

At the same time, he was also an active member of the Giordano Bruno Society, where exemplarily open-minded individuals met to discuss the leading issues of the day—from Haeckel to Hegel, and from psychology to the theory of inheritance. He was likewise a member of a leading cultural group called *Die Kommenden* ("The Coming Ones"), where he met such influential figures as the poet Else Lasker-Schule, the artist Kathe Kollwitz, and the ethnologist Leo Forbenius. No wonder, then, that Steiner felt that the new century was a summons to a spiritual awakening.

*

Such was the context of Steiner's entry into the Theosophical Society. Nietzsche had died on August 25, 1900. Recognizing the significance of the event, Steiner delivered three eulogies for him. Miss Schwab, a theosophist in the theosophical circle around Countess Brockdorff, heard (or heard of) the talks and suggested that Steiner be invited to speak on the same topic at the Theosophical Library—which he did, and with such success that he was invited to return the following week. As his topic, Steiner proposed Goethe's "Tale of the Green Snake and the Beautiful Lily." Thus, the following week, he spoke for the first time on the fairy tale, as he put it, "from a purely esoteric perspective." It was, as he said, "an important experience for me. I was able to speak with words created directly from the spiritual world." This lecture was then followed by two series of lectures, which subsequently became his first explicitly theosophical (anthroposophic) works: *Mystics after Modernism* (published 1901) and *Christianity as Mystical Fact* (published 1902).

In this way, a new path—indeed, a new life—in the world opened for Steiner, one that at first he engaged in simultaneously with his previous one. Feeling a sense of responsibility, he did not immediately abandon his old commitments. For instance, on January 12, 1902, Steiner appeared on the podium with Rosa Luxemburg at the Workers' Educational College in Spandau. Less than a week later, on January 17, he became a member of the Theosophical Society. In April, still continuing to give courses at the Workers' College, he was asked to become General Secretary of the German Section of the Theosophical Society. Throughout this time, he continued his non-theosophical activities, and even extended them. In fact, he did not give them up completely until 1905. Nor did his interest in social questions abate: in its first year of publication (1903), *Lucifer-Gnosis*, the theosophical journal he founded and edited, contained an essay by him on "Theosophy and Socialism." At the same time, of course, the work of building up the theosophical movement and taking on the enormous responsibilities and burdens of a spiritual teacher obviously occupied increasing amounts of his time. It should be noted, too, that Theosophists, generally speaking, were not interested in social questions. What is most striking is that, despite the lack of interest, in the very year that he stopped his non-theosophical, socially-oriented work, Steiner attempted to bring precisely those concerns explicitly into the Theosophical Society.

From the beginning of his theosophical life, then, we can say that the question of what a healthy social praxis might mean was Steiner's constant preoccupation. Given his audience, however, he would speak of it not so much in terms of economics and politics, but in terms of *community*, and even the primacy of community: that is, of the primacy of love, of service, as the only medicine able to transform the poison of egotism into the healing balm of the true "I" experienced in selfless encounter with another.

We see this aspect of Steiner's social teaching emerging in relation to several themes. First, very early he stressed the importance of Mani and Manicheanism as teaching not only the monistic intertwining of matter and spirit, good and evil, but also the path to their true redemption. Speaking of the basic Manichean myth in *The Temple Legend* in 1904, Steiner said:

> The profound thought is that the kingdom of darkness has to be overcome by the kingdom of light; not by means of punishment, but by gentleness, mildness, meekness; not by resisting evil but by uniting with it. Because a part of the light enters into the darkness, the evil itself is overcome.

In other words, love conquers all. As he put it in his lectures on the Apocalypse: "Good would not be so great a good if it were not to grow through overcoming evil. Love would not be so intense if it had not become love so great as to be able even to overcome wickedness in the face of evil people. Second, from the beginning, especially with regard to the community of the living and the so-called dead, he stressed the meaning of earthly life as the only place in the universe where relationships and love are developed. Third, especially after his separation from the Theosophical Society and the creation of the Anthroposophical Society in 1913, he related the creation of community to the fundamental meaning of Christ's deed and teaching.

While in this way continuously trying to encourage the creation of "community" within the Theosophical Movement, he also realized Theosophy would mean nothing if it did not engage the world. For instance, in a lecture entitled "Brotherhood and the Fight for Survival"(1905), invoking the theosophical principle of "Universal Brotherhood," he contrasted the guiding principle of Theosophy, namely "brotherhood"—"which is founded on an all-embracing love for all people without regard for race, sex, creed, or profession...and is the most noble fruit of deep inner knowing"—to the social Darwinist principle of "the fight for survival." On this basis, economists viewed "the fight of all against all in free enterprise" as the very engine of progress. Individualism, too, they interpreted in this light. True individualism for Steiner, however, was something quite different. Is it really true, he asked, that aggression makes a human being strong? Is it true that aggression and violence have been the motor of evolution?

To show the possibility of another view, Steiner invoked Peter Kropotkin's *Mutual Aid: A Factor of Evolution* (1902), in which Kropotkin drew on the research of the Russian zoologist Karl Kessler, who in the year before he died (1880) had delivered a famous paper on "The Law of Mutual Aid." Kessler argued that cooperation rather than conflict was actually the leading factor in evolution, pointing out that "the more individuals keep together, the more they mutually support each other, the better are the chances of the species surviving, as well as of making further progress in intellectual development." In his lecture, Steiner contrasted mutual aid in this sense with struggle or war, showing through examples like the free cities and guilds of the Middle Ages how "brotherhood/sisterhood" can provide a different paradigm than that embodied in the "struggle for survival." A certain amount of struggle (that is, egotism), he concluded, is perhaps necessary to stir innovation, but it must be tempered with the selflessness and idealism of mutual aid.

Steiner's efforts to develop true community within the Theosophical Society and later the Anthroposophical Society would be ongoing and ultimately frustrating. That this effort was connected with, and indeed inspired by, a concern for society as a whole is shown by the 1905 essay "Theosophy and the Social Question." In this work (which fell on deaf ears), he formulated for the first time what he would later call the "social axiom" or "basic principle of social science and social activity"; namely, the radical notion of separating human work from material compensation. As he put it later, during the period when he was work- ing for the threefolding of society: "It is essential to avoid associating the concept of work in any way ... with the concept of income."

The year 1905, of course, was one of great crises and trials. In Germany, there were major strikes by miners in the Ruhr district. Meanwhile, in Russia, strikers achieved revolutionary status on

"Bloody Sunday," which led to a general strike and the creation in October of the first soviet or "socialist council" in Ivanovo. And, astonishingly, on that very October day (October 21), at the Berlin House of Architects, Rudolf Steiner gave his first talk on the theme of "Theosophy and the Social Question." A second and then a third followed. Finally Steiner wrote them all up in a long essay, published in two parts in *Lucifer-Gnosis* under the title "Spiritual Science and the Social Question"; the first appeared in October 1905, and the second in January 1906. Already in the first talk, he was completely clear in which direction evolution was moving:

> Evolution is moving in the direction of totally uncompensated work. No one rejects the idea, and no one can change it. Whereas Greek workers performed their work in bondage to their master, and modern workers are compelled to work for pay, in the future all work will be performed freely. Work and income will be completely separated. That is the healthy state of social conditions in the future. You can see it already today. (Berlin, October 26, 1905)

"Spiritual Science and the Social Question" (the written text) was a major statement. It was the first complete formulation of what he would call "The Fundamental Social Law." Steiner did not pull these ideas out of thin air. They had emerged slowly and painfully as the fruit of thirty years' experience of observing, thinking about, and participating in the quandaries and painful problems posed by the pressing social, political, and economic issues of his time—and ours. It was his last attempt (until the "threefold" moment, beginning in 1917) to awaken Theosophists/Anthroposophists to the need, indeed, the duty to engage—or at least take an interest in—apparently exoteric social life. He put everything into the effort—all his experiences at the Workers' College, his whole life. Sadly, it failed, as did a slightly later attempt to raise interest in education. That too would have to wait. At that time (and perhaps still), as Steiner himself noted, Theosophists and, later, Anthroposophists, were much more interested in Devachan than in understanding what ground rent meant.

Here, some extracts from this complex text, which speak for themselves, must suffice:

> Right doing is the outcome of right thinking, and wrong doing is the outcome of thinking wrongly—or of not thinking at all....

> All evils that may rightly be called social evils, originate in human deeds. In this respect, not the individual, but humanity as a whole is most certainly the "forger of its own fate".... Undeniable as this is, it is no less true that, taken on a large scale, no considerable section of humankind, no one caste or class, has deliberately, with evil intentions, brought about the suffering of any other section.

> Considering such things, it is well to take particular instances. On the face of it, someone may very likely appear to be an oppressor because he or she is able to keep a smart establishment, travel first class on the railway, and so forth. And the oppressed will be those who are obliged to wear shabby coats and travel third class. But simple plain thinking may lead one to see the following: no one is oppressed or exploited through my wearing one sort of coat or another, but only from the fact of my paying the workman who makes the coat too low a wage in return. The poor workman who buys his cheap coat at a low price is, in this respect, in exactly the same position toward his fellows as the rich man, who has his better coat made for him. Whether I am poor or rich, I am equally an exploiter when I purchase things that are underpaid.

> When this line of reflection is pursued, it becomes evident that "rich" and "exploiter" are two notions that must be kept entirely distinct. Whether one is rich or poor today depends on one's own energies, or the energies of one's ancestors, or on something at any rate quite different. That one is an exploiter of other people's labor-power has nothing whatever to do with these things, or not directly at least. It is very closely connected,

however, with something else: namely, it has to do with the fact that our institutions, or the conditions of our environment, are built up on personal self-interest. One must keep a very clear mind here; otherwise one will have quite a false idea of what is being actually stated. If today I purchase a coat under existing conditions, it seems perfectly natural that I should purchase it as cheaply as possible; that is, I have only myself in view in the transaction. This indicates the point of view from which the whole of our life is carried on.

You may introduce any number of ameliorations for the better protection of one particular class of labor and thereby do much, no doubt, to raise the standard of living among this or that group of human beings. But the nature of the exploitation is not thereby essentially changed or bettered. For it still depends on the fact that one person, from self-interest, obtains for himself the labor-products of another.

Suppose I purchase a factory in order to make as much as possible for myself out of it; then I shall take care to get the necessary labor as cheaply as possible. Everything that is done will be done from the view of my personal self-interest. If, on the other hand, I purchase the factory with the view of making the best possible provision for two hundred human beings, then everything I do will take a different coloring. Practically, in the present-day, there will probably be no such very great difference between the second case and the first, but that is solely because one single selfless person is powerless to accomplish very much inside a whole community built up on self-interest. Matters would stand very differently if non-self-interested labor were the general rule.

Theosophy [Anthroposophy], in fact, shows that all human suffering is purely a consequence of egotism, and that in every human community, at some time or other, suffering, poverty, and want must of necessity arise if this community is founded in any way upon egotism.

There is, then, a fundamental social law that Theosophy [Anthroposophy] teaches us, which is as follows:

In a community of human beings working together, the well-being of the community will be the greater, the less that individuals claim the income from their own accomplishments for themselves, that is, the more they contribute this income to their fellow workers and the more their own needs are met not through their own efforts but through the efforts of others.

Every institution in a community of human beings that is contrary to this law will inevitably engender in some part of it, after a while, suffering and want. It is a fundamental law that holds good for all social life with the same absoluteness and necessity as any law of nature within a particular field of natural causation. It must not be supposed, however, that it is sufficient to acknowledge this law as one for general moral conduct, or to try and interpret it into the sentiment that everyone should work for the good of their fellows. No: this law finds living, fitting expression only in actual reality, when a community of human beings succeeds in creating institutions of such a kind that one can never claim the results of one's own labor for oneself, but that they all, to the last fraction, go wholly to the benefit of the community. And that each one, in turn, must then be supported by the labors of his or her fellows. The important point is, therefore, that working for one's fellow human beings, and the object of obtaining a certain income, must be kept apart, as two separate things.

How is one to translate this law into actual fact? Obviously, what it amounts to is this: *human welfare is the greater, in proportion as egotism is the less.* This means that, for its practical translation into reality, one must have people who can find the way out of their egotism. Practically, however, this is quite impossible if the individual's share of weal and woe is measured according to that person's labor. Whoever labors for himself or herself cannot help but gradually fall a victim to egotism. Only a person who labors solely and entirely for the rest of the community can, little by little, grow to be a worker without egotism.

One thing is needed to begin with. If a man works for another, he must find in this other man the reason for his work; and if a man works for the community, he must perceive and feel the meaning and value of this community, and what it is as a living, organic whole. He can do this only when the community is something other and quite different from a more or less indefinite totality of individuals. It must be informed by an actual spirit in which each single person has a part. It must be such that each single one says, "The communal body is as it should be, and I will that it be thus." The whole communal body must have a spiritual mission, and each individual member of it must have the will to contribute toward the fulfilling of this mission.

("Spiritual Science and the Social Question")

*

It would be ten years, more or less, before Steiner would again turn his energies explicitly to social, economic, and political questions. But this is not to say that in a deeper sense these same questions ever ceased to exercise their influence. In the interim, two areas of research, one more "esoteric" and one more "scientific"—though these distinctions do not really hold—must certainly have helped frame what would become the general theory of the "threefolding" of society, as well as the particular application of threefolding to the economic sphere as manifested in the economics course.

First, "esoterically," there was the continuous deepening of his understanding of the Mystery of Golgotha or the "Christ event." Beginning with his extraordinary series of lectures on the spiritual realities lying behind the canonical Gospels and culminating, initially at least, in his spiritual researches into what he called *The Fifth Gospel*, his understanding became increasingly and explicitly "Christocentric" in a phenomenological and, we might say, "post-religious" way.

What this meant in practice was the painful realization that the deed and teachings of Christ were endangered if human beings did not find concrete inspiration to walk the path of selflessness and sacrifice in the world as he had laid down by his example. *Selflessness*, as Steiner saw it, was an evolutionary necessity. In his words:

> We need a school of selflessness. Only a schooling in selflessness can bring about a renewal of morality, a deepening of human moral life; and, in accord with the conditions of our present cycle of time, we can attain such a schooling in selflessness only if we make the understanding of real selflessness our own.

In other words, to deepen moral life, on which everything else depends, we are called to take real selflessness—that is, a life lived for the sake of others and without the exercise of power—as epitomized in the deed of Golgotha, into all spheres of life. This what the entire cosmos called out for:

> Amen.
> The evils reign,
> Witness of egoity, separating itself,
> Guilt of selfhood incurred through others,
> Experienced in the daily bread
> In which the will of heaven does not reign,
> Because humanity separated from your kingdom
> And forgot your names,
> You Fathers in the Heavens.

These somber, painful words, heard by Steiner as he meditated on Jesus' life (and heard Jesus hearing them) affirm that we are all responsible, all guilty, each for everyone and everyone for the whole. These words are known either as the "macrocosmic world prayer" —because it presents the objective situation as viewed by the gods—or the "cosmic Our Father"—because its reverse structure clearly shows that it is the call, the need, to which the Lord's Prayer is the answer or response. As Steiner confessed, these words moved him to the quick. As for their continuing relevance, he knew too that one needed only to look around to see that nothing had changed: the spiritual world is still forgotten; evils still reign; and egotism and the ego's illusion of separateness and autonomy still rule and are continually reinforced in materialized, objectified power relationships. Thus, the essential thing became the overcoming of egotism, which elsewhere he spoke of as the sole source of evil in the world, and as what could destroy us.

He also understood that egotism is secondary, in a sense, to the reality of suffering. We must look suffering in the eye. As Steiner said:

> The details of the story are less important: what matters is that we get a real feeling for what the Jesus soul went through…how he took up the suffering and pain of humanity…You need to gain an idea of the sufferings undergone by Jesus and let your heart be deeply moved. He had to go through this pain and suffering before he came to the Mystery of Golgotha, so that the Christ impulse might enter Earth evolution.
>
> (CW 148, *The Fifth Gospel*)

And, Steiner added: "The Christ impulse comes alive in our minds when we bring those sufferings to life in ourselves." He put it this way in a meditation that he gave to nurses in the First World War:

> As long as you feel pain
> that I do not feel,
> Christ remains unrecognized
> in cosmic being;
> for weak is the spirit
> that can feel suffering
> only in its own body.
>
> (*Das Geheimnis der Wunde [The Secret of the Wound]*)

In other words:

The more strongly we practice and develop this fully conscious devotion to the other being, the greater our selflessness becomes, and the greater our love for that being must be. In this way we feel the ability becoming ever stronger to live in another being, instead of in ourselves; that is, to step out of our own being into that of another. We achieve intuition, which means that we no longer experience only ourselves. Instead we learn to experience the other in complete selflessness while fully maintaining our individualization. (CW 84; untranslated)

The path of return, then, which overcomes egotism and transforms it into love, is a path of active suffering, of entering into the belly of the beast. In the words of Etty Hillesum: "We should be willing to act as a balm for all wounds." Or, as the first rule of the Rosicrucian Order puts it: we should have "no profession but to heal, and that gratis." Here, then, is a new ethic, or the primordial ethic in a new form; a new way of thinking about the primacy of human relationships, including economic relationships—selflessness in our ethics, in our understanding of the world, in our soul's activity.

*

From a more scientific perspective, in March 1917, just before Steiner was to embark on the "threefold project" after more than thirty years of research into the subject, he gave two lectures in Berlin on "The Human Soul and the Human Body." In these he first described the way in which the soul—in its threefold activity of thinking, feeling, and willing—penetrates and works in the body in a threefold way through the nervous (nerve-sense) system, the circulatory/respiratory/heart system, and the metabolic/limb system. Here, without going into details, we might note the correspondence between economics (the flow of money) and the circulatory/respiratory/heart system, which suggests the primacy of economics in any understanding of the social organism. The heart, after all, is what makes us human; it is the first functioning organ to appear in the development of the embryo. For Steiner, rather than being a kind of "pump," this organ is actually a manifestation of the rhythmic, warm flow of the blood; and in the lectures, he likens the flow of money to the circulation of the blood. As an essentially rhythmic system (and "rhythm" being relationship, in a sense), the heart-blood-breathing system selflessly maintains the balance between the nerve-sense system and the dynamic metabolic-limb system. Here again the analogies (and they are only analogies) with economics, as Steiner reimagines it, are striking and worth exploring. This is especially so when one bears in mind his emphasis, during the last years of his life—that is, the period of the economics lectures—on the reality that the Christ is to be experienced above all in community, face to face, "when two or more are gathered together in my name." Thus, too, we are reminded that the word *economy* was appropriated and transformed during the early Christian centuries to refer to the dual "economy" of the Trinity and the Incarnation.

*

Returning to history: by 1917 the First World War, "a terrible catastrophe that partially exposes the social riddle in its original form," was coming to an end. For Steiner, the war made it evident that what he had feared had indeed happened. In the period leading up to 1914 economic activity had expanded "not only beyond our political-legal system but also [beyond] our cultural activity," with the result that economics had "swamped everything…with hypnotic effects on human thoughts, perceptions, and passions." The war was the result. Economic activity (ambition, imperialism, egotism) had brought Europe to the brink of disaster. Any hope of an improved human future, and any possibility of anything resembling lasting *peace*, depended upon rethinking the nature of the social contract— "threefolding" it—in such a way that the political-legal, economic, and cultural spheres could be autonomous, free, and independent in relation to one another.

Such, then, was the context in which, in late May or June 1917, Steiner was asked to draft ideals for a new social order for Germany— one that could also perhaps lay the ground for possible future peace negotiations. Initial negotiations had failed in December and January 1916–1917, after which Germany began unrestricted U-boat attacks on French and British vessels, resulting in the United States' terminating peace negotiations. Two months later, the United States entered the war. In making this decision, the U.S. president Woodrow Wilson did so as a "moral judge," turning what had been a war into a matter of ideologies. As he saw it, the United States was entering the conflict to protect the forces of democracy throughout the world. He was standing up for the liberation of the oppressed—sentiments that would later be fleshed out in his Fourteen Points. Meanwhile on March 8, worker unrest in Saint Petersburg climaxed in outright revolt, bringing Valdimir Lenin home to Russia by November to lead the Bolshevik Revolution. By summer, it was clear the U-boat attacks had failed in their mission, leading to chaos and confusion in Berlin, where Steiner then was.

Among the Berlin Anthroposophists, Otto Graf von Lerchenfeld, a member since 1907, was a well-connected member of the Bavarian court, and the Bavarian ambassador and delegate to the German Parliament. Unable to stand the confusion, von Lerchenfeld turned to Steiner in desperation. After listening to his description of the situation, Steiner asked him to return the following afternoon. When he did so, Steiner unfolded the idea of "threefolding" and detailed some of the specifics. After their meeting, Lerchenfeld noted in his diary (as cited by Lindenberg):

Spent three hours today at Dr. Steiner's. The solution to everything now stands before me. I know that no one else can provide it. He called it the threefolding of the social body. Its effect on me was like the egg that allowed Columbus to imagine the world as round.

Steiner's first point was the need to counter Woodrow Wilson's "propaganda," which created the impression that the West stood for the health of humanity, while Central Europe stood for militarism. What was needed was a "Central European program." This, he wrote in the first "Memorandum on the Threefold Social Order," would be a "program of human liberation." The focus would be on individual freedom, because only individuals could be free, not peoples or nations. For this reason, bearing in mind the multiple ethnicities within the Central European sphere, he proposed placing "all matters of jurisprudence, education, and spiritual life" in the realm of "individual freedom"—in other words, "the complete freedom that comes to expression in federal autonomy for ethnic groups." "National feelings," he wrote "arise out of freedom, not freedom out of nationalism." "A purely democratic parliament would address only matters that are truly political. Economic decisions likewise would be uncoupled from politics and placed in the hands of an "economic parliament," and a "form of senate would be elected out of the three bodies."

Here it should be noted that, regarding the position of the Kaiser and the adoption of Western style democracy, Steiner was ambiguous, both as a matter of temperament and with an eye to appealing to more conservative elements. As he put it in the "Memorandum":

German and Austrian undertakings would not become more intelligent simply because they were decided by a gathering of some 500 delegates instead of a couple of statesmen. One cannot imagine anything more discouraging than the superstitious belief that the adoption of their democratic model, in addition to everything else we have acquired from England, will have a magical effect.

Indeed, as Christoph Lindenberg puts it:

Steiner, who never cast his vote in an election and who fervently supported human rights and the well-being of the workers, was not a believer in democracy in the modern sense of the word. Being able to vote had no meaning for him; he was concerned with individual freedom—he looked upon any form of ruling power skeptically.

After several meetings, a first Memorandum was prepared, which fell upon deaf ears. Following some further developments, a second

Memorandum, much less restrained in tone, was drafted and circulated. At the beginning of January 1918, Steiner discussed it with
Prince Maximilian von Baden, who was convinced of the feasibil-
ity and appropriateness of the idea of threefolding. As Steiner had
anticipated, von Baden was appointed chancellor in October 1918
and asked to negotiate an armistice, which he intended to do on
the basis of the Memorandum. Before he could do so, however, the
leading German General, Erich Ludendorff, assessing the German
situation in the field, insisted that an armistice had to be negotiated
within twenty-four hours. Although later Ludendorff would admit
that he had been mistaken about the situation, this left von Baden
with no time to develop an alternative based on the threefold idea. He
was forced to negotiate on the basis of Woodrow Wilson's Fourteen
Points. Thus, tragically, on June 28, 1919, at the treaty of Versailles,
the die was cast; we still live with the consequences.

The moment, however, was still opportune. A "top down
approach" having failed, Steiner took his message to the people, as
well as Anthroposophists, to awaken them to the overall situation.
Then, somehow—it is unknown how—the Memorandum found its
way to a certain Major Fessman, and through him into the hands of
Emil Molt, a Stuttgart Anthroposophist and self-made businessman.
The Memorandum, as Molt put it, "became his destiny." Joining with
friends, he began to take initiatives to form an industrialists' coalition
to create jobs for returning soldiers. He also envisioned creating a
school for the children of his factory workers. This would become the
first Waldorf school. At the same time, filled with questions about the
details of the threefold social order, Molt and his friends approached
Steiner. Many long conversations ensued on topics such as banks,
money, currencies, taxation, socialization, factory management,
payments to entrepreneurs, ownership, and credit—not precisely
themes Steiner was yet thinking about explicitly. What seemed most
pressing to him at that moment was "to work toward a threefold
structure." In response to this need, he began to write, first his broad-
side, *A Call to the German People,* and subsequently his fundamental
book on the "Threefold Commonwealth," *Towards Social Renewal.*
The *Call* was successful, garnering many signatures. Soon the

Association for a Threefold Social Order was formed. Social initiatives proliferated; in 1919 the first Waldorf school came into being. Then, in 1920, two public corporations, operating along threefold lines, were created to promote economic and spiritual undertakings: *Der Kommende Tag* ("The Coming Day") in Germany and *Futurum AG* in Switzerland. Manifold books and lectures were published on threefold themes, and Steiner traveled indefatigably, giving public lectures to large numbers of people, as well as holding seminars and workshops with workers and business leaders.

At the same time, as the possibility of any large-scale success in the attempt to "threefold" society was waning fast, if it was not already gone, many other tasks were calling Steiner. Among them was the institution of anthroposophical college courses; and generally the need to address the influx into Anthroposophy of young, educated people; while at the same time trying to bring the older members, with their fixed expectations, into the brave new postwar world. In a sense, Anthroposophy was being reborn (or becoming what Rudolf Steiner always had intended). It was changing from an esoteric society (occultist-theosophical-mystical in its origins) largely turned inward, to a still esoteric but more outward-oriented society, a "new Mystery Center"—in other words, an esoteric spiritual society practicing spiritual scientific research with a civilizational mission.

*

The year of the economics lectures (1922) was not a good year. The question of how Germany could meet its reparation obligations stipulated by the Treaty of Versailles dominated the country. Gaining control of the budget required extreme austerity measures and radically increased taxation, which accelerated the already rapid depreciation of the currency. At the same time, international loans had to be continuously negotiated and renegotiated. Then, on June 24, Walther Rathenau, the minister for foreign affairs, was assassinated by anti-Semitic nationalists, leading to a further economic downturn. Despite all this, the postponement of reparations payments and a proposed reduction in monthly payments were at first refused—though finally accepted. Nevertheless, the depreciation of the DM (German mark) continued, reaching an astonishing level of hyperinflation by the end of the year. Such circumstances made it virtually impossible to gain any kind of financial control. As a result, unrest—strikes, violence, riots— became endemic. Meanwhile, internationally, French and Belgian troops were threatening to occupy the Ruhr (which they did). Such was the context in which Rudolf Steiner gave his economic lectures.

One of the few accounts of the event comes from Emil Leinhaus, a businessman, long-time Anthroposophist, and one of those closest to Rudolf Steiner in the threefold movement:

> Soon after the Vienna Congress [June 1-12, 1922], Rudolf Steiner's economics course for students of economics took place from the end of July to the beginning of August [1922]. I was able to take part in this with a few other practical business managers. For the rest, this course was intended less for practi-tioners of business management than for economics students. The course took off very steeply from certain fundamental economic concepts. The intention was to lead participants to a true understanding of the functions of modern business and economics in relation to the whole threefold social organ-ism. Important perspectives into a future world economy were produced in the process. Rudolf Steiner's explanations were so perfectly suited to promote the insight that world economics and business demanded a complete reversal of economic think-ing—the taking up of a global or world economic mentality in the theory and practice of economic life—that the course should actually have been called "World Business Course." When I once expressed this to Rudolf Steiner, he agreed, but added: "But it doesn't depend on what you call it."
>
> The "Economics Course" demanded of the participants an understanding of extraordinary difficulties—things that could be only partly raised, even during the seminar-like practical discus-sions that took place between Rudolf Steiner's lectures. Because of the defects in the stenographic transcription, the text is inad-equate in many important places. Unfortunately, too, even my

accounts—written immediately on the conclusion of the course and appearing in *Das Goetheanum* and later in *Die Drei*—did not succeed in communicating a real understanding of the course. The thoughts contained in the course were in that moment much too difficult to survey in their all-encompassing meaning.... The course contains a wealth of new points of view, in which those who will work with the intellectual and consciousness assumptions of a coming world economy in the future, will find an inextinguishable source of valuable suggestions. (*Aus der Arbeit mit Rudolf Steiner [From the Life and Work of Rudolf Steiner]*)

*

Leinhaus had worked personally with Steiner from the beginning in the threefold movement, and so should have been familiar with and at home in the material. That he found the economics lectures difficult and resistant to paraphrasing is indicative of the unique nature of the course, which, it must be admitted, in certain ways is both difficult and extraordinarily tight, and demands great inner flexibility on the part of the reader (and re-reader). It is not difficult, however, on account of the material, which on the face of it is self-explanatory. It is difficult because of the sustained level of focused thinking that it requires to follow and penetrate it. Without presenting any new information, it demands that the reader have the willingness to think in a new way—to rethink economics from the ground up. "Today another language is necessary," as Steiner put it. For those willing to do so, the consequence of learning this language is entry into a wholly new way of thinking about the world, which is at once practical and ethical.

At the same time, of course, the lectures are bursting with radical and fascinating new ideas and observations; for instance, that economics is essentially an "associative" activity; that there are three kinds of money (purchase, loan, and gift); and that money should be perishable (that is, should go out of date after a certain time). But such ideas, suggestive and inspiring in themselves, are not meant to be in any way prescriptive— only indicative of the possibilities of the new way of thinking. This is to say that they cannot be understood out of *context*.

And *context,* the reality that nothing exists on its own, that every-thing comes into being in relation, in *circulation*—which is to say, as part of a *living* process—is Steiner's guiding principle here. New thinking in economics, then, is "process thinking" and starts from the presumption that economics is a living process and that the economy is a living organism. The thinking that hopes to enter into it must therefore be extraordinarily flexible, unprejudiced, holistic, relational, and process-oriented. In fact, what Steiner was attempting in these lectures was to lead his audience phenomenologically—by means of a series of detailed thought experiments—to experience in thought the circulatory processes that are economics. To do this is not easy. In the words of the anthroposophic economist Stephan Eisenhut: "One can view this course as a kind of legacy or testament [on the part of Rudolf Steiner] because it illuminates the fundamental forces of modern economic life in such a way that one can enter *meditatively* into economic processes. But such a meditation or contemplation can arise only if the person, who wishes to do so out of his or her own free will, simultaneously also opposes another force, which guides his or her concepts from a clotted, dead form to a free, living one"—in other words, one that makes dead concepts live in a new way or resur-rects them.

*

Although it is a ninety-year-old historical document, Rudolf Steiner's course on economics is still as vital and relevant as it was when it was delivered—if not even more so. Prophetic in 1922, its call for the need for new thinking is presciently contemporary in the second decade of the twenty-first century. This is not surprising: the crisis has not abated; it has intensified—perhaps to the breaking point.

As confirmation, William Ophuls writes in *Plato's Revenge: Politics in the Age of Ecology* (2011), calling for a radical change in public philosophy from a quite different starting point than Steiner's: "If our problems have been created by a certain way of thinking, then the only real solution is to adapt a new way of thinking and not to devise clever political or economic 'mousetraps' based on the old one."

According to Ophuls, who writes from the perspective of one facing humanity's present ecological abyss, old thinking has created an "anti-ecological Titanic." Any and every "green" solution—"making the deck chairs recyclable, feeding the boilers with biofuels, installing hybrid winches and windlasses"—is doomed to failure, because the problems are not solvable by the application of "band-aids" created by the same thinking that brought about the problems in the first place. At the same time, Ophuls believes paradoxically that these problems, which he calls "the five Great Ills"—"ecological exploitation, military aggression, economic inequality, political oppression, and spiritual malaise"—are not new. Though clearly intensified by the thinking through which we think them, they have marked civilization from its inception. At the end of his book, he concludes:

> The problem lies with our notion of liberation... True liberation comes from within. Rousseau epitomized this understanding when he wrote: "For the impulse of appetite alone is slavery; and obedience to the law one has prescribed to oneself is freedom." Ergo, real freedom is paradoxically obtained only when we willingly obey some higher law.
>
> ... Only a politics of consciousness rooted in the moral vision of ecology can create a civilization worthy of the name—an ecological civilization in which humankind lives in harmony with nature, a conscious civilization in which men and women measure wealth in spirit and not in property, and a political civilization in which "the liberty, equality, fraternity of the ancient Roman Gentes" can flourish once again.

Steiner's approach, as I say, is very different, though points of convergence indicate both the timeliness and radical nature of the thinking he proposes. The difference itself is twofold. Ophuls, impelled primarily by the ecological crisis, draws on traditional sources (Plato, Rousseau) against an American background (Jefferson, Thoreau), with a strong Jungian and anthropological bias. Steiner, on the other hand, views the individual as the determining, central factor, not only of social and ethical life, but also of evolution as a whole. From Steiner's approach implicitly arises thinking of the social aspect as based on its necessarily human nature. From Steiner's anthroposophical perspective, the human is not simply an emergent epiphenomenon added to nature, but is coeval with it, even in some sense its arche or source. From his point of view, as any examination of Anthroposophy will reveal, the human is present from the beginning; and nothing in nature or the cosmos is to be considered without simultaneously considering the position and evolutionary task of the human being within it. As he points out in a lecture course for those about to go out to promote the ideas of threefolding:

> ... The human being has, in fact, been slowly removed from consideration in our modern worldview. You will find that the human being has actually been cut out everywhere. You find this above all in the most narrowly spiritual realm—that of science.... [Science] never starts by looking at the human being as such. It presents the human being only as the conclusion of animal evolution.... But this is merely a symptom of the casting out of the essence of the human being from our thinking and feeling....
>
> You can also see how the human being is disabled in the institutions that lie at the core of modern spiritual life. We are held fast by regulations that do not come from us, or we are tossed into the effects of forces coming from economic life, but very, very little worth is placed on the real existence of the human being as a human being in social life... And this is how people arrive at a definition of all manner of things—capital, labor, commodities. The human being falls completely out of these considerations....
>
> You see, if we want to consider the unified process, the process of social life as a whole, we can do this only by placing the human being at the center, by relating everything back to the human being.... Only in this way can the concepts of commodity, capital, and labor receive their proper meaning, just as natural scientific concepts receive their proper meaning only when we bring the human being into all of cosmic evolution....

Thus, whatever the question, the essence and nature of the human being—both the individual human being and the extended web or ecology of relationships that constitute all humanity—is always the implicit motivating center and ground of Steiner's research and thinking, whether it be cosmic and evolutionary as in his *Outline of Esoteric Science* (1910) or, as here, most down-to-earth, as in the question of economics. And he includes not only humanity, for in a larger sense the web of human relationships also includes and is intimately interwoven with—and indeed is a part of—nature and the earth, as well as the invisible worlds within which they are situated. Between all these, the human being mediates and creates the transformational/transfigurational work of culture and society. In this human work, economics, arising from the diverse associations of human beings, plays a fundamental and originary role, for without it nothing else is possible. The fundamental question therefore becomes: for whose sake—toward what end—is our economics, or humanity, to be oriented? In Otto Scharmer's phrase: is it to be ego-centric or eco-centric? The answer depends on our vision of the human being and the place of the human being in the whole. Above all, it depends on our understanding of the true nature of the self: selfishness, or selflessness leading to liberation from selfishness and the experience of the true "I am." In other words: does the whole exist for the sake of the human being, or does the human being exist for the sake of the whole? And if the latter, what does this require of us? Reading between the lines of Steiner's lectures on economics begins to give an answer.

FURTHER READING

Assenza, Gaudio, *Beyond the Market: Economics for the 21st Century.* London: New Economy Publications.

Barfield, Owen. "Equity," *Anthroposophy, A Quarterly Review of Spiritual Science*, No 2, 1932 Vol 7. London: Anthroposophical Publishing Company.

——"The Relation Between the Economics of C. H. Douglas and Those of Rudolf Steiner." *Anthroposophy, A Quarterly Review of Spiritual Science*, No. 3, 1933, Vol. 8. London: Anthroposophical Publishing Company UK/NY.

Beuys, Joseph. *What is Money.* London: Clairview Press.

Bloom, John. *The Genius of Money: Essays and Interviews Reimagining the Financial World.* Great Barrington: SteinerBooks.

Budd, Christopher. *Prelude in Economics*. London: New Economy Publications.

—— *Finance at the Threshold: Rethinking the Real and Financial Economies*. London: Ashgate.

König, Karl. *Becoming Human: A Social Task, The Threefold Social Order*. Edinburgh: Floris Books.

Lamb, Gary. *Associative Economics: Spiritual Activity for the Common Good*. AWSNA.

Ophuls, William. *Plato's Revenge: Politics in the Age of Ecology*. Cambridge, MIT Press.

· Perlas, Nicanor. *Shaping Globalization: Civil Society, Cultural Power and Threefolding*. Manilla: Center for Alternative Development Initiatives (CADI).

Preparata, Guido Giacomo. "Perishable Money in a Threefold Commenwealth: Rudolf Steiner and the Social Economics of an Anarchist Utopia." *Review of Radical Economics* 38/4 (Fall 2006), pp. 619–648.

Selg, Peter. *The Fundamental Social Law: Rudolf Steiner on the Work of the Individual and the Spirit of Community*. Great Barrington: SteinerBooks.

——*The Culture of Selflessness: Rudolf Steiner, the Fifth Gospel, and the Time of Extremes*. Great Barrington: SteinerBooks.

Spence, Michael. *Freeing the Human Spirit: The Threefold Social Order, Money & the Waldorf School*. AWSNA.

Steiner, Rudolf. *Anthroposophy and the Social Question: Three articles by Rudolf Steiner*. Spring Valley: Mercury Press.

—— *Brotherhood and the Struggle for Existence*. Spring Valley: Mercury Press.

—— "Das Geheimnis der Wunde. Aufzeichnungen zum Samariterkurs." *Beiträge zur Rudolf Steiner Gesamtausgabe*, no. 198, 1992, p. 8.

—— *Education as a Force for Social Change*. Great Barrington: SteinerBooks.

—— *The Esoteric Aspect of the Social Question: The Individual and Society*. London: Rudolf Steiner Press.

—— *The Fifth Gospel*. London: Rudolf Steiner Press.

—— *Freedom of Thought and Societal Forces*. Great Barrington: SteinerBooks.

—— *The Influence of the Dead on Destiny*. Great Barrington: SteinerBooks.

—— *Intuitive Thinking as a Spiritual Path [The Philosophy of Freedom]*. Great Barrington: SteinerBooks.

—— *The Social Future*. Great Barrington: SteinerBooks.

—— *Social Issues: Meditative Thinking & the Threefold Social Order*. Great Barrington: SteinerBooks.

—— *Social and Political Science*. London: Rudolf Steiner Press.

—— *The Time-Sequence and Spiritual Foundations for Threefolding: Two lectures*. Spring Valley: Mercury Press.

—— *Towards Social Renewal*. London: Rudolf Steiner Press.

Wilken, Folkert. *The Liberation of Capital*. London: Allen & Unwin.

RETHINKING ECONOMICS

Rudolf Steiner

PART I

Fourteen Lectures Held in Dornach, Switzerland

JULY 24–AUGUST 6, 1922

Lecture 1

From Industrialism to World Economy

DORNACH, JULY 24, 1922

Today I intend a kind of introduction. In tomorrow's lecture, we shall begin to try to give a more or less complete picture of the questions of social and political economy that humanity today must set before itself.

The subject of economics, as we speak of it today, is in reality a very recent creation. It did not arise until the time when the economic life of modern peoples had become extraordinarily complicated in comparison with earlier conditions. As this course is intended primarily for students of political economy,[†] it is necessary by way of introduction to point out this peculiarity of the economic thinking of today.

After all, we need not go very far back in history to see how much economic life has changed, even during the nineteenth century. We need only consider this one fact: England, for example, already had during the first half of the century what was, practically speaking, the modern form of economic life. There was comparatively little radical change in the economic structure of England in the course of the nineteenth century. The great social questions that arise out of economic questions in modern times were being asked in England as early as the first half of the nineteenth century; and those who wanted to think about social and economic questions in the modern sense could pursue their studies in England at a time when in Germany, for instance, such studies would have remained unfruitful. In England, above all, the conditions of trade and commerce on a large scale had already come into being by the first third of the nineteenth century. Through the great development of trade and commerce in the economic life of England, a foundation was already there in the form of trade capital. In England, there was no need to seek for any other starting point for modern economic life. They simply had to go on with the trade capital resulting from the consolidation of trade and commerce, even as early as the first third of the nineteenth century. Starting from this time, everything took place in England with a certain logical consistency; we must not forget that the whole of this English economic life was possible only on the basis originally given by England's relation to her colonies, especially to India. The whole of the English economic system is unthinkable without the relationship of England to India. In other words, English economic life, with all its facility for evolving large sums of capital, is founded on the fact that there lies in the background a country that is, as it were, virgin economic soil. We must not overlook this fact, especially when we pass from England to Germany.

If you consider the economic life of Germany, you will see that in the first third of the nineteenth century it still essentially corresponded to economic customs that had arisen out of the Middle Ages. The economic customs and relationships within Germany in the first third of the nineteenth century were absolutely old: consequently the whole pace of economic life was different in Germany from what it was in England during the first third, or even the first half, of the nineteenth century. In England, during the first half of the century, there was already what we may call a reckoning with quickly changing habits of life. The main character of economic life remained essentially the same, but it was already adaptable to quickly changing habits. In Germany, on the other hand, habits of life were still conservative: economic development could afford to advance at a snail's pace, for it had to adapt itself only to technical conditions that had remained more or less the same over long periods, and to human needs that were not rapidly changing.

But in this respect a great transformation took place in the second third of the nineteenth century. Then there rapidly took place an approximation to English conditions: a development of the industrial system. In the first half of the nineteenth century, Germany had been in all essentials an agrarian country—now it was rapidly transformed into an industrial country, far more rapidly than any other region of the earth.

But there is an important fact in this connection. We might describe it thus: In England the transition to industrial life took place instinctively; nobody knew exactly how it happened. It came as a natural event. In Germany, it is true, the medieval character still existed in the first third of the nineteenth century. Germany was an agrarian country. But while the outer economic conditions were taking their accustomed course in a way that might almost be called medieval, human thinking was undergoing a fundamental change. It came into the consciousness of human beings that something altogether different must now arise, that the existing conditions were no longer appropriate for the time. Thus the transformation of economic conditions that arose in Germany in the second third of the nineteenth century took place far more consciously than in England. In Germany, people were far more aware of how they entered into modern capitalism; in England, people were not aware of it at all. If you read today all the writings and discussions in Germany during that period concerning the transition to industrialism, you will get a remarkable impression, a strange impression, of how the people in Germany were thinking. They actually looked upon it as a real liberation of humanity; they called it liberalism, democracy. Moreover, they regarded it as the very salvation of humanity to get right out of the old connections, the old binding links, the old kind of corporation, and pass over to the fully free position (for so they called it) of the individual within the economic life. Hence in England you will never meet with a theory of economics such as was developed by the people who received their education in Germany at the height of the period that I have just characterized. Schmoller, Roscher,† and others derived their views from the ideal of this "liberalism" in economics. What they built up was altogether in accord with this ideal, and they built it with full consciousness. The English would have thought such theories of economics stale and boring; they would have thought that one should not trouble to think about such things. Look at the radical difference between the way in which people in England talked about these things (to mention even a man like Beaconsfield, who was theoretical enough in all conscience) from the way in which Richter or Lasker or even Brentano† were speaking in Germany. In Germany, therefore, this second period was entered into with full consciousness.

Then came the third period, the period essentially of "the state." It is true that as the last third of the nineteenth century drew near, the German state was consolidated purely by means of external power. What was consolidated was not what the idealists of 1848, or even of the 1830s and on, had desired; no, it was the state that was consolidated, and moreover by sheer force or power. And this state gradually laid claim to the economic life for its own purposes, with full consciousness. Thus, in the last third of the nineteenth century, the structure of the economic life was permeated through and through by the very opposite principle as had been in the previous period. In the second third of the century, economic evolution had been subject to the ideas of liberalism. Now its evolution became altogether subject to the idea of the state. This was what gave the economic life in Germany, as a whole, its stamp. It is true that there were elements of consciousness in the whole process, and yet in another sense the whole thing was quite unconscious.

But most important is that through all these developments a radical contrast, an antagonism of principle, was created, not only in thought but in the whole conduct of economic life itself between the English and the Central European economies. And the manner of their economic interchange depended on this contrast. The whole economy of the nineteenth century, as it evolved into the twentieth, would be unthinkable without this contrast between the West and Central Europe. The way in which people sold their goods, the way in which they found a market for their goods, the way in which they manufactured them—all of this would be unthinkable without this contrast.

The course of development was as follows. First, the economic and industrial life of England became possible on the basis of England having possession of India; next, it became possible for the whole of economic activity to be expanded on the basis of the contrast between the Western and the Central European economic life. In effect, economic life is founded not on what one sees in one's immediate surroundings, but on the great reciprocal relationships in the world at large.

Now it was with this contrast that the world as a whole was entering the state of world economy—and could not enter! For the world continued to depend on the instinctive element that had evolved from the past, the existence of which I have just indicated in describing the antithesis between England and Central Europe. In the twentieth century, though the world was unaware of the fact, we stood face to face with this situation. The antithesis became more and more immediate, it became deeper and deeper, and we stood before a great riddle. The economic conditions had evolved out of these antitheses or contrasts and, having done so, they were carrying the contrasts themselves ever more intensely into the future. And yet, if the contrast were to go on forever increasing, economic dealings would become impossible. This was the great riddle of the twentieth century. The contrast had created the economic life; the economic life had in turn enhanced the contrast. The contrast was calling for a solution. The question was how these contrasts or opposites would be resolved. The further course of history was destined to prove that human beings were incapable of finding the answer.

It would have been practical to speak in words like these in 1914, in the days of peace. But, in place of a solution, there came the result of a failure to find such a world historic solution. Such was the disease that then set in, seen from the economic perspective.

You must recognize that the possibility of all evolution always depends fundamentally on contrasts or antitheses. I will only mention one example. Through the fact that the English economic life had been consolidated far earlier than the Central European, the English were unable to make the price of certain goods as low as was possible in Germany. Thus, there arose a great contrast of competition, for "made in Germany" was simply a question of competition. And when the war was over, the question could arise: Now that people have knocked in each other's heads instead of seeking a solution for existing contrasts, how can we deal with the matter? At that time, I could not but believe in the possibility of finding human beings who would understand the contrasts that must be brought forth in another domain. For life depends on contrasts, and can exist only if contrasts are there, interacting with one another. Thus in 1919 one could come to the point of saying: Let us now draw attention to the real contrasts or contra positions towards which world-historic evolution is tending—those of the economic life, the political life of rights, and the spiritual-cultural life—the contra positions of the threefold social order.

What, after all, was the actual situation when we believed that we must bring the threefold social idea to the awareness of as many human beings as possible? I will describe it only externally today. The important thing would have been to bring the idea of three-folding to the awareness of as many individuals as possible before the economic consequences ensued, which afterward did take place. You must remember that when the idea of threefolding was first mentioned, we did not yet stand face to face with the monetary difficulties of today. On the contrary, if the threefold social order had been understood at that time, these difficulties could never have occurred. Yet once again we were faced by the inability of human beings to understand such a thing as this in a really practical sense. When we tried to bring the threefold social idea home to them, people would come and say, "Yes, all of this is excellent. We see it perfectly. But, after all, the first thing needed is to counteract the depreciation of the currency." All that one could answer was that it is contained in the threefold social order. Adjust to work with it; that is the only means of counteracting the depreciation of the currency. People were asking how to do the very thing that the threefold social order was meant to do. They did not understand it, however often they declared that they did.

And now the situation is such that if we are to speak again to people today, we can no longer speak in the same forms as we did then. Today another language is necessary, and that is what I want to give you in these lectures. I want to show you how one must think about these questions today, especially if one is young and can still have an opportunity to play a part in shaping the immediate future.

Thus, on the one hand, we can characterize a certain period—the nineteenth century—in terms of world-historic economic contrasts. But we might also go still farther back and include the time when people first began to think about "political economy," as it was then called, at all. If you take the history of economics you will see that earlier everything took place instinctively. It was only in modern times that there arose that complexity of economic life, in the midst of which human beings felt it necessary to think about these things.

Now I am speaking, in effect, for students. I am trying to show how students of economics should find their way into this subject. Let me, therefore, now relate the most essential thing on which it all depends.

You see, the time when individuals had to begin to think about economics was just the time when they no longer had the thoughts to comprehend such a subject. They simply no longer had the requisite ideas. I will give you an example from natural science to show that this is so.

We as human beings have our physical bodies, which have weight just like any other physical object. Your physical body will be heavier after a midday meal than before; we can even weigh the difference. That is to say, we partake in the general laws of gravity. But with this gravity, which is the property of all ponderable substances, we could do very little in our human body; we could at most go about the world as robots, certainly not as conscious beings. I have often explained what is essential to build any valid concept of these matters. I have often said what we need for our thinking. The human brain, if we weigh it alone, weighs about 1,400 grams. If the weight of these 1,400 grams were to press directly on the veins and arteries, which are situated at the base of the skull, it would destroy them. You could not live for a single moment if the human brain were pressing downward with its full 1,400 grams. It is indeed fortunate that the principle of Archimedes holds true. I mean that a body loses as much of its weight in water as the weight of the fluid that it displaces. A body that has a certain weight loses as much of its weight in water as a body of water of equal size would weigh. The brain swims in the cerebrospinal fluid, and thereby loses 1,380 grams: for such is the weight of a body of cerebrospinal fluid of the size of the human brain. The brain presses downward onto the base of the skull with a weight of only 20 grams, and this weight it can bear. But if we now ask ourselves what the purpose of all this is, we must answer that with a brain that was a mere ponderable mass, we could not think. We do not think with the heavy substance; we think with the buoyancy. The substance must first lose its weight. Only then can we think. We think with what flies away from the earth.

But we are also conscious in our whole body. How do we become thus conscious? In our whole body there are some 25 billion red blood cells. These 25 billion red cells are very minute. Nevertheless, they have weight; they have weight because they contain iron. Every one of these 25 billion red cells swims in the serum of the blood, and loses weight exactly in accordance with the fluid it displaces. Once again, therefore, in every single blood cell an effect of buoyancy is created—25 billion times. Throughout our body we are conscious by virtue of this upward-driving force. We may also say that whatever food we consume must first, to a very large extent, be divested of its weight; it must be transformed in order to serve us. Such is the demand of the living organism.

To think in this way, and to regard this way of thinking as essential, are the very things individuals ceased to do just at the time when it became necessary to think in terms of economics. Thereafter, they reckoned only with ponderable substances; they no longer thought of the transformation that a substance undergoes in a living organism—as to its weight, for example, through the effect of buoyancy.

And now another thing. If you call to mind your studies of physics, you will remember that the physicist speaks of the "spectrum." This band of colors is created with the help of the prism: red, orange, yellow, green, blue, indigo, violet. So far (from the red to the violet), the spectrum appears luminous. But, as you know, before the area that shows a luminous effect, what we call the infrared rays are assumed to exist; and, beyond the violet, the ultraviolet rays. If, therefore, one speaks merely of light, one does not include the totality of the phenomenon. We must go on to describe how the light is transformed in two opposite directions; we must explain how, beyond the red, light sinks into the element of warmth and, beyond the violet, into chemical effects. In both directions the light, as such, disappears. If, therefore, we give a theory of light alone, we are giving a mere extract of the greater whole. (The current theory of light is, in any case, not a true one. It is significant that at the very time when humankind had to begin to think consciously of economics, human thinking on physics was in such a condition that it resulted, among other things, in an untrue theory of light.)

I have, however, mentioned the matter here because there is a valid analogy. Consider for a moment not the economy of peoples, but, let us say, the economy of sparrows or the economy of swallows. They too, after all, have a kind of economy. But this—the economy of the animal kingdom—does not reach far up into the human kingdom. Even in the case of the hamster we may indeed speak of a kind of animal capitalism. The essence of animal economics is that nature provides the products, and the animal as a single creature takes them for itself. Humanity does indeed reach down into this animal economy; but we have to emerge from it.

The true human economy may be compared to the part of the spectrum that is visible as light. What reaches down into nature would then be comparable with the part of the spectrum that extends into the infrared. Here, on the one hand, for example, we come into the domain of agriculture, of economic geography, and so forth. The science of economics cannot be sharply defined in this direction: it reaches down into a region that must be grasped by very different methods. This is one side of the situation.

On the other hand, just under the influence of the very complicated relations of today, it has gradually come to pass that our economic thinking fails us once more in another direction. Just as light ceases to appear as light, as we go on into the ultraviolet, so does human economic activity cease to be purely economic. I have often characterized how this came about. The phenomenon began only in the nineteenth century. Until then, the economic life was still more or less dependent on the capability and efficiency of the individual human being. A bank prospered if some individual in it was a thoroughly capable person. Individuals were still of real importance. I have often related, as an amusing example, the story of the ambassador of the King of France who once approached Rothschild,† trying to raise a loan. Rothschild happened to be in conversation with a leather merchant. When the ambassador of the King of France was announced, he said, "Ask him to wait a little while." The ambassador was terribly upset. Was he to wait, while a leather merchant was in there with Rothschild? When the attendant came out and told him, he simply would not believe his ears. "Go in again and tell Herr Rothschild that I am here as the ambassador of the King of France." But the attendant brought the same answer again, "Will you kindly wait a little?" Thereupon he himself burst into the inner room. "I am the ambassador of the King of France!" Rothschild answered, "Please, have a seat." "Yes, but I am the ambassador of the King of France!" "Please, then, take two seats!"

You see, what took place in the economic life in that time was placed consciously within the sphere of the human personality. But things have changed since then. Now, in the "great" affairs of economic life, very little indeed depends on the individual personality. Human economic functioning has to a very large extent been drawn into what I am here comparing with the ultraviolet light. I refer to the workings of capital as such. Accumulations of capital are active as such. Over and above the economic, there lies an ultra economic life, which is essentially determined by the peculiar power inherent in the actual masses of capital. If, therefore, we wish to understand the economic life of today, we must regard it in this way. It lies in the midst of two regions, of which the one leads downward into nature and the other upward into capital. Between them lies the domain that we must comprehend as the actual economic life.

Now from this you will see that people did not even possess the necessary concept to enable them to define the science of economics and set it in its proper place within the whole domain of knowledge. As we shall presently see, it is a curious thing, but this region alone (which we have compared to infrared light)—this region, which does not yet actually reach up into the sphere of economics—this alone is intelligible to the human intellect. We can consider with ordinary thinking how to grow oats or barley, and so forth; or how best to obtain ore in mining. Basically, that is all that we can really think about with the intellect as we have grown accustomed to apply it in the science of modern times.

This is a fact of immense significance. Think back for a moment to what I have just indicated as the concept that we need in science. We consume as food, substances that have weight. That they can be of use to us depends upon the fact that they continually lose their weight within us. That is to say, within the body they are totally transformed. This is not all. They are changed in a different way in each organ; the liver acts upon the substances differently than the brain or the lungs. The organism is differentiated, and the conditions are different for each substance in each single organ. We have a continuous change of quality along with the change from organ to organ.

Now, it is approximately the same when, within a given economic domain, we speak of the value of a commodity. It is nonsense to define some substance as carbon, for example, and then to ask how it behaves inside the human body. The carbon, even regarding the way it is to be considered, becomes something altogether different depending on where it is in the outer world. Likewise, we cannot simply ask, what is the value of a commodity? The value is different according to whether the commodity is lying in a shop, or whether it is transported to this or that place.

Thus, our ideas in economics must be quite mobile. We must rid ourselves of the habit of constructing concepts with the intention of defining things once and for all. We must realize that we are dealing with a living process, and must transform our concepts within the living process. But what the economists have tried to do is to grasp such things as value, price, production, consumption, and so forth, with ideas such as they had in ordinary science. And these were of no use.

Fundamentally speaking, therefore, we have not yet attained a true science of economics. With the concepts to which we have grown accustomed thus far, we cannot truthfully answer the question, for instance, "what is value?" Or, "what is price?" Whatever has value must be considered as being in perpetual circulation; likewise we must consider price, which corresponds to value, as something in perpetual circulation. If you ask about the simple properties of carbon, you will still know absolutely nothing of what goes on in the lungs, for example, although carbon is also present in the lungs. For the whole configuration of carbon becomes quite different in the lungs. In the same way, iron, when found in the mine, is something altogether different from what it is in the economic process. Economics is concerned with something quite different from the mere fact that it "is" iron. It is with these unstable, constantly changing factors that we must reckon.

Forty five years ago, I met a certain family. They showed me a painting. I think it had been lying up in an attic for about thirty years. As long as it lay there, and no one was there who knew any more about it than that it was the kind of thing one throws away in the corner of an attic, it had no value in the economic process. Once its value had been recognized, it was worth 30,000 gulden—quite a large sum of money in those days. What did the value depend on in this case? Purely and simply on the opinion people formed of the painting. The painting had not been removed from its place; rather, individuals had simply arrived at different thoughts about it. And so, in no case does value depend on what a thing "is" directly. You can never develop concepts of economics in reference to the mere external reality. No, you must always develop them in reference to the economic process as a whole. And within this process each thing is continuously changing. Therefore we must speak of the economic process of circulation before we can arrive at such things as value, price, and so forth.

In the economic theories of today, you will observe that they generally begin with definitions of value and price. That is quite wrong. First it is necessary to describe the economic process. Only then do those things emerge with which the theorists of today can begin.

Now, in the year 1919, when everything had been destroyed, one might have thought that people would realize the need to begin with something fresh. Alas, it was not the case. The small number of people who did believe that there must be a new beginning very soon fell into the comfortable reflection: "After all, there is nothing to be done." Meanwhile, the great calamity was taking place: the devaluation of money in Eastern and Central Europe, and with it a complete revolution in the social strata; for it goes without saying that with each progressive devaluation of money, those who live by what I have here compared to ultraviolet light must be impoverished. And this is happening today, far more perhaps than people are yet aware. And it will happen more and more completely. Here, above all, we are directed to the idea of the living, social organism. For it is evident that this devaluation of money is determined by the old state restrictions and limitations. The old state restrictions and limitations are interfering with the economic process. The latter must indeed be understood, but we must first gain an understanding of the social organism. Yet all economic systems—from Adam Smith[†] to the most modern—reckon, after all, with small regions as if they were complete social organisms. They do not realize that, even if one is only using an analogy, the analogy must be correct.

 Have you ever seen a complex, full-grown living organism, such as the human being, for instance, in this drawing?—immediately beside this human being a second one, and here a third, and so forth. These human organisms would be quite charming, attached to one another in this way; however, with complex, full-grown organisms there is no such thing.

Yet, with the separate states and countries, this is the case. Living organisms require an empty space around them—empty space between them and other living organisms. You could at most compare single states or countries with the cells of the organism. It is only the whole earth that, as an economic body, can truly be compared with a living organism. This ought surely to be taken into account. It is quite palpable ever since we have had a world economy that the single states or countries are at most to be compared with cells.

The whole earth, considered as an economic organism, is the social organism.

Yet this is nowhere being taken into account. It is precisely owing to this error that the whole science of economics has grown so remote from reality. People want to establish principles that are meant to apply only to an individual cell. Hence, if you study the French theory of economy, you will find it differently constituted than English or German or other economic theories. But as economists, what we really need is an understanding of the social organism in its totality.

So much for today by way of introduction.

Lecture 2

The Fluid Nature of Economic Processes

DORNACH, JULY 25, 1922

PARTICULARLY in the sphere of economics the first concepts and ideas that we must develop cannot but be a little complicated—and for a quite objective reason. You must imagine the economic process, considered even as a world economy, as a thing of perpetual movement. As the blood flows through the human being, so do goods, as merchandise or commodities, flow by every conceivable channel through the whole economic body. And we must conceive, as the most important thing within this economic process, all that takes place in buying and selling. That, at least, is true of the economic life of today. Whatever else there may be—and we shall of course have to consider the most varied impulses contained in economic life—the subject of economics comes home to us directly when we have anything to buy or sell. In the last resort the instinctive thinking of every naïve person on economic matters culminates in the process taking place between buyer and seller. Fundamentally, this is what is important.

Think about what counts when buying and selling are considered in the economic process. The thing that people care about is the price of a commodity, the price of the piece of goods in question. In the last resort all the most important economic considerations really merge in this question of price. All the impulses and forces that are at work in economics culminate at length in price. We shall, therefore, first have to consider the problem of price, but it is by no means a simple problem. You need only consider the most simple case. At a given place, *A*, we have a certain commodity; at place *A* it has a certain price. But suppose it is not bought there but is transported to another place, *B*. Our endeavor will then be to add to the price whatever transport charges had to be paid from *A* to *B*. Thus the price changes in the process of circulation. There we have the simplest—if I may put it so, the most trite—instance. Of course, there are far more complex cases.

Assume, for instance, that at a given date a house in a large town costs a certain amount. Fifteen years later the same house may perhaps cost six times as much. Let us not imagine that the main cause of the rise in price lies in the devaluation of money. On the contrary, let us assume that this is not the case. The rise in price may simply lie in the fact that in the meantime many other houses have been built around it. The other buildings, now situated in its neighborhood, greatly increase the value of the house. Of course, there may be ten or fifteen other circumstances accounting for the rise in price. In reality, we are never in a position to apply some general statement to the specific case, to say, for instance, that the price of houses, or iron ware, or grains, can be explicitly determined, at a given place, from any particular condition. To begin with, we can say little more than that we must observe how the price fluctuates with place and time. Then, perhaps, we can trace some of the conditions through which at a given place a given price actually emerges as it does. But there can be no such thing as a general definition stating how the price of a thing is composed: that is an impossibility. Again and again one is astonished to find price discussed in the commonly found works on economics, as though it were possible to define it. We simply cannot define it, for a price is always concrete and specific. Precisely, in economic matters, it is impossible to get anywhere near the realities with definitions.

I once witnessed the following case. In a certain district where land is comparatively cheap, there is an organization with a more or less famous man in its midst. The organization buys up all the cheap plots of land, and prevails upon the famous man to build himself a house there. Then the plots of land are offered for sale. They can be offered at a considerably higher price than the price at which they were bought, for the simple reason that the famous man has been persuaded to build himself a house there.

Such instances will show you how indeterminate are the conditions on which the price of a thing depends in the economic process. Of course, you may say, such developments must be counteracted. Land reformers and people with similar aims try to resist these things. Through various regulations they desire to establish a kind of just price for everything. Of course one can do so, but economically considered, the price is not changed thereby. In the above instance, for example, when the plots of land are sold at a higher price, one can take the money away again, in the form of a high property tax. Then the state will pocket the difference. People have not grasped this reality. In reality, the original price has increased because of the tax. You can resort to regulations, but they will only obscure the issue. The price will still be what it would have been without them. You only bring about a redistribution. And it is no true economic thinking to say that the land has not increased in price during the last ten years, simply because you have obscured the matter by regulations. Economics must stand firmly on a basis of reality. In economics we can speak only of the conditions existing at a given time and at the actual place to which we are referring. Those who desire the progress of humanity will come to the conclusion that things can be different. To begin with, however, things must be observed in their immediate reality at the particular moment. From all this you will see how impossible it is to approach such a thing as price—a most important concept in economics—by seeking to grasp it with a sharply defined idea. We can make no progress in economic theory by this means; quite other ways must be adopted. We must observe the economic process itself.

Yet the problem of price is the most important and all our efforts must be directed to it. We must observe the economic process, and try, as it were, to catch the point where (at any given place and time) the actual price of a given thing results from all the underlying economic causes.

Now if you follow ordinary economic doctrines, you will generally find three factors mentioned—three factors, through the interplay of which the whole economic process is supposed to take its course. They are nature,[†] labor, and capital. It is true that we can say to begin with that tracing the economic process we find what comes from nature, what is achieved by human labor, and what is derived from, or directed by means of, capital. But if we take nature, labor, and capital simply side by side in this way, we shall not grasp the economic process in a living way. On the contrary, we shall be led to many one-sided points of view—a fact to which the history of economic theory bears eloquent witness. Some say that all value is inherent in nature and that no special value is added to the substance of natural objects by human labor. Others believe that all true economic value is really impressed on a piece of goods, on a commodity, by the labor that, as they sometimes say, is crystallized in the commodity. Or again, the moment you place capital and labor side by side, you will find people saying, on the one hand, in reality it is capital that alone makes labor possible, and the wages of labor are paid out of the accumulated capital. On the other side it is said, no, the only thing that produces real value is labor, and all that capital obtains for itself is the surplus value resulting from the yield of labor.

The fact is that considering things from the one point of view, the one is right; considering them from the other point of view, the other is right. Over against the reality, such ways of thinking remind one of many a method in bookkeeping—put the item here and this will be the result; put it there, and that will result. One can speak, with strong apparent reasons, of surplus value, saying that this is deducted from the wages of labor and appropriated by the capitalists to themselves. But one can say with equally good reasons, that, in the whole connection of economic life, everything is due in the first place to the capitalists, who can pay their workers only from what they have available for the wages of labor. For both of these points of view there are very good and very bad reasons. In fact, none of these ways of thinking comes near to the reality of economics. Though excellent as a basis for agitations, they are of no importance in a serious economic science. Quite other foundations must be found if we would hope for progress in economic life.

Up to a certain point, of course, all these systems have their justification. Adam Smith, for instance, sees the real, original value-forming factor in the work or labor that is expended on things. Here again, excellent reasons can be brought forward in support of this view. Such a man as Adam Smith certainly did not think in a stupid or nonsensical way. Here again, nevertheless, there is the underlying idea of taking hold of something static and giving it a definition, whereas in the real economic process things are in perpetual movement. It is relatively simple to form concepts of the phenomena of nature—even the most complicated—as compared with the ideas that we require for a science of economics. Infinitely more complicated, variable, and unstable are the phenomena in economics than in nature—more fluctuating, less capable of being grasped with any defined or hard and fast concepts. In effect, an altogether different method must be adopted. You will find this method difficult only in the beginning; but as a result of it, you will presently see, the only real and possible foundation for a science of economics can be discovered.

To begin with, we may say that to this economic process, which we must now consider, three things contribute: nature, labor, and (thinking, at first, of the purely external economic aspect) capital. So, At first! Let us consider the middle one of these three, human labor. Let us try to form a conception of it by going down, as I indicated yesterday, into the sphere of animal life. Let us observe, instead of the economy of peoples, the economy of sparrows, the economy of swallows.

Here, you see at once, nature is the basis of economy. True, even the sparrow has to do a kind of work; at the very least, it must hop around to find its food. Sometimes it has to hop around a very great deal in the course of a day to find what it requires. The swallow building its nest also has to do a kind of work, and again it has much to do to build it. Nevertheless, in the true economic sense, we cannot call this "work," we cannot call it "labor." We shall make no progress in economic ideas if we call this labor. If we observe more closely, we shall have to admit that the sparrow and the swallow are organized precisely in such a way as to do the very things—fulfill the very functions—which they fulfill in finding their food, and so forth. They simply could not be healthy if they had no opportunity to move around in this way. It is part and parcel of their organization; it belongs to them, no less than their legs and wings. In seeking to build up economic concepts, we can therefore leave out of account what we might here call a mere apparent labor, a semblance of labor. In such cases nature is taken just as she is, and the single creature, merely to satisfy its own needs or those of its nearest kin, carries out the corresponding semblance of labor. If, however, we wish to determine what is value in the true economic sense, we must disregard this apparent labor. Thus, it is a matter first of all of approaching a true concept of economic value.

Consider the animal economy once more. There we may say that nature alone is the value-forming factor. If we now ascend to the human being, that is, to economy, it is true that we still have—from the side of nature—the same starting point of "nature-value." The moment human beings no longer provide merely for themselves or for their nearest kindred, however, but for one another, human labor, properly so-called, comes into consideration. Indeed, the moment we no longer use nature's products just for ourselves, but we stand in some relation to other human beings and trade goods with them, what we then do becomes, in relation to nature, labor. Here we arrive at the one aspect of value in economy. It arises in this way. Human labor is expended on the products of nature, and we have before us in economic circulation products of nature transformed by human labor. It is only here that a true economic value first arises. As long as the product is untouched, at the place where it is found in nature, it has no other value than it has, for instance, for the animals. But the moment you take the very first steps to put the product of nature into the process of economic circulation, the transformed nature-product begins to have economic value. We may therefore characterize this economic value as follows. An economic value, seen from this one aspect, is a product of nature transformed by human labor. Whether the human labor consists in digging or chopping, or merely moving a product of nature from one place to another, is irrelevant. If we are seeking the determination of value in general, then we must simply say: one value-forming factor is that of human labor, transforming a product of nature so as to pass it into the economic process of circulation.

If you consider this, you will see at once how very fluctuating is the value of a piece of goods circulating in the economic life. For labor is something always present, and is continuously expended on the goods. You cannot really say what value is; you can say only that value arises in a given place and at a given time, inasmuch as human labor transforms some product of nature. That is where value emerges. To begin with we cannot and do not want to try to define value, but want to simply point out the place where it appears. I will present this diagrammatically. Here on the left side of the drawing we have nature, as it were, in the background.

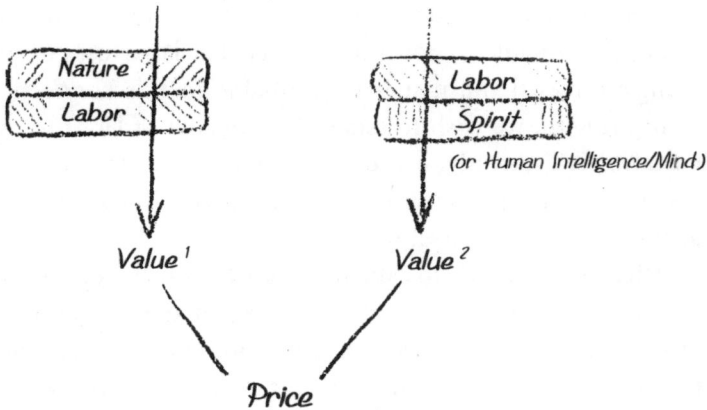

Human labor approaches nature. What then becomes visible—appearing, as it were, through the interplay of nature and human labor—is one aspect of economic value. It is by no means a faulty image if, for instance, we look at a black surface, or at anything black, through a bright medium and see it as blue. According to whether the luminous medium is thick or thin, we will see various shades of blue. According to how we shift it, its density will vary; it is continuously fluctuating. So it is with value in the economic life; it is really none other than the appearance of nature through human labor. That, too, is always fluctuating.

To begin with, we are gaining a few abstract indications and little more; but these will give us our bearings during the next few days and help us to reach more concrete concepts. After all, you are accustomed to this, for in all sciences one begins with what is the simplest.

You see, labor as such has no purpose at all in economics. A man may chop wood, or he may get onto a treadmill. The man on the treadmill may be doing just as much work as the one who chops wood. To consider labor as Marx[†] did, when he said that we should look for its equivalent in the amount that is consumed in the human organism by the labor, is colossal nonsense. The same amount is consumed whether someone chops wood or dances about on this machine. What happens in the human being is not the point in economics. We have already seen how the subject of economics borders on uneconomic matters. Speaking purely economically, it is quite unjustifiable to point to the fact that labor uses up the human being's forces. I mean it is unjustifiable in this connection, where, to begin with, we wish to establish a concept of labor in the sense of economics. Indirectly, it is of great significance, for on the other side the needs of people have to be cared for. But Marx's way of thinking at this point is a colossal nonsense.

What do we need, to take hold of labor in the economic process? It is necessary, to begin with, to disregard the human being and to observe how labor enters into the economic process. The labor on the treadmill does not enter into it at all; it simply adheres to the man himself. The chopping of wood, on the other hand, does enter the economic process. The one thing that matters is how labor enters the economic process. It is a matter of the fact, for everything being considered, that everywhere nature is changed by human labor; and only in so far as nature is transformed by human labor do we create real economic values from this one side. If, for instance, we find it necessary for our physical health, having worked upon nature in some way, to dance a little or to do eurythmy in the intervals, all this may of course be judged from another standpoint; but what we do in the intervals cannot be described as work or labor in the economic sense, nor can it be regarded as in any way a factor creating economic values. Seen from another side, it may well be creating values, but we must first get our concepts pure and clear concerning economic values as such.

Now there is an altogether different possibility for economic value to arise. It is that we turn our attention to labor as such, and we take labor as the given thing. To begin with, as you have seen just now, this labor, economically speaking, is something totally neutral and irrelevant. Yet, it becomes an economic value-creating factor the moment we let it be directed by human intelligence (the human mind or Spirit). I must now speak in a somewhat different sense from before. Even in the most extreme cases, you can imagine something that would otherwise not be labor at all being transformed into real labor by human intelligence. If it occurs to a man, in order to lose weight, to set up the apparatus that we spoke of in his bedroom and practice on it, there will be no economic value in it. If somebody winds a rope around it, however, and uses it to drive some machine, the moment this is done, what would not otherwise be labor at all, in the economic sense, receives value through Spirit. The fellow on the treadmill will incidentally lose weight just the same, but the essential point is that through Spirit—by intelligence, reflection, perhaps even speculation—labor is given a certain direction and the various units of labor are brought into certain mutual relations.

We may say that here we have the second aspect of the value-forming factors in economics. Here labor stands in the background, and in the foreground stands Spirit, which directs the labor. Labor shines through Spirit (or human intelligence), and this creates once more economic value. As you will soon see, these two aspects are present everywhere. Having shown in this diagram how an economic value emerges when we have nature appearing through labor [see diagram, p. 21, left side], if we now wish to represent diagrammatically what was just explained, we shall have to put labor in the background and in the front of it Spirit, which gives it a certain modification [right side].

These are the two essential poles of the economic process. There are indeed no other ways in which economic values are created. Either nature is modified by labor, or labor is modified by Spirit (human intelligence/mind). The outer expression of Spirit, in this connection, is in the manifold formations of capital. Economically, Spirit must be looked for in the configurations of capital: these at any rate are its outward expression. We shall realize the facts more clearly when we come to consider capital as such, and then capital as a monetary medium.

So you see there can be no question of arriving at a definition of economic value. Once more you need only consider on how many circumstances—on the cleverness or stupidity of how many different people—the modification of labor by the Spirit in any given instance will depend. There is every kind of fluctuating condition. Nevertheless, this fact will always be in evidence—the value-creating factors in the economic process will always be found at these two opposite poles.

Suppose now we find ourselves at any given point within the economic process. The economic process takes its course in the activities of buying and selling. Buying and selling are essentially an exchange of values. There is, in fact, no other exchange than that of values. Properly speaking, it is wrong to speak of an exchange of goods. The "goods" that play a part in the economic process—whether they appear as modified products of nature or modified labor—are always values. It is always the values that are exchanged. Whenever a process of buying and selling takes place, values are exchanged. Now what is it that emerges in the economic process when value and value, as it were, impinge on one another in the process of exchange? It is price. Wherever price emerges, it is always through the impact of value on value in the economic process. For this reason you cannot think truly about price if you have in mind the exchange of mere goods. If you buy an apple for a penny, you may say that you are exchanging one piece of goods for another—the apple for the penny. But you will make no progress in economic thinking along these lines. The apple has been picked somewhere and then transported, and it may well be that various other things have been done around it. All this is labor that has modified it. What you are dealing with is not an apple but a product of nature transformed by human labor, representing an economic value. In economics we must always take our start from values. Similarly, the penny represents not a piece of goods but a value, since after all (or so at any rate we must suppose) the penny is but the sign for the fact that there is present in a man who buys the apple another value that he exchanges for it.

Today I am anxious for you to get a clear insight into the fact that in economics we must not speak of goods but of values as what is elementary. It is wrong to try to consider price in any other way than by envisaging the interplay of values. Value set against value gives you price. If, as we saw, value itself is a fluctuating thing, incapable of definition, may we not say that when you exchange value for value, price, which arises in the process of exchange, is a fluctuating thing raised to the second power?

From all this you may see how futile it is to try to take hold of values and prices with the idea of finding a firm and fixed ground in economics. It is still more futile, if your object is to influence the economic process in practice. Something altogether different is needed, something that lies behind all these things. This can be seen from a very simple observation.

Consider this for a moment: nature appears to us through human labor. Suppose we obtain iron at a given place under extraordinarily difficult conditions. The value that is thus produced through human labor is a modified object of nature. If at a different place iron is produced under far easier conditions, it may happen that an altogether different value will result. You see, therefore, that we cannot grasp the reality in the value itself; we must go behind the value. We must go back to what creates the value. Here alone can we gradually find our way to the more constant conditions on which we can exercise a direct influence. The moment you have brought the value into economic circulation, you must let it fluctuate with the economic organism as a whole. Consider the finer constitution of a blood cell; it is different in the head and in the heart and in the liver. You cannot say, "We will now seek the true definition of blood." In the human organism, the most you can do is to consider what are the more favorable foods to consume in the one case and in the other. Likewise, there is no point in talking round and round about value and price. The important thing is to go back to the primary factors, back to what, if rightly formed, will actually bring forth the proper price. The proper price will then emerge of its own accord.

In the study of economics it is quite impossible to stop short at definitions of value and price. We must always go back to the real origins whence the economic process is nourished, on the one hand, and by which, on the other hand, it is regulated—nature on the one hand, Spirit on the other.

In all economic theories of modern times, this has been the difficulty: they have always tried at the outset to hold fast what is really fluctuating. As a result, those who can see through these things find themselves confronted not with wrong definitions—scarcely any of them are wrong; they are generally quite right! (Though, it is true that one must indeed miss the mark to say that the amount of labor corresponds to what has been expended and has to be restored in the human body; that it corresponds, therefore, to the expenditure of substance. Such a statement is really a blunder; one has really failed to see the simplest things.) No, the point is that even those of considerable insight have stumbled again and again over this obstacle in developing their theory of economics. They have tried to observe things that are always in a state of flux as if they were at rest. For the objects of nature, one can and must often do so. In nature it suffices to observe the state of rest in a quite different way. All we have come to do in the natural science of today to observe a state of movement is to regard the movement as though it were composed of a multitude of tiny states of rest, and jump from one to the other. For when we integrate, we regard even movement as if it were composed of states of rest.

On the model of such a science, however, we cannot study the economic process. This, therefore, must be said: The first thing needed in grappling with the science of economics is to consider how, on the one hand, value appears because nature is transformed by human labor—nature is seen through human labor—while, on the other hand, value appears because labor is seen through Spirit. These two origins of value are the real polar opposites. They differ, as in the spectrum, the one pole—the luminous or yellow pole— differs from the other—the blue or violet pole. You may well hold fast this image: as in the spectrum the warm colors appear on the one side, so on this side there appears the nature-value that will show itself more in the formation of rents.† On this side we perceive nature transformed by labor. On the other side there appear to us instead those values that are translated into capital; here we see labor transformed by Spirit. Then, indeed, price can arise, inasmuch as values of the one pole impinge on values of the other. Or again, the several values within the one pole come into mutual interaction. The point is that wherever it is a question of price formation, there will be a mutual interaction of value and value. We must therefore disregard everything to do with the substances and materials themselves; we must look away from all this and begin by seeing how values are formed on the one side, and on the other. Then we shall be able to press forward to the problem of price.

Lecture 3

Economics and Egotism

DORNACH, JULY 26, 1922

In economic science, as I explained yesterday, one is essentially trying to take hold of something that is always fluctuating, namely, the circulation of values and the mutual interplay of fluctuating values in the forming of price. Bearing this in mind, our first need is to discover what is really the proper form of the science of economics. A thing that fluctuates cannot be taken hold of directly. There is no real sense in trying by direct observation, to take hold of something that is forever fluctuating. The only sensible procedure is to consider it in connection with what really lies beneath it.

Let us take an example from life. For certain purposes we use a thermometer. We use it to read various degrees of temperature, which we have grown accustomed, in a certain sense, to compare with one another. For instance, we estimate 20° of warmth in relation to 5°, and so on. We may also construct temperature curves. We plot the temperatures, for instance, during the winter, followed by the rising temperatures in summer. Our curve will then represent the fluctuating level of the thermometer. We do not come to the underlying reality, however, until we consider the various conditions that determine the lower temperature in the winter, the higher temperature in the summer months, the temperature in one district, the different temperature in another, and so forth. We have something real in hand, so to speak, only when we refer the varying levels of the mercury to that which underlies them. To record the readings of the thermometer is in itself a mere statistical procedure. In economics it is not much more than this when we merely study prices and values, and so forth. The procedure begins to have a real meaning only when we regard prices and values much as we regard the positions of the mercury—as indications, pointing to something else. Only then do we arrive at the realities of economic life. Now this consideration will lead us to the true and proper form that economic science must have.

By ancient usage, as you are probably aware, the sciences are classified as theoretical and practical. Ethics, for instance, is called a practical science; natural science a theoretical one. Natural science deals with what is; ethics with what ought to be. This distinction has been made since ancient times between the sciences of what is and the sciences of what should be. We mention this here only to help define the concept of economic science. We may well ask ourselves if economics is a science of what is, as Lujo Brentano, for instance, would assert. Or is it a practical science—a science of what ought to be? That is the question.

Now, if we wish to arrive at any knowledge in economics it is undoubtedly necessary to make observations. We have to make observations, just as we must observe the readings of the barometer and thermometer to ascertain the state of air and warmth. So far, economics is a theoretical science. At this point, nothing has yet been done. We achieve something only when we are really able to act under the influence of this theoretical knowledge.

Take a special case. Let us assume that by certain observations —which, like all observations, until they lead to action, will be of a theoretical nature—we ascertain that in a given place, in a given sphere, the price of a certain commodity falls considerably, so much so as to give rise to acute distress. In the first place, then, we observe— theoretically, as I have said, this actual fall in price. Here, so to speak, we are still only at the stage of reading the thermometer. Now what are we to do if the price of a commodity or product falls to an undesirable extent? We shall have to go into these matters more closely later on. For the moment I will simply indicate what should be done and by whom, in the case that the price of some commodity shows a considerable decrease. It will be a matter of finding guidelines or regulations that counteract the sinking prices. There may be many such measures, but one of them will be to do something to accelerate the circulation, the commerce or trade in the commodity in question. This will be one possible measure, though naturally it will not be enough by itself. For the moment, however, we shall not discuss whether it is a sufficient measure, or even the right measure to take. The point is that if prices fall in such a way, we must do something of a kind that can increase the turnover.

It is, in fact, similar to what happens when we observe the thermometer. If we feel cold in a room, we do not go to the thermometer and try by some mysterious method to lengthen out the column of mercury. We leave the thermometer alone and stoke the fire. We get at the problem from quite a different angle; and so it must be in economics too. When it comes to action, we must start from quite a different angle. Only then does it become practical. We must conclude, therefore, that the science of economics is both theoretical and practical. The point will be how to bring the practical and the theoretical together.

Here we have one aspect of the form of economic science. The other aspect is one to which I drew attention many years ago, though it was not understood then. It was in an essay I wrote at the beginning of the century, which at that time was entitled "Theosophy and the Social Question."† It would have had real significance only if it had been taken up by politicians, and if they had acted accordingly. But it was left altogether unnoticed; consequently, I did not complete it or publish any more of it. We can only hope that these things will be more and more understood, and I hope these lectures will contribute to a deeper understanding. To understand the present point, we must now insert a brief historical reflection.

Go back a little way in the history of humanity. As I pointed out in the first lecture, in former epochs, even as late as the fifteenth or sixteenth century, economic questions such as we have today did not exist at all. In Eastern antiquity economic life took its course instinctively, to a very large extent. Certain social conditions existed—caste-forming and class-forming conditions—and the relations between people that arose out of these conditions had the power to shape instincts for the way in which the individual must play a particular part in economic life. These things were very largely founded on the impulses of the religious life, which in those ancient times were still of such a kind as to aim simultaneously at the ordering of economic affairs. Study Eastern history and you will see there is nowhere a hard and fast dividing line between what was ordained for the religious life and what was ordained for the economic; the religious commandments very largely extend into the economic life. In those early times, the question of labor, or of the social circulation of labor-values, did not arise. Labor was performed, in a certain sense, instinctively. In pre-Roman times, whether one person was to do more or less never became a pressing question, not at any rate a pressing public question. Such exceptions as there may be are of no importance, compared to the general course of human evolution. Even in Plato we find a conception of the social life wherein the performance of labor is accepted as a complete matter of course. Only those aspects are considered that Plato beholds as wisdom-filled ethical and social impulses, excluding the performance of labor, which is taken for granted.

In the course of time, the situation gradually changed. As the immediately religious and ethical impulses became less effective in creating economic instincts, they became increasingly restricted to the moral life. These impulses became mere precepts about how people should feel for one another or relate themselves to extra-human powers. There arose more and more the feeling that, pictorially stated, might be expressed, "*Ex cathedra*, or from the pulpit, nothing whatever can be said about the way a person should work!" Only then did labor, as the incorporation of labor into the social life, become a question.

Now this incorporation of labor into the social life is historically impossible without the rise of all that is comprised in the term "law" or "rights." We see emerge at the same historical moment the assignment of value to labor in relation to the individual human being, and what we now call law. Go back into very ancient times of human history and you cannot properly speak of law or rights as we conceive them today. You can do so only from the moment when the law becomes distinct from the "Commandment." In very ancient times there is only one kind of command or commandment, which included at the same time all that concerns the life of rights. Subsequently, the "Commandment" was restricted more to the life of the soul, while law made itself felt with respect to the outer life. This again took place within a certain historic epoch, during which definite social relationships evolved. It would take us too far afield to describe all this in detail, but it is an interesting study—especially for the first centuries of the Middle Ages—to see how the relationships of law and rights on the one hand, and on the other, those of labor, became distinct from the religious organizations with which they had formerly been more or less closely merged. I mean, of course, religious organizations in the wider sense of the term.

Now this change involves an important consequence. You see, so long as religious impulses dominate the entire social life of human-kind, egotism does no harm. This is a most important point, notably for an understanding of the social and economic life. Human beings may ever be so egotistical, but if there is a religious organization (and these, it should be noted, were very strict in certain districts in Oriental antiquity) such that in spite of their egotism individuals are fruitfully placed in the social life, it will do no harm. Egotism does begin to play a part in the life of the people, however, the moment human rights and labor emancipate themselves from other social impulses or social currents. Hence, during the historical period when labor and rights are becoming emancipated, the spirit of human-ity strives unconsciously to come to grips with egotism, which now begins to make itself felt and must in some way be integrated with the social life. This striving culminates in nothing other than modern democracy—the sense for the equality of human beings—the feel-ing that each must have influence in determining legal rights and in determining the labor that one contributes.

Simultaneously with this culmination of the emancipated life of rights and human labor, another element arose—though it undoubt-ably existed in former epochs of human evolution—which had quite a different significance in those times because of the religious-social impulses. In European civilization, during the Middle Ages, this element existed only to a very limited degree, but it reached its zenith at the very time when rights and labor were emancipated most of all. I refer to the division of labor.

In former times the division of labor had no particular significance because it too was embraced in the religious impulses. Everyone, so to speak, had an assigned place. It was very different when the democratic striving united with the tendency toward the division of labor—a process which only began in the last few centuries and reached its climax in the nineteenth century. Then the division of labor gained very great significance.

The division of labor entails a certain economic consequence. (We shall yet, of course, learn to know its causes and the course of its development.) To begin with, if we think it abstractly to its conclusion, we must say that in the end it leads to this: none of us uses what we ourselves produce. Economically speaking, however, what does this mean? Let us consider an example.

Suppose there is a man who is a tailor. Given the division of labor, he must, of course, be making clothes for other people. But while he may intend to make clothes for others, he may also make his own clothes. He will then devote a certain portion of his labor to making his own clothes, and the remainder—by far the greater portion—to making clothes for other people. Superficially considered, one may think that it is the most natural thing in the world, even under the system of the division of labor, for a tailor to make his own clothes, and then go on working as a tailor for other people. But, economically, how does the matter stand? Through the very fact that there is division of labor, and that one does not make all one's own things—through the very fact that there is a division of labor and one person always works for another—the various products will have certain values, and consequently, prices. Now the division of labor extends, of course, into the actual circulation of the products. Let us assume, therefore, that by virtue of the division of labor, extending as it does into the circulation of the products, the tailor's products have a certain value. Will those he makes for himself have the same economic value? Or will they possibly be cheaper—or more expensive? This is the most important question. If he makes his own clothes for himself, one thing will certainly be eliminated. They will not enter into the general circulation of products. What he makes for himself, then, will not share in the lowering of the cost that takes place through the division of labor. It will, therefore, be more expensive. Though he pays nothing for it, it will be more expensive. On those products of his labor that he uses for himself, it is impossible for him to expend as little labor—compared to their value—as he expends on those that pass into general circulation.

This may require a closer consideration, I admit; nevertheless, it is so. What one produces for oneself does not enter into the general circulation, which is founded on the division of labor. Consequently, it is more expensive. Thinking the division of labor to its logical conclusion, we must conclude that a tailor who is obliged to work only for other people will tend to obtain for his products the prices that ought to be obtained. For himself, he will have to buy his clothes from another tailor, or rather, he will get them through the ordinary channels. He will buy them at the places where clothes are sold.

These things considered, you will realize that the division of labor tends towards this result that no one any longer works for oneself at all. All that is produced by an individual's labor is passed on to others; and what one requires oneself must come, in turn, from the community. Of course, you may object that if the tailor buys his suit from another tailor, it will cost him just as much as if he were to make it for himself; the other tailor will not produce it any more cheaply, nor more expensively. If this objection were true, we would not have division of labor—or at least not a complete division of labor. It would mean that the maximum concentration of work, because of the division of labor, could not be applied to this particular product of tailoring. In effect, once we have the division of labor, it must inevitably extend into the process of circulation. It is, in fact, impossible for the tailor to buy from another tailor; in reality he must buy from a merchant, and this will result in quite a different value. If he makes his own coat for himself, he will "buy" it from himself. If he actually buys it, he buys it from a merchant. That is the difference. If division of labor, in conjunction with the process of circulation, lowers the cost, his coat will, for that reason, cost him less from the merchant. He cannot make it as cheaply for himself.

To begin with, let us regard this as a line of thought that will lead us to the true form of economic science. The facts themselves will, of course, have to be considered again later.

Meanwhile, it is absolutely true, and indeed self evident, that the more the division of labor advances, the more it will come about that one always works for others—for the community in general—and never for oneself. In other words, with the rise of the modern division of labor, the economic life as such depends on egotism being extirpated, root and branch. I beg you to take this remark not in an ethical but in a purely economic sense. Economically speaking, egotism is impossible. I can no longer do anything for myself; the more the division of labor advances, the more must I do everything for others.

The summons to altruism has, in fact, come far more quickly through purely outward circumstances in the economic sphere than it has been answered on the ethical and religious side. This is illustrated by an easily accessible historical fact.

The word "egotism," you will find, is a relatively old one, though not perhaps with the negativity that we attach to it today. Its opposite, however—the word "altruism," "to think of another"—is scarcely a hundred years old. As a word, it was coined very late. We need not dwell exceedingly on this external fact, though a closer historical study would confirm the indication. We may truly say that human thought on ethics was far from having arrived at a full appreciation of altruism at a time when the division of labor had already brought about its appreciation in the economic life. Taking it, therefore, in its purely economic aspect, we see at once the further consequences of this demand for altruism. We must find our way into the process of modern economic life, wherein one does not have to provide for oneself, but only for others; and so each individual will, in fact, be provided for in the best possible way.

This point of view could easily be taken as idealism, but I ask you to observe once more that in this lecture I am speaking neither idealistically nor ethically, but from an economic point of view. What I have just said is intended in a purely economic sense. It is neither God, nor a moral law, nor an instinct that calls for altruism in modern economic life—altruism in work, altruism in the production of goods. It is the modern division of labor, a purely economic category, that requires it.

This is approximately what I desired to set forth in the essay I published long ago:† In recent times our economic life has begun to require more of us than we are ethically, religiously, capable of achieving. This is the underlying fact of many a conflict. Study the sociology of the present day and you will find that the social conflicts are largely because as economic systems expanded into a world economy it became more and more necessary to be altruistic, to organize the various social institutions altruistically; while, in their way of thinking, people had not yet been able to get beyond egotism and therefore kept on interfering in a clumsy, selfish way with the course of things.

We shall arrive at the full significance of this only if we observe not merely the plain and obvious fact, but the same fact in its more masked and hidden forms. Because of this discrepancy in the mentality of present-day humanity—the discrepancy between the demands of the economic life and of ethical and religious ability—the following state of affairs is largely predominant in practice. To a large extent, in present-day economic life, people are providing for themselves. That is to say, our economic life is actually in contradiction to what, by virtue of the division of labor, is its own fundamental demand. The few who provide for themselves on the model of our tailor do not so much matter. A tailor who manufactures his own clothes is obviously one who mixes into the division of labor something that does not properly belong to it. This is open and unmasked. The same thing is present in a hidden form in modern economic life where, though people by no means make products for themselves, people have little or nothing to do with the value or price of the products of their labor. Quite apart from the whole economic process in which these products are contained, people simply have to contribute, as a value to the economic life, the labor of their hands. Basically, all wage earners in the usual sense provide for themselves. They give only so much as they want to earn. In fact, they cannot at all give as much to the social organism as they could give, for they want to give as only much as they want to earn. In effect, to provide for oneself is to work for one's earnings, to work "for a living." To work for others is to work out of a sense of social necessity.

To the extent that the demand which the division of labor involves has been fulfilled in our time, altruism is actually present—namely, to work for others. But to the extent that the demand is unfulfilled, the old egotism persists. Egotism has its roots in the fact that people are still obliged to provide for themselves. That is economic egotism. In the case of the ordinary wage earner we generally fail to notice this fact because we do not think about what values are really being exchanged for in this case. The things that the ordinary wage earner manufactures have, after all, nothing to do with the payment for their work—absolutely nothing to do with it. The payment—the value that is assigned to their work—proceeds from altogether different factors. They, therefore, work for their earnings, work "for a living." They work to provide for themselves. It is hidden, it is masked, but it is so.

One of the first and most essential economic questions, therefore, comes before us. How are we to eliminate from the economic process this principle of working for a living? Those who to this day are still mere wage earners—earners of a living for themselves—how are they to be placed in the whole economic process, no longer as such earners but as people who work out of social necessity? Must this really be done? Assuredly it must. If this is not done, we shall never obtain true prices but always false ones. We must seek to obtain prices and values that depend not on the human beings but on the economic process itself—prices that arise in the process of fluctuation of values. The cardinal question is the question of price.

We must observe prices as we observe the degrees of the thermometer. Then we can come to the underlying conditions. Now to observe a thermometer we need some kind of zero-point, from which we go upward and downward. For prices, a kind of zero level does in fact arise in a perfectly natural way.

It arises in this way. Here, we have nature on the one side [see diagram, page 21]. It is transformed by human labor, and thus we get the transformed products of nature. This is one point at which values are created, *Value 1*. On the other side, we have labor itself.

It, in turn, is modified by the spirit, and from here arises the other kind of value, *Value 2*. As I said on a previous occasion, price originates through the interaction of *Value 1* and *Value 2*. We will progress even farther in grasping these economic views.

Now these values on either hand—*Value 1* and *Value 2*—relate to one another as polarities. And we may put it as follows. If people are working in this sphere, for example [diagram, p. 21, right side], or mainly so—in an absolute sense it is of course impossible, but I mean mainly in this sphere—if in the main their work is of the type that is organized by Spirit/mind, then it will be to their interest that the products of nature should decrease in value. If, on the other hand, people are working directly on nature, it will be to their interest that the other kind of products should decrease in value. This "interest" becomes an effective process, for if it were not so, the farmers would have very different prices, and vice versa; the actual prices on both sides are, of course, very "hidden." When this process happens, we may be able to observe a kind of "mean price" midway between the two poles where we have two persons (there must always be two, for any economic dealings) with little interest either in nature or Spirit [applied capital p. 60].

Where is this in practice? We have the case in practice if we observe a wholesaler, a pure trader, buying from and selling to another wholesaler. Here, prices will tend towards a mean. If under normal conditions (we shall yet have to explain this word "normal") a wholesaler trading in boots and shoes buys from a wholesaler trading in clothes, and vice versa, the prices that emerge will tend to assume the mean position. To find the mean price level, we must not refer to the interests of those producers who are on the side of nature, nor of those who are on the side of Spirit/mind [in the diagram, p. 21]. We must go to where wholesalers trade with wholesalers, buying and selling. Here it is that the mean price will tend to arise. Whether there be one wholesaler more or not is immaterial.

This argument does not contradict what we have said before. After all, look at the typical modern capitalists. Are they not, all of them, traders? Economically speaking, industrialists are, after all, traders. Incidentally they are producers of particular goods, but economically they are traders. Commerce has developed very largely on the side of production. In all essentials, the industrial capitalist is a trader. This is important. In actual fact, modern conditions amount to this. All that arises here in the middle [where "price" is written, diagram, p. 21] rays out to the one side and to the other. On the one side, you will soon recognize it when you study the typical business undertaking, and we shall see how it appears on the other side in the course of the next few days.

Lecture 4

Labor and Value

DORNACH, JULY 27, 1922

Yesterday I chose from the economic life a somewhat extreme example as an illustration. It appears that this illustration has caused some of you a good deal of "brain wracking." I refer to the example of the tailor, who, as I said, works less cheaply if he makes his own suit of clothes for himself than he would if, while making clothes for other people, he bought his own from a merchant in the ordinary way like the rest of us. Now it is only too easy to miss the point of such a crude example. For it is quite natural to work it out in this way. Merchants, in order to make some profit, will buy clothes from the tailor more cheaply than they will sell them. Hence, it goes without saying that if the tailor buys a suit of clothes, he will pay more for it than he would if he made it for himself. He will, in fact, have to pay the merchant's profit in addition. This objection is so obvious that it is bound to occur; nevertheless, I purposely chose this rather crude example because I wished to illustrate how necessary it is, for present-day economic life, to think not in terms of household economics, but in terms of the economic life as a whole. We must, in fact, reckon with all that arises from the division of labor.

The important thing is not to consider how the tailor will stand directly after he has finished making the suit of clothes. It is true enough that if he proceeds to sell the suit to a merchant, and then buys another suit for himself, he will have sustained a loss. That is not the point, however; the point is, how will he stand when he makes up his accounts after a certain lapse of time? Will he be in a better position if he made his own suit for himself, or will he be in a better position if he refrained from doing so?

In effect when the division of labor works, it makes products cheaper in the right way; they become cheaper, through the division of labor, precisely in the whole system of economic relationships. If we work against the division of labor, we force down the price of one particular class of products; but this forcing down of prices will itself go against the main stream of the economic process. In other words, though the tailor may save something on that particular suit, he will—by a very small figure to begin with—force down the price of clothes. If many tailors do the same, the effect will be multiplied; clothes will become cheaper and the result will be that the tailor will have to supply other suits at a lower price. It will only be a question of time. After a certain time, he will observe in his balance sheet how much less income he has derived from the other suits than he would have derived if he had not thus forced the prices down.

We must not confuse the issue by thinking in the narrow spirit of household economics. I did not mean that the tailor has not a perfect right to make his own clothes for himself or that he might not quite properly have a taste for doing so, only that he must not imagine that it will save him anything in the long run—on the contrary, it will be more expensive. Taking his total balance after a certain lapse of time, he will find that it is more expensive. I admit that in this crude example the effect will be comparatively slight, for the amount by which the price is forced down will become evident only after a considerable lapse of time. The tailor will have to make a large number of other suits before the very small fraction by which they are cheapened becomes effective. Nevertheless, sooner or later it will appear in his general balance sheet.

The economic process does indeed consist in an infinite number of interdependent factors. The single phenomenon is the outcome of an untold number of factors, all of which work into one another. To understand it, it simply will not do to think so very near at hand, if I may put it so. All your thinking on economics will lead to disaster if you let your thoughts be guided only by what lies in the immediate neighborhood of the individuals who are engaged in it. You will never come to grips with the economic process in this way. You must learn to envision the social organization in its totality. If you do so, you will also feel impelled to illustrate the facts by such extreme examples, where the effect, though it does not become apparent in a day, may make itself felt very strongly, say, in a decade.

We must indeed take our start from such half-absurd examples, to detach our thinking from familiar habits and lead it into a mode that comprehends wide issues and, losing its hard and fast contours in the process, gains the power to grasp what is continuously fluctuating. What lies close to us we can grasp in sharp outline, but our task is to achieve a real insight, an insight that gives us always mobile ideas, which never correspond to those we can gather in our immediate neighborhood.

Today I especially want to mention this, for, while we take our start from comparatively simple matters, we shall have to realize nevertheless how the economic process is built up little by little of the most manifold factors. We must come nearer and nearer to the possibility of grasping the problem of price. With this end in view, we shall today once more consider the economic process as such from a particular aspect.

Let us begin today with nature. In the first place, human labor must set to work on nature, transforming nature's products. A product of nature thus receives the stamp of human labor; as transformed by human labor, it receives an economic value. In economics we are not dealing with the substance; the substance, as such, has no economic value. Coal, as substance, lying in mines under the earth, has no economic value; nor would it gain an economic value if it walked of its own accord from the mine into the house of the person who uses it for heating. What turns the substance into a value is the labor that has been impressed upon it; that is to say, all that had to be done to bring it to the light of day, to prepare the mines themselves, to transport the coal, and so forth. It is only the human labor impressed upon the substance of the coal that gives it economic value, and this is all that we must concern ourselves with in economics.

You cannot grasp any phenomenon of economic life if you do not start from such ideas as these. In the application of human labor to nature, we now come, with the further evolution of the economic life, to the division of labor. The division of labor arises whenever people work together in any task that has significance for economic life.

Let us take a perfectly simple example. Suppose that in a certain district a number of men are working, and suppose that it is a very primitive time. From the various places where they live, the workers have to walk to the common scene of their labor—to a place where some particular product is extracted from nature. The workers have no other means of arriving at the place where they do this work. Then someone conceives the idea of making a cart, and using horses to pull it. Henceforth, what formerly had to be done by each one alone will now be done by each individual in conjunction with the man who provides the cart. A certain part of the work is now divided; what is done, which is labor in the economic sense, is now divided. It will, of course, happen in this way, that everyone who makes use of the cart will have to pay a certain quota to the enterprising individual who provided it.

The inventor of the cart, however, thereby enters the category of the capitalist. For him, the cart is now genuine capital. Wherever you look, you will always see that this is so. The point of origin of capital always lies in the division, the qualitative division, of labor. How was the cart invented? It was invented by the mind or Spirit. Every such process, indeed, consists in the application of Spirit to labor. In one respect or another, human labor is permeated by Spirit. It is *labor-permeated-by-Spirit* that arises in the process of the division of labor. Where we see capital arise in the course of the division of labor, we have, in the first place, nothing other than labor penetrated by Spirit. The first phase of capital always consists in this. Where human labor hitherto was determined only by nature, it is now organized, divided, and so forth, by Spirit.

It is indeed necessary to see capital and its formation very clearly from this point of view. Only from this point of view can we understand the function of capital in the economic process. The forming of capital is always a concomitant of the division—that is to say, the qualitative, organic division—of labor.

In this process, however, something of the direct, immediate connection that the human being has with nature when working upon the earth is always loosened. You see, so long as the economic life consists merely in the elaboration of nature, all that we deal with are the products of nature, which, being transformed by human labor, acquire an economic value. The moment the human Spirit organizes labor, however—organizes, that is to say, labor as such (for, after all, to the man who creates capital with his cart, it will matter nothing to what end or for what purpose he transports the workers from one place to another)—an emancipation from nature begins to take place.

Here, [referring to diagram p. 21, left] if I may put it so, we still see nature shining through human labor at all points. Although the value is constituted not by the coal as a substance but by the human labor that is stamped upon it, nevertheless the nature-product still shines through the human labor. This is one side from which economic values originate.

The other side is this. Whatever in human labor is organized by Spirit emancipates itself from nature, is lifted away from nature, until at length we have the capitalist, to whom the relation of the labor to nature that is being organized may be a matter of complete indifference. This, after all, may happen in a very simple way. Suppose a man has hitherto been driving people from many places to, say, some fields to do agricultural work. He may suddenly prefer to take his cart away and drive people to a quite different place and a quite other kind of work. Wherever Spirit is applied, you will inevitably find the organized division of human labor becoming emancipated from its foundation in nature. Here, then, you have the emancipation of capital from the nature-foundation of economic life.

From various points of view the idea has been expressed in economics that capital is stored labor power. But this is no more than a definition that will fit the facts only at a certain stage, because things are always fluctuating. So long as the organization due to Spirit is narrowly bound to a certain kind of labor, nature will still shine through. The moment we emancipate ourselves, thinking only of how to make fruitful what we gain by application of Spirit—the moment we do this, the more we shall observe the labor becoming indistinct within the total mass of capital. In its particular and specific character, the labor vanishes.

Suppose you have been amassing capital for a considerable time and this capital continues to work in the economic process. The man who to begin with had only a single cart can extend his economic activity by acquiring a second cart, and so on. His capital is working in the economic process; but there is really nothing left in it of the nature of labor. Look at a miner, for example, in him you still see very much of the nature of labor. In capital, however, you see less and less of it. We may go still further. Suppose the man with the carts hands the whole business over to another man. The transfer will very likely mean that the newcomer will be concerned only with fructifying what has thus been brought about by Spirit. The nature of the labor that is thus organized will be a matter of indifference to him. He is concerned only with organizing, no matter what kind of labor.

In other words, we have here a real process of abstraction. Precisely the same thing that we do inwardly in our logical thinking, in the process of abstraction, is here accomplished outwardly. The specific quality disappears. The specific qualities, both of the substance of nature and of the different kinds of labor, gradually disappear in the masses of capital. As you will presently see, if we follow the economic process still further, nothing whatsoever is left of the human labor that was originally organized. The further development of the economic process will be somewhat as follows. The man who built the cart did at least stamp his own Spirit upon the whole invention; but now he earns more values than he can manage by himself. Are these values to remain unused in the whole economic life? Of course not. Another man must come along, able to manage them by means of a different kind of Spirit. He will then turn the values to good account—he will make them valuable—in quite a different way.

After a time, for instance, the values created by the inventor of the cart—the fructification which has thus resulted—may pass over to a blacksmith. The blacksmith has the Spirit, the intelligence, to erect a workshop; but with his Spirit alone he can do nothing. The other man has already created certain economic values; these he must now transfer to his fellow man, the blacksmith. Here you have, indeed, in the outer world of reality, the most complete imaginable process of abstraction. It is essential, moreover, if the process is to go on at all (for how else could the cartwright transmit his values to the black-smith?)—it is essential for something to be there that is related as an abstract element to all the specific elements that are contained in the economic process. What is this something? It is, of course, in the first place, money. Money is nothing but the externally expressed value that is gained in the economic process through the division of labor and transmitted from one person to another.

Thus, we see that capitalism arises in the process of the division of labor; and in the process of capitalism (at a relatively early stage), the financial system, money, economics [*die Geldwirtschaft*]. In relation to all the particular economic processes, money is completely abstract. If you have five francs in your pocket, you can buy a supper, just as well as an article of clothing. Regarding the money itself, it is irrelevant what you acquire with it, or what it is exchanged for in the economic process. Money is the thing absolutely indifferent to the single factors in the economic life, in so far as they are still influenced by nature. For this very reason money becomes the means of expression, the instrument, the medium for Spirit to enter into the economic organism in the division of labor. Without money being created, it is absolutely impossible for Spirit to enter in and play its part in the economic organism, which depends on the division of labor. We may say then that what in a primitive economic condition is originally all together—what one does in egotism for oneself—is now divided up among the whole community. Such is the division of labor. With capital, the single parts are gathered up again into a total, collected process. The forming of capital is a synthesis. Those who first emerge as creators of capital, being able to change it into money capital (since money must necessarily appear at this stage), become lenders to others, who possess nothing but their Spirit. The latter now receive the money, which is the true and proper representative of economic values created by Spirit.

We must really consider this thoroughly from the point of view of economics. However evil money may be from a religious or ethical point of view, in the economic sense money is Spirit at work in the economic organism. It is so indeed. Once more then, money must be created in the economic process if Spirit is to progress at all from the initial point where it applies itself merely to nature. Spirit would remain in an altogether primitive condition if it could do no more than this. To pour again into the economic process what has been achieved by the application of Spirit, Spirit must be realized in the form of money. Money is the realization of Spirit. But the concrete quality comes back into it again. In the first place, money is an abstract thing, for, as we said before, to money it is a matter of indifference whether for the five francs in my pocket I buy an article of clothing or get my hair cut (several times, if you like). The moment money returns to the individual human being, that is, to the individual human Spirit, it becomes economically active once more as a concrete and specific fact. The Spirit is economically active in the money.

Now at this point a very special relationship arises. The one who acquired the money to begin with becomes the lender, the creditor. The other, who receives the money—the individual, the man, we will suppose, who has only Spirit—becomes the debtor. You have here a relationship between two human beings. The same relationship will also come about if the lenders are a whole number of people who hand over their extra capital to the man, so that a higher synthesis is brought about by his intelligence (Spirit). He is then the debtor, and works on a foundation entirely emancipated from the basis of nature. What he actually receives from the original capitalists themselves is a nonentity in his hands. He will have to give it back again after a time—it does not really belong to him. In effect, it is only from one side that he works economically as a debtor. From the other side he is economically responsible as a creative individual. Truth to tell, this is perhaps one of the healthiest relationships—and this point is especially important in relation to the social question—for the one who works out of the sphere of human intelligence or Spirit: being enabled to work for the general community through the giving of the necessary money by the general community. (So far as he is concerned, it is the community.) How property, possession, and the like enter into the matter is a question we shall have to consider another time; our present object is only to trace the economic process as such. Here it is a matter of indifference whether or not you conceive of the lender as the real owner, and whether or not you conceive of the debtor as jurisprudence does. For the moment we are concerned only with this question: How does the economic process take its course?

Here, then, we have a part of the economic process where the work is founded purely on what has already been spiritually-culturally achieved and acquired. That is to say, the very foundation of the work is already emancipated from the basis of nature. True, it originated in the organization of labor; but we are now at the second stage, and if at this second stage—where worker out of the Spirit works as a debtor—you would still describe the borrowed capital that he receives as "crystallized labor" or the like, you would be talking—economically—sheer nonsense. It is immaterial to the economic process how the capital that he owes originated. The important thing now is the Spirit, the intelligence, of the one who receives the money. Will this person be able to lead it over into fruitful economic processes? The original labor through which the capital arose no longer has an economic value. The Spirit that is applied in turning the money to good account, giving it value—this alone will have economic value at this stage. Whatever the amount of labor you conceive as being stored up in the capital, if a fool gets hold of it and "scatters it all to the winds," it is an altogether different thing than if a clever person gets hold of it and starts a fruitful economic process with it. At this second stage, therefore, where we have to do with lender and debtor, we are dealing with capital from which the labor has already disappeared. What then is the economic significance of this "capital from which the labor has disappeared?" It is twofold. In the first place it has been possible to raise and collect the capital for lending purposes, and in the second place the capital thus raised can be given value by spiritual-cultural means. Therein lies its true economic significance.

The reality that emerges from the process is the relation between the debtor and the creditors. In the economic process to which the debtor now gives rise, the debtor stands in the middle. On the one hand we have the person as a debtor; on the other hand, we have what proceeds from this person as a spiritually-cultural productive individual. What on the one hand is "lent" or "invested" capital—through the very fact that it becomes "owed" or " borrowed" capital—passes over into the second stage of the economic process.

This is simply the circulation of capital—nothing else. This circulation is part and parcel of a social-organic activity, just as you have the blood in a human or animal organic activity when it flows through the head and is used for what the head produces. I may put it in this way. What is it that is brought about through this relationship of lenders and debtors? It is very similar to the "difference of level" we meet with in physics. If you have water up here, it will flow down there, simply through the difference of level. In like manner, there is a social difference of level between the first position of the capital—the position of the lender who does not know what to do with it—and the second position of the debtor who can make good use of it. This difference works as a difference of level.

But you must pause a moment to consider the active driving force in this difference of level. The active principle is not simply the Spirit, which is at work in the whole process. It is the diversity of human talents and dispositions. That is the determining factor in the difference of level. If a lazy-minded person possesses capital, then, in a healthy economic organization, that person will be above, while the clever person will be below. The result is a "drop," or difference of level, and the capital flows downward to the clever person. It is through the difference of level between the talents of individuals that capital is brought into flow. It is not even the positive activity of individuals; it is simply the human qualities of those who are united together in the social organism that produce this "difference of level" and, in so doing, carry forward the economic process.

Look at this economic process quite concretely and you will conclude that we start from nature, which has as yet no value. Clearly it has no value, for the sparrow, satisfying its needs from nature, pays nothing for it. This is evident from the contrast of sparrow economy and human economy. Economic value begins when human labor unites itself with nature. Next, the economic process is continued through the division, the differentiation of labor. Let us take it to begin with in an absolutely general way. We have human labor applied to nature. I will put it down as follows (though the full economic meaning of this will emerge only in the further course of these lectures). Let us designate what arises at this stage by *N1*—"nature taken hold of by human labor." What is it, economically speaking? It is, as we have already seen, a value. I will call it "nature taken hold of by human labor, and thus made into a value"—$N1^v$. That is one side.

Now comes the division of labor. What does it signify? It signifies a dividing up of those processes that were performed in the first place as single completed labor processes applied to nature, that which now live a separate life. If I make a whole stove, I shall be performing many and varied labor processes; if I now introduce the division of labor, I peel and part the labor processes one from another. I divide. If $N1^v$ is "nature-product transformed by labor and made into a value," then what arises by the division of labor (of course, we might denote it in many different ways) will be $N1^{v1}$, $N1^{v2}$, and so on.

Now if all this is a real process, how shall we express what happens when the division of labor makes its appearance? Clearly, we should express it by a division, by a fraction. When the value that I have here written down passes over into the division of labor, the thing that is there in the reality must in some way be divided. By what is it divided? What is the dividing principle? What is it that divides up the process? We must now look to the other side. In pure mathematics we take only what is given as number; but when we are to seek such arithmetical processes in the world of reality itself, we must look for the real divisor, the real dividing principle. Now, as you will remember, we found, on the other side of the picture, "labor taken hold of by the Spirit." Over against this ($N1^v$) we may, therefore, place labor taken hold of by the Spirit. This becomes a value on the other side: Ls^v. But we have today reached a certain conclusion concerning this "labor taken hold of by the Spirit." We have seen what must arise if it is to work on beyond a certain point in the economic process and if this ($N1^v$) is divided and is to work on in the economic process—we have seen what enters the process for this Ls^v (labor organized by the Spirit and made into a value). It is money.

Money appears at this point not in its fully abstract nature; it is abstract, to begin with, if I may put it so (abstract, as the substance to which Spirit first applies itself), but it grows highly individualized, highly specific, when Spirit takes hold of it and uses it for this or that purpose. In doing so, it is Spirit as such that determines the value of the money. Here, you see, money begins to gain a concrete and specific value. Whether a person is a fool and throws the money away on something that turns out to be unfruitful, or whether the person applies it in a useful way—this now emerges as a very real value in the economic process. For your denominator, therefore, you will here get something that has to do with money; while your numerator, I need hardly say, will have to do with the fact that you have before you that into which the substance of nature has been transformed. What is a substance of nature, transformed by labor and present in the economic process? It is a commodity. This, then, is the numerator; and for the denominator, corresponding to "labor organized by Spirit," you will have money.

$$\frac{N1^v}{Ls^v} = \frac{Commodity}{Money}$$

New values come to light: the commodity value and the money value. In the economic process founded on the division of labor, we must recognize this truth. The quotient of the total commodities present in the economic organism and the money present in the economic organism (taking as "money" not what is counted in the registers, but what is actually taken hold of by Spirit in human beings) will represent a real interaction. Money is the divisor. This interaction, which cannot be represented by a subtraction but only by a division, represents the real health of the economic process. To understand of what this health consists, we must learn to understand what is at work in the numerator here and in the denominator. We must understand more and more wherein the essential nature of a commodity on the one hand, and of the medium of circulation, the money, on the other hand, consists. The most essential economic question cannot be solved at all unless we proceed in this exact way. We must not forget that whatever appears in the economic life will always be fluctuating. The moment the commodity is taken from one place to another, the numerator here will change. I can do nothing other than point out, at every turn, how fluctuating all things are in the economic process.

There is a great difference between the wallet with five francs that I have in my pocket and the wallet with five francs another person has. It is not a matter of indifference whether the five francs are in the one pocket or the other. This too must be taken as belonging to the real economic process. You will get, otherwise, only a few rigid, abstract, arbitrary concepts of price, value, commodity, production, consumption, and so on; you will get nothing to lead you to a true understanding of the economic process.

This is what is infinitely sad in the present day. For many centuries humankind has grown accustomed to sharply outlined concepts, but such are inapplicable to a living process. Today we are called upon by the facts of life to welcome movement into our concepts, so as to penetrate the economic processes with conscious understanding—but we cannot do so. This is what we must attain: mobility of thinking, so as to be able to think a process through to its end quite inwardly. True, in ordinary science we also contemplate processes, we "think them through," if you will; but we always see them from outside, and that is of no avail in economics. To contemplate the economic process as the chemist contemplates chemical processes, from outside, you would have to go far up above the earth in a balloon. The economic processes are distinguished by the fact that we ourselves are in them; therefore we must see them from within. We must feel ourselves *within* the economic processes, just like a being that is inside a chemist's retort where something is being concocted with a great generation of heat. The being in the retort, that I am now comparing with ourselves, cannot of course be the chemist. The being would have to be taking part in the heat, boiling with it, as it were. The chemist cannot do this; to the chemist the whole thing is external. In natural science, we stand outside the process. The chemist could not take part in it, with the temperature in the retort far above boiling point.

The economic process is different, however; we ourselves partake in it inwardly at every point. Therefore, we must understand it inwardly as well. A mathematician may well object that we have written something like a formula; but mathematicians are not used to building up mathematical formulas in this way. This is true enough; usually we build up a mathematical formula only as a result of contemplating natural processes from without. We must evolve a faculty of insight to get a numerator and denominator in this way, or to understand that it must be something like a division—that it cannot be a subtraction in this case. We must try to think our way into the economic process. For this very reason I chose that crude example yesterday. I did not introduce to you a tailor and a merchant from outside, as a scientist would. What is essential could not have been found in that way. With our thinking accustomed to seeing things only as the natural scientist does from outside, we feel it is strange to get inside a process. Nevertheless, we must conceive inwardly the countless processes that intervene between the tailor and the effects that follow in the economic process.

I would not be true to the task you have set me if I described these things in any other manner. I am well aware that this makes it somewhat difficult from the outset.

Lecture 5

Production and Consumption

DORNACH, JULY 28, 1922

WE ARE NOW going to pursue a little further the sequence of events within the economic process that we considered yesterday. The economic process, as we have seen, is set in motion by human labor working upon nature, so that from the mere raw natural product—which has as yet no value in the economic process—we get the product of nature transformed by human labor. At the next stage, labor is, as it were, caught up by capital, which divides and organizes it until it eventually disappears in the capital. For the further advance of the economic process, therefore, capital itself must labor. This labor of capital is not labor in the old sense; rather the capital is taken up by a purely "spiritual" activity. The economic process now goes forward by the Spirit "making good" the capital, giving it additional value, as I described in the last lecture.

We must try to understand more and more the formula that was indicated yesterday. To this end, let me now describe diagrammatically—symbolically, as it were—what I explained yesterday. We may say that nature goes under in human labor [see diagram, opposite]. We have, therefore, this stream from nature into labor. Nature disappears in labor. Labor continues to evolve. Then the values that evolved stream onward, as it were, until labor vanishes in capital. You can easily continue this process, which I have traced to this point, for yourselves. The cycle must necessarily be completed in some way. The capital cannot merely be blocked at this point, for otherwise

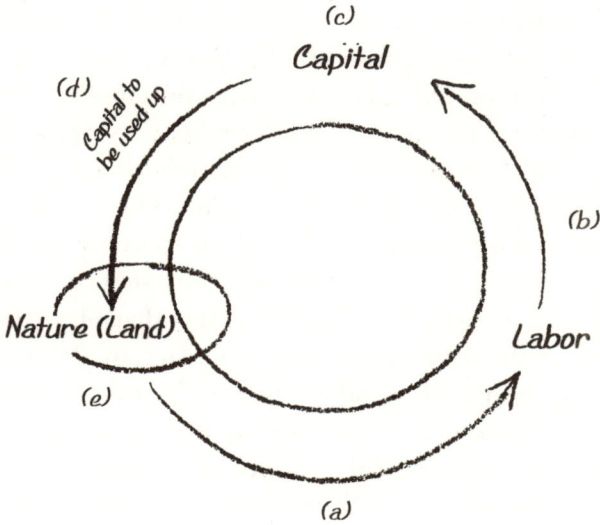

we should be dealing not with an organic process but with one that would die and end in capital. The capital must disappear once more into nature. You must first call to your aid another idea, however, if you wish to understand this rightly.

Consider for a moment the economic process as we have traced it up to the present. First the elaboration of nature by human labor, then the organizing of labor by Spirit, and with it the rise of capital, for capital is a concomitant of the organizing of labor by the Spirit. Then the existence of capital as such. Capital passes over from the Spirit, which organized the labor. The capital becomes independent. The labor disappears in its turn, and now the Spirit works in the capital as inventive Spirit in connection with the whole social life. The technical aspect of invention need not concern us here; this will come into question only at a later stage.

If you now review all that I have described, you will see that I have presented everything from one side only. This was inevitable because, apart from a few occasional hints, I have been speaking only of production. I have indeed included, now and then, ideas that had to do with consumption, especially when we were trying to approach the question of price. Apart from that, you will have found practically nothing about consumption in our discussions thus far. I have been speaking of production. Yet, the economic process does not consist merely of production—it consists also of consumption.

A simple reflection will show you that consumption is exactly the opposite pole to production. We have been trying to find, on one hand, the values that arise in the economic process within the sphere of production. Consumption, on the other hand, consists in a continual elimination of these values. In consumption they are constantly being used up; that is to say, consumption consists in a constant devaluation of the values. It is this that plays the other important part in the economic process—this constant devaluation of values. It is just through this, indeed, that we have a certain right to call the economic process an organic one, an organic process in which Spirit then intervenes. It is of the essence of a living organism that something is continually being formed and again unformed. In any organism there must be a continual production and consumption, and this must be so in the economic organism too. There must be a constant producing and a using-up of what is produced.

At this point we begin to see in a different light, and from a different point of view, the value-creating forces that we have been considering. Before this point, we have shown only how values arise as the process of production takes its course. At this point, every time a value approaches its moment of devaluation, the whole movement that we have been witnessing thus far will change. So far, we have been observing a progressive, forward movement. Values thus arise through the application of labor to nature; values arise through the application of the Spirit to labor; and values arise through the application of the Spirit to capital. All of this is a forward movement.

In fact, we have been observing the value-creating movement in the economic process. As the *de*valuing factor of consumption enters into the process at every point, there will be something else as well. There will be a development of values that arises between production and consumption themselves. When a value enters the process of consumption, however, it no longer moves forward. It does not attain a higher degree of value, it no longer moves; for something now stands over against it. This is consumption—with its development of need. Here the value enters into a very different sphere from the one we have so far been studying. We have been considering the value in its progressive, forward movement [in the diagram, p. 55]. Now we must imagine its moving up to a certain point and being stopped there. Every time a value is stopped, there arises not a further value-creating movement, but a value-creating tension.

This is the second element in the economic process. In the economic process we have not only value-creating movements but also value-creating tensions. We can observe such value-creating tensions most conspicuously and simply where a consumer stands face-to-face with a producer or merchant, and in the very next moment the creation of value comes to an end, passing over into devaluation. Here there arises a tension—a tension that is maintained in equilibrium by the human need on the other side. Here the value-creating process is stopped. Human need or consumption confronts it, and there arises the tension between production and consumption.

This tension is also most decidedly a value-creating factor—albeit one that is comparable to a force that is restrained, held in equilibrium, rather than to a force that is working itself out. There is here a true analogy with the contrast in physics between kinetic and potential energies—between kinetic energies and those energies of position where an equilibrium is brought about. If you do not take into account these energies of tension, these potential energies, in the economic process, you will be driven to the strangest misconceptions. Developing the ideas indicated here, one gains an intelligent conception of every economic relationship; otherwise, one is led into the greatest confusion. If, for example, you limit yourself to considering the movements of economic energies, you will never understand why the diamond in the king of England's crown has such an immense value. Here you are at once obliged to have recourse to the idea of economic tension-value. Many economists take into account the rarity of particular products of nature; but we can never understand rarity as a value-creating factor if we regard the movement in the economic process as the only creator of values. We must also learn to understand how there arises here and there—most of all through consumption, but through other relationships as well—what I would call the creation of value by tensions, situations, equilibria.

You see, then, that devaluation can also take place in the economic process, which as I said, you can therefore regard as an organic process—an organic process in which Spirit constantly intervenes. There must be—or rather, there is—constant devaluation. As the values proceed on their way from nature through labor to capital, they will be accompanied by a continual process of devaluation.

What would happen if this corresponding devaluation could not take place? You can see this from the diagram. To make it clear, let us consider the question of credit. To place capital into the service of the Spirit in the sense that I explained yesterday, the man who produces by means of Spirit becomes a debtor. It is only through his having credit that he becomes, or can become, a debtor. At this point in our diagram credit steps in—what may be properly called "personal credit." A man has credit. The credit can be expressed in numbers. The capital that many others advance to him is, so to speak, his personal credit. As you know, this personal credit has a certain consequence, at least if we consider it within our present economic conditions. Its economic effect is connected with the rate of interest.

Assume that the rate of interest is low. If by using Spirit to create in the economic process, I become a debtor—that is to say, if I ask for credit—I shall have to pay only a small sum for it. Having less interest to pay, I can produce my goods more cheaply. I shall thus have a cheapening effect on the economic process. We may say, therefore, that personal credit cheapens production when the rate of interest falls. So long as the capital continues to be turned to good account or made valuable by the Spirit in the economic process, it is always so. When the rate of interest goes down, those who require credit have more freedom of movement. They can play their part far more intensively in the economic process—more intensively, that is to say, for their fellow human beings. If they lower the cost of their commodities they are playing a fruitful part in the process—at least from the point of view of the consumer.

Let us now take the other side. Assume that credit is given on land— "real credit." When credit is given on land, the situation is essentially different. Assume that the rate of interest is 5%. A person borrowing capital on the security of land must pay 5%. Capitalizing this, you will get the capital corresponding to the particular piece of land—that is to say, you will get the amount which would have to be paid to buy the piece of land outright. Assume now that the rate of interest falls to 4%. More capital can then be "credited into" the land—at least this is what actually happens. We then see everywhere, as a result of a falling rate of interest, land becoming not cheaper but more expensive. When the standard rate of interest goes down, land does not become cheaper but more expensive. "Real credit" makes things more expensive, while "personal credit" makes things cheaper. Real credit makes land more expensive, while personal credit makes commodities cheaper. This is very important in the economic process. It means that when capital returns to nature and simply unites with nature in the form of real credit (in other words, when there is a union of capital with land, that is to say, with nature), then the economic process will tend more and more in the direction of dearness.

The only sensible thing, therefore, will be for the capital at this point [see diagram: c] not to preserve itself in nature, but rather to vanish into nature. How then can capital vanish into nature? So long as it is at all possible to unite capital with nature—that is to say, so long as you can make nature in its original unelaborated condition more and more expensive through the accumulation of capital—so long as this is possible, capital cannot vanish into nature; on the contrary, it penetrates into nature and maintains itself there. In all countries where the law of mortgage makes it possible for capital to unite with nature, therefore, we shall find a congestion of capital in nature, that is, in the land. Instead of the capital being expended at this point [see diagram: d]—instead of its disappearing at this point, instead of a value-creating tension arising—there is a further value-creating movement, which is harmful to the economic process. There is only one way of preventing this. In a healthy economic process we must not and cannot give "real credit"—credit based on the security of land—even to a person working on the land. Only personal credit should be given—that is to say, credit that will enable the person to turn the capital to good account through the land. If we simply unite the land with the capital, the capital will become congested the moment it arrives again at nature. If, on the other hand, we unite the capital with the capacities of Spirit of those who administer the land and further the economic process by working upon it, then, you see, the capital vanishes. As it reaches nature at this point, it will not become congested; it will not be preserved, but will go right on through nature, back again into labor, and will begin the cycle once more. It is one of the worst possible congestions in the economic process when capital is simply united with nature. Tracing the economic process hypothetically from its initial stages, after labor and capital have evolved from the starting-point of nature, when the capital is enabled to take hold of nature instead of losing itself in nature, we see that economic congestion occurs.

At this point you may, of course, make a serious objection. In the course of this movement, you may say, the capital has come into being. Suppose it now arrives again at nature and there is too much of it. (It would be different if we were able to lead it over into labor—if we were able, let us say, to invent new methods so as to further the processing of raw materials. For in such a case we would be uniting not nature but labor with the capital. If we arrive at this point with our capital and process the raw materials in a more economical way, or open out new sources or the like, then we are leading the capital directly over into labor). Suppose, however, there is too much capital. The numerous owners of capital will become painfully aware of the fact; they will not be able to start anything with their capital. This is indeed the case if you look into the matter historically. In actual fact, too much capital did arise, and the only way out that it could find was to preserve itself in nature. We thus witnessed in the economic process the so-called rise in the value of land.

By contrast, consider the matter in our present, larger context. Land reformers always describe these things in an inadequate way, so that the thing cannot be understood. Consider it in a larger context and you will notice that if I unite capital with nature, the value of nature will of course be enhanced. The more something is mortgaged, the more you will eventually have to pay for it. The value is constantly increased. But is this increase in the value of land a reality? No, it is no reality at all. By its nature, land can never receive a greater value. It can, at most, receive a greater value by being worked upon in a more rational and scientific way; and in that case it is the labor that increases the value. To imagine the land itself, however, the land as such, increased in value is absurd. It is absolute nonsense. If you do improve the quality of the land, you do so only by working upon it. In so far as it is only nature, the land can have no value at all. All you can do is to give it a fictitious value by uniting capital with it. We may say then, that what is called the value of land in the sense of present-day economics is in real truth nothing other than capital fixed in the land. Capital fixed in the land is not a real value but an apparent value—a semblance of a value. That is the point. In the economic process it is high time that we learn to understand the difference between real values and apparent values.

Notice that if you have an error in your system of thought, you do not observe its full effect to begin with. Many disturbing processes in an organism are, in fact, connected with error in thought, but the connection is recognizable only by spiritual science; it escapes the rudimentary natural science of today. People are unaware, for instance, how digestive troubles and similar problems in our peripheral organs arise as a result of such errors. In the economic process, the errors and semblances become real and have real consequences. Economically speaking, it makes no essential difference whether, for example, I issue money that has no foundation in reality but represents a mere increase in the amount of paper money, or whether I assign capital value to the land. In both cases I am creating fictitious values. By inflating the currency, I increase the prices of things numerically; but in the reality of the economic process, I effect absolutely nothing except a redistribution, which may do immense harm to individuals. In the same manner, the above described capitalizing of land does harm to those who are involved in the economic process.

It would make a very interesting study to compare, for example, the mortgage laws existing before World War I in the Central European countries with the English mortgage laws. On one hand, in the Central European countries it was possible to ratchet the so-called value of land up and up and up without limit. The law itself made this possible. In England, on the other hand, it is true to say, in a certain sense, that this was not so. Compare the effect on the economic process in the one case and in the other. This comparison would make an interesting subject for a dissertation. It would make a very good subject, to compare statistically the working of the English mortgage laws with that of German laws.

The previous examples have illustrated the essential point in our present context. At this point, [diagram: e] nature simply must not be allowed to tend toward a preservation of capital. Capital must be allowed to work on, unhindered, into labor. What is to happen if capital is actually there—more of it than we are able to make use of? The only thing to prevent its being there in excess is to see that it is used up along this path [diagram: d], so that in the end, only as much of it is left at this point [diagram: e] as can enter once more into the work to be done upon the land. Only as much capital is left as is required for this work. The essential and obvious thing is that the capital should be used up, consumed, along this path. Indeed—assuming hypothetically that it could be so—it would be a most appalling thing if nothing were consumed along this whole path. We would have to carry all the products around with us. The process becomes organic only through the fact that things are used up. Just as the products of nature, transformed by human labor, are used up; just as the labor which has been organized by capital is used up. So in its further path, the capital itself simply must be used up—properly used up. This using-up of capital is something that absolutely must be brought about.

This proper using-up of capital can be brought about only if the whole economic process from beginning to end—that is, right up to its return to nature—is ordered rightly. There must be something there like the "self-regulator" in the human organism. The human organism, at any rate when it is functioning normally, manages to prevent indiscriminate deposits of unused food products. If unused food products are deposited here or there, we become ill. Suppose, for instance, that in the process of digestion, substances are deposited in the head, that is to say, an irregular digestive process arises in the head. The substances that are deposited are no longer carried away—that is to say, their consumption is not properly regulated. Then we get migraine conditions. In a similar way, you will see the same principle at work in all parts of the human organism. The cause of illness lies in inadequate absorption and the inadequate removal of what was not digested. It is just the same in the social organism, when what ought to be used up at a certain point is accumulated. It is a matter of sheer necessity for the capital to be used up along here [diagram: d], in order that it may not unite with nature and so become nonliving—a petrified deposit, as it were, in the economic process. For capitalized land is, in fact, an impossible deposit in the economic process.

Let me state expressly that there can be no question here of any sort of political agitation. I simply unfold these matters as they take shape out of the natural process itself. We are only considering the scientific aspect. A science that deals with human actions, however, cannot possibly be pursued without indicating the kinds of sicknesses that can arise, just as we cannot study the human body without indicating the various possible manifestations of illness. There must, therefore, be a proportionate using-up, consumption, of capital—certainly not a total consumption, for it is necessary that a certain amount should pass on, so that nature can be further worked upon.

This again I can make clear to you by a picture. Consider a farmer in his economic life. He must certainly try to sell the yield of his acres, but he must also keep sufficient seed for the next year. Seed must be preserved. This is a very apt comparison, and we may well apply it to the process we are now considering. Capital must be used up, until what remains we may conceive of as a kind of seed to kindle the economic process anew—once more from the starting point of nature. That alone must remain which may be necessary for a more scientific processing of natural resources—of raw materials, or for an improvement of the land, let us say, by the creation of better manures, and the like. In every such case labor must be applied. It is that amount of capital which can work on as labor that must be withdrawn from consumption. Before this point in the diagram is reached (e), the surplus capital, which would otherwise unite with nature in an inorganic way, must be used up.

You may say, well, tell us, how it is to be done. How is it to be brought about that only just enough capital arrives at this point for use as a seed for the future?

In the science of economics we stand on the ground, not of logic, but of reality. We cannot give the kind of answers that are sometimes given, for example, in the theory of ethics. In the theory of ethics, if we admonish a criminal very soundly, then we shall have done all that is required. But the economic process happens—it must go on—and we must speak out of the reality of this. When we spoke of production, showing how it creates economic values, we were indeed speaking of realities. That consumption is a reality, everyone is well aware. In economic science one must always speak of realities. Ideas by themselves have no effect in the real world. What will rightly regulate the economic process, at this point in the diagram, finds expression in what I called the "real associations" in my book *Towards Social Renewal.*†

If you make the economic life independent; if you bring together, in associations that are suitably composed, the human beings who are actually taking part in the economic life—whether as producers, as merchants, or as consumers—then, through the economic process itself, these human beings will find it possible to restrain the formation of capital if it is too intense and to stimulate it if it is too feeble.

This approach, of course, implies a right observation of the economic process. For instance, if at any point a certain kind of commodity becomes too cheap or too expensive, those concerned must be able truly to observe the fact. The mere fact in itself is not the point. When, through experiences that can grow only out of the concerted counsels of the associations, they are able to say, as a result of such experiences, "Five units of money for so and so much salt are too little or too much—the price is too low or too high," then and then only will they be in a position to take the necessary steps.

If the price of a commodity becomes too low, so that those who produce it can no longer receive sufficient remuneration for their excessively cheap services and their excessively cheap products, it will be necessary to assign fewer workers to this particular commodity. Workers will therefore have to be diverted to another kind of work. If, on the other hand, a commodity becomes too expensive, workers will have to be led over into this branch of production. In this way, the associations will always be concerned with a proper employment of people in several areas of the economic life. We must be clear on this. A real rise in the price of a given economic article indicates the necessity for an increase in the number of those who are working on this article, while an undue fall of price calls for measures to divert workers from this field of labor to another. In reality we can speak of prices only in relation to the distribution of people among the several branches of labor in the given social organism.

The view that sometimes prevails today, in which people always have the tendency to work with concepts rather than realities, is illustrated by some advocates of "free money"[*Freigeldeute*]. To them it appears quite simple. If prices anywhere are too high, so that too much money has to be spent in purchasing a certain article, these advocates wish to ensure that the amount of money becomes less; then the commodities will be cheaper, and vice versa. If you think about it thoroughly, however, you will find that this signifies nothing for the economic process. In reality, it is as if by some mischievous device you were to cause the column of mercury to rise when the thermometer indicates that the room is too cold. You are only trying to cure the symptoms. By giving the money a different value you create nothing real.

You create something real if you regulate the labor—that is to say, the number of people engaged in a certain kind of work. The price depends on the number of workers engaged in a given field of work. To try to regulate these things bureaucratically, through the state, would be the worst form of tyranny. To regulate through free "associations" that arise within the social sphere, where everyone can see what is going on—either as members, or because their representative sits on the association, or they are told what is going on, or they see for themselves and realize what is required—that is what we must aim for.

Of course this proposal also involves quite another social need. We must see to it that workers are not restricted to only one skill throughout their lives, but are able to turn their hand to other things. Know that this flexibility will be necessary, moreover, if only for the reason that otherwise too much capital would arrive at this point in the diagram (e). You can use up the surplus capital, which

would be excessive at this point, to instruct and educate the workers in one thing or another, to be able to transplant them into other
callings. You see, therefore, the moment you think in a rational way,
the economic process will correct itself. That is the essential thing.
It will never correct itself if you think that by employing this cr
that measure, by inflation or by the issue of any official instructions,
things will improve. By such means the economy will never improve.
It will be improved only by enabling the economic process to be
clearly and transparently observed at every place, assuming always
that those who make the observations are in a position to follow them
out to their logical conclusions.

I wanted to reach this point in our study today in order that you
might see that there is no question of starting any agitations with
the "threefold social impulse" as it was intended, and to show what
follows from a real and true study of the economic process itself.

Lecture 6

Price, Culture, and Gift

DORNACH, JULY 29, 1922

You know, perhaps, that in my book *Towards Social Renewal* I tried to express in a formula how we may arrive at a conception of "true price" (as we will call it to begin with) in the whole economic process. Needless to say, such a formula is only an abstraction. It is the object of these lectures—which, I believe, in spite of the short amount of time, will really form a whole—it is our very object in these lectures to work the whole science of economics, at any rate in outline, into this abstraction.

The formula that I gave in my *Towards Social Renewal* was as follows. "A 'true price' results when individuals receive, as counter-value for the product they have made, sufficient recompense to enable them to satisfy the whole of their needs, including of course the needs of their dependants, until they will again have completed a like product." Abstract as it is, this formula is nonetheless exhaustive. In setting up a formula, it is always necessary that it should contain all the concrete details. I do believe, for the domain of economics, that this formula is no less exhaustive than, say, the Theorem of Pythagoras is for all right-angled triangles. But the point is that just as we have to introduce into the Theorem of Pythagoras the varying proportions of the sides, so shall we have to introduce many, very many more variables into this formula. Economic science is precisely an understanding of how the whole economic process can be included in this formula.

Today I intend to start from one essential feature of the formula. It is this: The formula does not point to what is past but to what is going to happen in the future. For I say in it, deliberately, that "the counter-value must satisfy the individual's needs in the future, that is, until he or she will have made a like product again." This is an absolutely essential feature of the formula. If we were to demand a countervalue, literally, for the product that is already finished—if we expected this to be true to the real economic facts—it might well happen that we would receive a value that would satisfy our needs, say, for only five-sixths of the time we need to finish the new product. The economic facts alter from the past into the future. Those who imagine that they can draw up any kind of table from the past, will invariably go wrong in economics. Economic or business life essentially consists in setting future processes in motion with the help of what went before. Where past processes are thus used to set future ones in motion, it inevitably happens in some cases that the values are considerably shifted. Indeed, they are constantly shifting. Hence in this formula it is essential to say that "If someone makes a pair of boots, the time taken to make them is not the determining factor in the economic sense. The determining factor is the time required to make the next pair of boots." That is the point, and we must now try to understand its fuller implications within the whole economic process.

Yesterday we brought before our minds the cycle: nature, labor, capital—that is, capital imbued with value by Spirit. [diagram, p. 55, c; also diagram p. 72] At this point, instead of "capital," I might just as well write "Spirit." To begin with we followed out the economic process in this direction, counterclockwise, and we found that at this point, with nature, [diagram p. 55, e] congestion must not be allowed to occur, but only so much must be allowed to go through as will act as a kind of seed to carry on the process. A state of economic congestion must not be allowed to arise through a fixation of capital in ground rent; as I said, fundamentally speaking, the return for land when it is sold—that is, when land is given a value in the economic process—works in direct opposition to the interests of those engaged in the manufacture of valuable goods. If people wish to manufacture valuable goods with the help of capital, it is to their benefit that the rate of interest should be low. Having less interest to pay, they will be less hampered in their use of the capital they have borrowed. The landowners, on the other hand (I will go fully into these things, as they are of economic significance), the landowners, or those who have an interest in the land's becoming more expensive, will be able to make it more expensive simply by a reduction in the rate of interest. If they have a low rate of interest to pay, the value of their land will grow; it will become more and more expensive. By contrast, those engaged in the manufacture of valuable commodities will be able to make them for less because of a low rate of interest. Commodities, therefore, which depend mainly on manufacture, become less expensive when the rate of interest is low. Land, on the other hand, which gives a yield without first having to be manufactured, becomes more expensive when the rate of interest is low. You can easily work it out. It is an economic fact.

It would appear then to be necessary to arrange for two different rates of interest: We ought to have a rate of interest as low as possible for building the work for the production of valuable commodities and a rate of interest as high as possible for everything that falls under the heading of "land." This follows directly from what we said before. We want a rate of interest as high as possible for all that comes under the heading of "land." This cannot easily be carried out, however, in practice. A slightly higher rate of interest for capital advanced on land might be practicable, but this would be of little help. A considerably higher rate of interest—say, for instance, the rate of interest that would keep the land at an ever-constant value, that is, 100%—would be extremely difficult to realize in practice without taking additional steps. 100% interest for money borrowed on land would mend matters at once, but it cannot be carried out in practice. In all such cases, the first point is to see with full clarity into the economic process. When we do so, we soon realize that the life of the associations is the only thing that can make the process healthy, because if seen correctly, the economic process will lead to our being able to direct it in the right way.

In the economic process we must speak, as I indicated yesterday, of production and consumption. We must observe both the producing and the consuming processes. The contrast between them has played a great part recently in various widely held economic theories, which in due course have been used for purposes of agitation. There has especially been much dispute of the question of whether spiritual-cultural (intellectual) work, as such, is in any way value-creating in the economic sphere.

Those who work out of the sphere of human intelligence or Spirit are certainly consumers. Whether they are also producers in the economic sense is a question that has been much discussed. Extreme Marxists, for example, have again and again cited that unlucky fellow, the Indian bookkeeper, who has to keep the accounts for his village community. He does not till the fields or do any other productive work; he merely registers the productive work done by others. The Marxists deny him the faculty of producing anything. They declare that he is simply and solely maintained out of the surplus value that the productive workers create. This worthy bookkeeper is worked as hard in economics as Caius is in the formal logic that we studied at college. Caius's job is proving the mortality of the human being. You may remember, "All human beings are mortal; Caius is a human being; therefore Caius is mortal." His everlasting function of proving the mortality of the human being has made him immortal in the world of logic. The same thing has happened in Marxist literature to the Indian bookkeeper who is maintained simply by the surplus value of the productive workers. He has become a classic.

This question is, if I may say so, extraordinarily full of snags, in which we very easily get caught when we try to work it out economically. I refer to the question, "To what extent (if at all) is spiritual-cultural work economically productive?" Now here it is especially important to distinguish between the past and the future. If you consider and reflect statistically on only the past, with respect to the past and to all that is only the unbroken continuation of the past, you will be able to prove that spiritual-cultural work is unproductive. From the past within the material sphere, only purely material work and its effects can be held to be productive in the economic process. It is quite a different matter when you turn your eye to the future. As we have said, to be engaged in economics is to be working from the past into the future.

You need think only of this simple instance. Assume that in some village a craftsman falls ill. Under certain given circumstances—let us say, if he falls into the hands of an unskilled doctor—he will have to lie in bed for three weeks, during which time he will be able to do nothing. Then, he will disturb the economic process to no small extent. If he is a shoemaker, for three weeks his boots and shoes will not be brought to market, taking the word "market" in the widest sense. But now suppose he gets a very skillful doctor who makes him well in a week. He can go back to work again in a week. In all seriousness you can now decide the question, "Who made the boots for the difference of the fourteen days, the shoemaker or the doctor?" In reality it was the doctor. Now the situation is altogether clear. As soon as you take into account the future from any given moment onward—toward the future—you can no longer call the spiritual/cultural unproductive. In relation to the past, the spiritual/cultural—or rather, those human beings who work in the spiritual-cultural sphere—are consumers only. In relation to the future they are decidedly productive; indeed they are the producers, for they transform the whole process of production and make it substantially different for the economic life. You can see this from the example of a tunnel. What happens when tunnels are built nowadays? They could not be built unless differential calculus had been discovered. To this day, therefore, Leibniz† is helping to build all tunnels. The way prices work out in this case has really been determined by that exertion of his spiritual-cultural forces. You can never answer these questions in economics if you consider the past in the same way as the future. Life does not move toward the past, nor does it even prolong the past; it goes on into the future.

Hence no economic thought is real that does not reckon with what is done by spiritual-cultural work, if we may call it so; that is to say, fundamentally, what is done by thinking. But spiritual-cultural work is not easy to comprehend. It has its own peculiar properties, which are not at all easy to grasp in economic terms. Spiritual-cultural work begins the moment work itself—that is to say, labor—is organized. The organizing work of thinking begins the very moment labor itself is organized and divided. Thenceforward, it grows more and more independent. Consider the spiritual-cultural work of those who direct some undertaking within the material sphere. You will see that they apply an immense amount of spiritual-cultural work. Nevertheless they are still working with the resources with which the economic process provides them from the past. Even on quite practical grounds, you cannot ignore the fact that the sphere of spiritual-cultural activity (if I may now call it "activity" instead of work or labor) also includes the entirely free kind of activity. When someone invents differential calculus, and even more so when someone paints a picture, there we have a case of entirely free spiritual-cultural activity. Relatively speaking, at least, we can call it free. Whatever materials are derived from the past—the paints and the like—they no longer have the same significance in relation to the eventual products as do the raw materials, for example, purchased for manufacture.

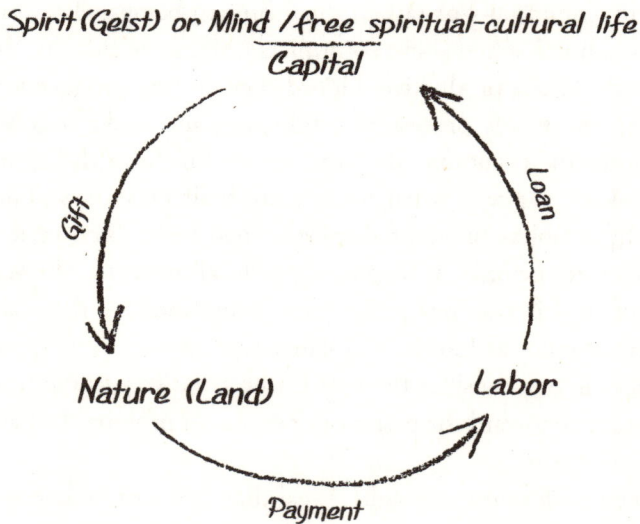

Spirit (Geist) or Mind / free spiritual-cultural life
Capital

Gift

Loan

Nature (Land)

Labor

Payment

Passing into this region, therefore, we come into the sphere of the completely free spiritual-cultural life [see diagram above]. In this sphere we find, above all things, teaching and education. Those who teach and educate undoubtedly stand within the sphere of the completely free spiritual-cultural life. For the purely material economic process, it is especially these (free spiritual-cultural workers) who are, in relation to the past, absolutely and exclusively consumers. Of course, you may say, they produce something; and, if they are painters, for example, they are even paid something for what they have produced. In appearance, therefore, the economic process is the same as when I manufacture a table and sell it. The process is essentially different as soon as we cease to consider buying and selling by the individual and turn our attention to the economic organism as a whole—and this is what we must do in the present advanced stage of the division of labor.

There are also pure consumers of another kind within a social organism; namely, the young and the very old. Up to a certain age, the young are pure consumers; and those who are on pensions are again pure consumers. Very little reflection will suffice to convince you that if there were no pure consumers in the economic process— mere consumers who are not producers at all—the process could not go forward at all. If everyone were producing, not all that is produced could be consumed, and the economic process would not be able to go forward. It is as human life is, and human life is not purely economics; it must be taken as a whole. The real advancement of the economic process is possible only if it includes pure consumers.

We must now illumine from a different angle this fact: that we have pure consumers within the economic process. You see, this circle (in the diagram) can be very instructive. We can endow it with all manner of properties, and the challenge will always be how to bring the several economic processes and facts into this circle, which represents for us the cycle of the economic process. Something very important happens when in buying and selling in the market I pay on the spot for what I get. The point is not that I pay for it with money; I might equally well barter it for a corresponding commodity that the other person is willing to accept. The point is that I pay at once. It is this that constitutes "paying" in the proper sense of the word.

Here once more we must pass from the ordinary, everyday conception to the true economic conception. In the economic life, several concepts constantly play into one another. The total phenomenon, the total fact, results from the interplay of the most diverse factors. You may think it is conceivable that some regulation should be made so that no one need ever pay cash down. Then there would be no such thing as "paying at once"; one would pay only after a month or after some other interval of time. The point is that I am forming my concepts altogether wrongly if I think that someone should hand me a suit of clothes, and I pay for it after a month. The fact is that after a month I no longer pay for this suit of clothes alone. In that moment, I am paying for something quite different. I am paying for something that circumstances, by raising or lowering prices, may have made quite different. I am paying for an ideal element in addition. In fact, we cannot do without the concept of "immediate payment." This is the concept that holds good in cases of simple purchase. A thing becomes a commodity on the market, moreover, through the very fact that it is paid for at once. This is generally the case with those commodities that are "nature-transformed-by-labor." For such commodities I pay. Here payment plays the essential part. There must be such payment. I pay at the very moment when I open my wallet and give away my money; and the value is determined in the very moment at which I give away the money or exchange my commodity for another. That is payment. That is one thing that must be in the economic process.

The second factor, which plays a similar part to payment, is the factor to which I drew attention yesterday. It is lending. This, as I said, does not interfere with the concept of payment as such. Lending, once more, is an altogether different fact, a fact which simply exists. If I have money lent to me, I can apply my Spirit to this loaned capital. I become a debtor, but I also become a producer. In this way, lending plays a real economic part. If I have intellectual/ spiritual capacities in some direction, it must be possible for me to obtain loaned capital. No matter where I get it, I must have it. Thus, in addition to payment there must be loan [see diagram, p. 72]. Here then we have two very important factors in the economic process: payment and loan.

By a simple deduction—we must verify it here (see diagram)—by a very simple deduction you can find the third. You will not doubt for a moment what the third factor is. We have had payment and loan. The third factor is gift. Payment, loan, and gift—this is a real trinity of concepts, essential to a healthy economy. There is a prevailing disincli- nation to include "gift" in the economic process as such; but if there is not an act of giving somewhere, the economic process cannot go on at all. Imagine for a moment what we should make of our children if we gave them nothing. We are constantly giving gifts to our children. If we consider the economic process as a whole—as a process that goes on and on continuously—gift is part of it. There is no escaping the fact. It is wrong to regard the transfer of values from hand to hand, representing a process of gifting, as something inadmissible in the economic process as such. Precisely this one of the three is found—with horror by some people—worked out in my book *Towards Social Renewal.* There it is shown how values are to be transferred—how means of production, for instance, are to be transferred to one who has the faculties necessary for managing them further by a process that is really identical with giving. Provision must, of course, be made that the giving is not done in a haphazard way. In the economic sense they are nonetheless gifts, and such gifts are absolutely necessary.

You will find, more and more, this value transfer to be an economic necessity. The trinity of payment, loan, and gift is there in the economic process. Consider the matter thoroughly and you will agree that in every economic process this transfer must be contained. Otherwise, it would be no economic process; it would lead to absurdities at every point.

People may rebel against these things for a time, but we must remember that economic wisdom is today not very great. Those especially who want to teach it should be under no illusions on this point. Modern economic knowledge is by no means great. People are little inclined to go into the real economic relationships. This is an obvious fact—so obvious that if you look in today's *Basler Nachrichten* [the regional daily newspaper published in Basel] you will find, curiously enough, a reflection on this very fact. Neither governments nor private people nowadays, it says, are inclined to develop real economic thinking. I think we may take it that anything expounded in the *Basler Nachrichten* is likely to be obvious. It is indeed a palpable fact, and it is interesting to find it discussed in this way. The article is interesting, inasmuch as it endeavors to set in a glaring light the absolute impotence that prevails in the economic sphere. Interesting, too, is the statement that these things must be changed—it is time governments and individuals began to think differently. There the matter ends. How they are to think differently—on this you will, of course, find nothing in the *Basler Nachrichten*, which is also interesting!

It is possible to interfere in the economic process in a disturbing way, if one does not rightly relate the one thing with the other in this trinity. Many people today are enthusiastically demanding the taxation of legacies (which, of course, are also gifts). Such proposals have no deep economic significance. We do not lessen the value of the inheritance if, say, it has a value V and we divide the value V into two parts, V_1 and V_2, giving V_2 to some other party and leaving the legatee with V_1 alone. All it means is that the two together will now do business with the original value V, and the question will be whether the one who receives V_2 will husband it as advantageously for the economic life as would the original legatee who would otherwise have received V_1 and V_2 together. One of course may settle this question for oneself according to one's own taste: whether a single clever person, receiving the whole legacy, will husband it better, or whether it will be better for one to receive only part while the state receives the other part, so that the individual is obliged to do business in conjunction with the state.

This sort of thing definitely leads us away from pure economic thinking. It is a thinking based on resentment, on feeling. People envy the rich heir. There may be reason for it, but we cannot look at it only from this point of view if we claim to be thinking in an economic sense. The point is to find the right conception in the economic sense. Whatever else has to be done must take its start from this. You can, of course, conceive of a social organism becoming diseased through the fact that payment is not working together in an organic way with loan and gift, since one or the other is being obstructed and one or the other fostered. But they will still go on working together in some way. If you abolish giving on one side, you merely effect a redistribution, and the question to be decided is not whether this ought to be done, but whether it is necessarily advantageous. Whether the individual heir alone should receive the inheritance, or whether it must be shared with the state, is a question that must first be settled on economic grounds. Which is more advantageous? That is the point.

The important point is that a free spiritual-cultural life arises, almost of necessity, out of the entry of Spirit (mind) into the economic life.

As a result of this free spiritual-cultural life—freedom of mind—there will be pure consumers so far as the past is concerned. But what of free spiritual-cultural life (free life of the mind) in relation to the future? Here it is productive—indirectly, it is true—but nonetheless extraordinarily productive. Imagine a free spiritual-cultural life in the social organism—really freed—so that the individual faculties are always able to develop fully. Then free spiritual-cultural life will be able to exert an extremely fertilizing influence on the half-free spiritual-cultural life—that is, on the spiritual-cultural life that enters into the processes of material production. Considered in this light, free spiritual-cultural life takes on a decidedly economic aspect.

Those who can observe life with an unbiased mind will say to themselves that it is by no means a matter of indifference whether in a given place all who are active in the free spiritual-cultural life are eliminated (for instance, if they were given nothing to consume, the right to live being admitted only for those who work directly into the material process), or whether truly free spirits are allowed to exist within the social organism. Free spirits have the characteristic of loosening and liberating spirituality; they are the "inspiration," of the others. Their thinking is more mobile, and they are thus able to work into the material process more effectively. It is important to remember that the free spirits are living human beings. You must not try to refute me by pointing to Italy and saying that there is a great deal of free spiritual-cultural life there, yet the economic processes that proceed from Spirit have not been stimulated to any unusual degree. Granted, it is a free spiritual-cultural life. But it is one handed down from the past. There are statues, museums, and the like, but these do not have this effect. Only what is living is effective—that is to say, what proceeds from creative human beings and spreads into others who can produce spiritually, intellectually and creatively. This is what works as a productive factor into the future, even in the economic sense. It is certainly possible to exert a healing influence on the economic process by giving an open field of action to spiritual-creative people.

Suppose now that we have a healthy associative life in a community. The task of the associations will be to arrange production in such a way that when there are too many people working in any sphere, they can be transferred to some other work. It is this vital dealing with people, the process of allowing the whole social order to originate from the insight of the associations, that matters. When one day the associations begin to understand something of the influence of the free spiritual-cultural life on the economic process, we can give them a very good means of regulating the economic circuit. I mentioned this in my book *Towards Social Renewal*. The associations will find that when free spiritual-cultural life declines, too little is being given freely; they will grasp the connection. They will see the connection between too little giving and too little free spiritual-cultural work. When there is not enough free spiritual-cultural work, they will realize that too little is being given. When too little is being given, they will notice a decline in free spiritual-cultural work.

There is then a very definite possibility of driving the rate of interest on property right up to 100% by transmitting as much property as possible in the way of free gifts to those who are spiritually-culturally productive. In this way you can bring the land question into direct connection with what works particularly into the future. In other words, the capital that presses to be invested, the capital that tends to march into mortgages and stay there, must be given an outlet into free spiritual-cultural institutions. That is the practical aspect. Let the associations see to it that the money that tends to get tied up in mortgages finds its way into independent spiritual-cultural institutions. There you have the connection of the associative life with the general social life. Only when you try to penetrate the realities of economic life does it begin to dawn on you what must be done in the one case or in the other. I do not by any means wish to agitate that this or that *must* be done; I only wish to point out what *is*. This is undoubtedly true: what we can never attain by legislative measures— namely, to keep the excess capital away from nature—we can attain through the life and system of associations, diverting capital into free spiritual-cultural institutions. I only say that if the one thing happens, the other will happen too. Science, after all, has only to indicate the conditions under which things are connected.

Lecture 7

Price Formation

DORNACH, JULY 30, 1922

W E HAVE NOW SEEN how the economic system as a whole takes
its course; we have seen how purchase or sale, loan, and gift, act as
impelling factors, motivating factors, within this system. Let us realize
at once that there can be no economic system without this interplay
of purchase, loan, and gift. The influences that create the economic
values (of which we have already spoken from one aspect) and which
lead to the forming of price, will therefore proceed from these three
factors: purchase, loan, and gift. The important thing is to understand
how the three factors work in the forming of price. Only by perceiving
this shall we succeed to any degree in formulating the price problem.

It is quite necessary that we should have a distinct view of the real
nature of separate economic problems. In this respect our present
economic science is full of unclear ideas—ideas that, as I have often
explained, become confused mainly because they try to grasp what is
in constant movement as if it were at rest.

Granting then that purchase, loan, and gift are inherent in economic
movement, let us consider what in our present-day economy are (if
I may so call them) the principal factors of rest. Let us turn for a
moment to what is perhaps one of the most discussed topics nowadays
and a principal source of the errors that find their way into economic
science. People talk of "wages," and they talk of them in such a way as
to make them look like the price of labor. If the so-called wage earners
have to be paid more, they say that the price of labor has gone up. If

they have to be paid less, they say that labor is cheaper. They actually speak as though a kind of sale and purchase took place between the wage earners who sells their labor and those who buy it from them. But this sale and purchase is fictitious. It does not in reality take place. That is the trouble in our present economic conditions. We have everywhere hidden or masked relationships—relationships that develop in a way not in accordance with what, in a deeper sense, they really are. I have spoken of this before.

Value in the economic system, as we have already seen, can arise only in the exchange of products—in the exchange of commodities, or, more generally, of economic products. It cannot arise in any other way. But what follows? If value can arise only in this way, and if, moreover, the price of the value is to be arrived at along the lines laid down yesterday (that is, by seeing that the producers of a given product receive, as its counter-value, what they will require to satisfy their needs during the production of another like product)—if this is to be possible, the various products must, as it were, reciprocally determine one another's value. After all, it is not difficult to see that this is what actually happens in the economic process; only it is masked by the fact that money steps in between the objects exchanged. But the money is not the important thing. We would not take the slightest interest in money if it did not foster the exchange of products, making the process not only more convenient but less expensive. We would have no need of money if it were not for the fact that when people bring a product to the market, under the influence of the division of labor, they cannot be bothered to get what they need from wherever it is. They take money for it instead, so that they may supply their needs later on at their own convenience. Therefore we may say that it is the mutual tension arising between the various products in the economic process that must be concerned in the forming of prices.

Let us consider from this point of view the so-called wage nexus; that is, the labor nexus. We cannot really exchange labor for anything because between labor and anything else there is no possibility of reciprocal determination of value. We may fancy that we are paying for labor; we may even actualize this fancy by letting in the wage nexus. But we do not really do anything of the sort. In reality, even in the labor or wage nexus, it is values that are exchanged. Workers produce something directly and deliver a product, and it is this product that the entrepreneur [*Unternehmer*] really buys from them. In actual fact, down to the last penny, the entrepreneur pays for the products that the workers deliver. It is time we began to see these things in their right light. Entrepreneurs buy products from workers; and after they have bought the products it is their business to impart to them a higher value, by making use of the conditions present in the social organism and by their own enterprising or "undertaking" spirit. It is really this that gives them their profit. They gain on the transaction because, having bought the commodities from the workers, they are able by their "knowledge of the market" (we must not shirk unpleasant expressions) to enhance the value of the commodities.

In the labor nexus, therefore, we are dealing with a true purchase. We cannot speak of a surplus value arising through the labor nexus as such. All we can say is that in certain circumstances the price that the enterpriser pays is not according to the true price, of which we spoke yesterday. This is a situation we shall often find in the economic process—that, although the products reciprocally determine one another's values, although they have their real values, these values are not actually paid for in the course of commercial dealing. It is easy enough to see that all values are not really paid for. Take the case of a man who is a manufacturer on a small scale, who suddenly inherits a large legacy. Tired of the whole factory business, he decides to sell his stock in trade, and does so at an absurdly low price. That does not mean that the commodities decrease in value; it only means that the true price is not paid. In ways like this, prices are constantly being falsified in the actual economic process. We must not forget this. In the course of commercial dealing, prices may often be falsified. There is, nevertheless, a true price. The commodities sold by the man in the above example are worth just as much as the same commodities produced by someone else.

Now that we have tried to make it clear that the wage nexus does really involve a purchase, let us consider what is involved by rent—by the price of land. You see, the conditions under which the price of land originates are not those of a mature economy. To take an extreme instance, we may consider how a piece of land may have come under the control of particular people by conquest; that is, by the exercise of force. Even here, no doubt, the element of exchange will enter in to some extent; the invader will have granted certain portions of the conquered territory to those who helped him to victory. Here, then, at the starting point of an economic process we have something that is not properly economics. The process is not really economics; it is a process to which we can only apply the word "power" or "right." By means of power, rights are gained—rights, in this case, over land. We have the economic domain bordering on the one hand on these relationships of rights and power.

What is it that takes place under the influence of such relationships of rights and power? This is what happens continually. Those who have the free right of disposal over land look after themselves better than those others who are attached to them as laborers—who deliver the products by their labor. I am speaking now not of the labor, but of the products of the labor; it is the products of labor with which we are concerned. The laborers have to deliver more to the landowners than they deliver to other laborers. This, indeed, is only the prolongation of the conquest or rights relationship. What is this excess that is given to them over what they give? What is it, in other words, that falsifies the price relationship in this case? It is none other than a compulsory gift! Here, then, the relation of giving comes in, with the sole difference that those who are to make the gift do so not of their own free will, but by compulsion; it is in fact a compulsory gift. That is what happens in relation to the land. Through the compulsory gift, the price that farm products really ought to have in terms of other products is actually raised.

Thus the price of all things capable of subjection to such relationships of "rights" has an inherent tendency to rise above its true level. So, for instance, if foresters or hunters are living with farmers, the foresters and hunters will come off better than the farmers. Farmers, among forest people, have to pay higher prices to the foresters for what they give the farmers—higher prices, that is to say, than the true exchange prices as between their respective products. In forestry, more than anywhere else, it is as a pure matter of rights that the owners have the products of nature at their disposal and determine prices. Farming requires some real labor; but in forestry, hunting, and the like, we come very near to the pure "labor-less" valuation—a valuation proceeding solely from relationships of rights and power. Again, if skilled workers are living among farmers, the prices once again will tend to rise above their true level on the farmer's side; while on the other hand, they will sink beneath the true level against the skilled worker. Life is more expensive for skilled workers among farmers; life is comparatively less expensive for farmers among the skilled workers (assuming there are enough of them to make any appreciable difference). Skilled workers among farmers will find life comparatively more expensive. Thus, the sequence governing this tendency for prices to rise above or to sink below their true level is as follows. First forestry, then farming, then the skilled trades, and last, the completely free spiritual-cultural work. These are the lines along that we should approach the problem of price formation in the economic process.

There is a tendency, an inherent tendency, in the economic process to create rent. The economic process tends, as it were, of its own accord, to submit itself to this necessity of paying more for farm products than for other things. This tendency exists where there is division of labor—and all of our discussions refer to a social organism in which there is division of labor. This tendency is called forth through the fact (what I had to repeat twice, a few days ago, to the bewilderment of a large part of the audience) that those who provide for themselves live more expensively, and for that reason they must take more for their products, must estimate them at a higher value than those who get their products in independent commercial dealing from others. This circumstance simply does not enter into the process in the case of farming.

In relation to the various branches of industry, this principle of expense in providing for oneself has a very real meaning, though you may have to think a very long time to find your way to that meaning. With respect to agriculture and forestry, however, this principle has no meaning. We must never forget that when we are dealing with realities the various concepts hold good only for certain areas; they change for other areas. This is equally true in other walks of life.

What is a means of healing for the head is pernicious—is a means to disease—for the stomach, and vice versa. So it is in the economic organism. For example, if it were at all possible for farmers to not provide for themselves, the rules we apply for the general circulation of commodities would be right in their case too. The fact is, however, that they cannot help but provide for themselves; within the economic process, the entire agriculture of a social organism forms of its own nature an entity, a whole, however many individual landowners there may be. Accordingly, farmers must in every case keep back from the totality of their products what they need to provide for themselves. Even if they get it from another farmer, in reality they are still keeping it back. In reality, the farmers provide for themselves. Hence they are obliged to value their goods more expensively. The consequence is that prices must rise on their side.

It follows that there is an inherent tendency to create rents in the economic process. The only question will now be how these rents can be made harmless in the economic life. In the first place, we must know that this tendency to create rent exists. If you abolish rents, in one form or another they will be created again, for the simple reason that I have just explained.

You see, for the same reason that underlies the tendency in the economic process to create rent, there arises, on the other hand, the tendency of manufacturers to devalue capital, to make capital cheaper and cheaper. We shall best understand this tendency if we are clear, to begin with, that capital cannot really be bought. True, there are dealings in capital; people "buy" capital. Every such purchase of capital is once again merely a masked relationship; in reality we do not buy capital, we only borrow it. In the end, even if the relationship is apparently other, you will always be able to unmask it and expose the loan character of business capital. I say expressly of business capital, for if you extend the principle to rents it is no longer the case. It is certainly the case with business capital, for the simple reason that there is a constant tendency to undervalue, as compared with other things, what depends on human will—that is to say, craftsmanship or manufacture and entirely free spiritual-cultural work [at this point in the diagram, p. 72]. Business capital is altogether implicated in the independent spiritual-cultural work; hence, it is constantly being devalued. And we may say, on this side [diagram, p. 72], there is inherent in the economic process a tendency, while we create rents, to lower business capital—to make it lower and lower in value. Just as things become more and more expensive on the one side, on the side of ground rent, so do they become cheaper and cheaper on the other side, on the side of capital. Capital has a permanent tendency to go down in its economic value, or rather in its economic price; rents have a permanent tendency to rise in price.

There is also another reason from which you will see that business capital must inevitably go down. We said just now that in farming one cannot help providing for oneself. It is just by this self provision that the rise in the value of farm products is brought about. At the same time you will see that in the case of business capital, where the loan principle predominates, one cannot provide for oneself; one cannot provide for oneself with capital. What one does provide for oneself must be included in the balance sheet nowadays in precisely the same way as what one borrows—if the balance sheet is to be correct. Since, therefore, at this point [diagram, p. 72] one cannot provide for oneself, it follows that the opposite tendency obtains— the tendency towards lower prices.

Everything depends on our seeing clearly through these relationships in the economic process. Then we shall see that it is by no means easy to establish true prices. The true price is constantly being upset by the fact that, on the one hand, there are things appearing on the market that tend to be too high in price, while, on the other hand, there are things appearing that tend to be too low in price. Since the price is settled by exchange, being in the middle, between the two, it is continually exposed to these disturbing influences. You can observe this very clearly in the economic process. In the same measure in which the products of forestry and agriculture grow more expensive, those produced by free cultural activity grow cheaper. In this way, there arise those relationships of tension that give rise to social unrest and discontent. This, therefore, is the most important question in relation to the formation of price. How can we deal with the natural tension that exists in the creation of prices, between the values accruing to goods arising out of our free will, and the values accruing to those goods in the production of which nature participates? How can we get at this tension? How can we balance the one, the downward, tendency with the other, upward tendency?

Through division of labor, more and more highly differentiated products arise. You need only remember how simple the products are that arise, let us say, among a hunting or forest community. Here the price difficulty scarcely comes into question; but as soon as agriculture is added to forestry, the difficulty begins. In effect, the difficulty lies in the differentiation; the further the division of labor extends, and new needs arise in the process, the more does the differentiation of products increase, and the more do difficulties connected with price formation accumulate. The more varied the products are, the more difficult it becomes to bring about their reciprocal valuation—and the valuation can only be reciprocal. This may be seen from the following comparison. There is a reciprocal valuation even in the case of products only slightly differentiated from one another—say, for instance, wheat, rye, and other agricultural products. Follow this process over a long period of time and you will find that the relationship of reciprocal valuation between wheat, rye, and other cereals remains fairly stable. If wheat goes up, the other grains go up; if wheat goes down, the other grains go down with it. This is because there is comparatively little differentiation between these products. As soon as the differentiation becomes greater, this constancy no longer exists.

It may well happen, through various events in the social organism, that some product that someone has been accustomed to exchange for another suddenly shoots up in price, while the other may go down at the same time. Think what shifts are thus brought about in economic relationships. Altogether the things that happen in the economic sphere depend far more on mutual rising and failing prices than on any other circumstance. It is by the mutual rise and fall in prices that the difficulties of life itself are introduced into the economic sphere. As to whether the products as a whole rise or fall— if they all would rise or fall uniformly, this would concern us very little. What interests people is that the different products rise or fall to a different extent. This fact is emerging in a very tragic way just now, under the present economic conditions. Products rise and fall in varying measure. Money values, especially, are rising and falling, but in the money values we simply have stored what were once real values. By this rising and falling, an entire mingling and confusion is now being brought about in society.

From this we can see that there is another way, too, in which we must look at the factors operative in the economic organism. We took our start from the several factors that are enumerated by orthodox economics, but we saw that the mere enumeration of nature, capital, and labor leads us no farther. Precisely when you add what we have said today to what has been said before, you will see that the pricing or valuing of the products of nature comes about not only through purely economic relationships, but also through relationships of rights or title. On the other hand, the valuing of business capital is influenced by the free human will with all that it unfolds when it is active in public life. Consider all that is necessary in order to collect a sum of capital for a given purpose. Here the free human will comes in. Where lending is concerned, free human will has a very great part to play—indirectly perhaps, because those who want to have savings are naturally going to invest those savings. Whether they ever save at all, or not, is an expression of their will. Here, then, the free human will plays a real part. If we take this into account, we shall find yet another classification of the economic factors in addition to the one that we have been considering thus far.

Up until now I have given you a diagrammatic classification in which I showed the following: There is nature, but value arises only through nature elaborated—it arises only when nature moves in the direction of human labor; and, again, value will arise through human labor only when it moves on toward capital, that is, toward Spirit. In this way the tendency arises to return to nature. This, as we saw, can be prevented by leading the excess capital, not into nature, where it would become fixed, but into independent spiritual-cultural undertakings, where it vanishes except for the remnant, which must continue as a kind of seed by which the economic process can be maintained.

In addition to this movement, which begins on the left and moves anticlockwise [diagram, p. 72], there is another movement. The former movement, as we have seen, gives rise to elaborated nature, organized or articulated labor, and emancipated capital—capital, that is to say, that figures only within undertakings dependent on mind or spirit—active capital. The second movement does not lead to the creation of values in this way (the preceding element always being taken on by the next element), but goes in the opposite direction. The first movement runs counterclockwise, the second clockwise. Here, in the first movement, something arises through the former member that is always working on into the next; in the second movement something arises through the fact that what flows in one direction receives, as it were, what is flowing in the other direction, and embraces it. You will soon see what I mean. Remember that capital is, properly speaking, Spirit realized in the economic process; so I can write at this point "Spirit." We now have nature, labor, and Spirit. When the Spirit absorbs and receives the elaborated nature (nature transformed by labor)—when it does not merely lead elaborated nature on into the economic process in the continued counterclockwise movement, but absorbs it—means of production arise. What we call means of production is something different from a product of nature that has been elaborated for consumption—it is in quite an opposite process of movement. Means of production is a product of nature taken

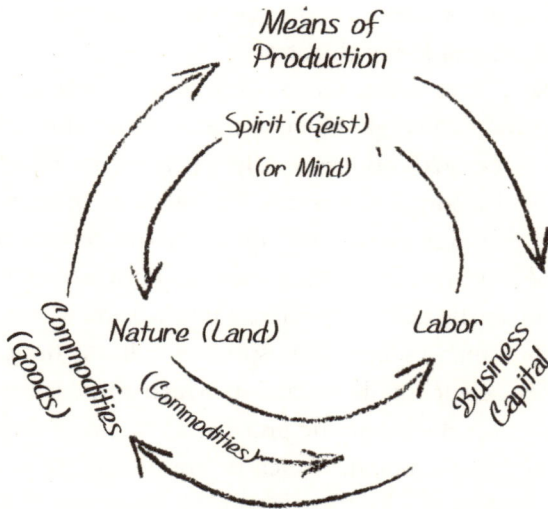

Means of Production

Spirit (Geist) (or Mind)

Nature (Land)   Labor

Commodities (Goods)

Commodities

Commodities

Business Capital

charge of by Spirit—a nature-product that Spirit needs. From the pen that I possess as my means of production, to the most complicated machinery in a factory, means of production are nature grasped by spirit. Nature can be elaborated and sent on in this direction, in which case it becomes capital; or it can be sent in the other direction, in which case it becomes means of production.

What arises at this point with the help of means of production can move on, and human labor can take charge of it. Just as nature is here received by the Spirit, so can the means of production (in the widest sense of the term) be received in turn by labor. What have we then, when labor receives the means of production—when means of production and labor are united? It is business capital, for in effect business capital consists in this very union. If you follow the process farther, you get a movement whereby means of production and business capital coalesce.

If this movement is now continued, so that nature (albeit a different portion of nature from what is the consumption process) continuously receives what has been produced with the help of means of production and business capital, then, and then only, does there arise in the economic process what we may call commodity in the proper sense. The commodity is at once taken over by the process of nature. Either it is eaten, in which case it is taken up very strongly by nature, or it is used or otherwise worn-out. In short, a product becomes a commodity by the very fact that it returns to nature.

We may say, therefore that we have now traced out the movement that is inherent in the whole economic process, and that contains the three factors: means of production, business capital, and commodities. Here, at this third point in the diagram, the distinction becomes unusually difficult. When the thing we are seeking is shifting back and forth in the process of exchange proper (that is, in purchase and sale), it is extraordinarily difficult to distinguish whether it is moving in this direction or in that—whether it is a commodity, or something that cannot be called a commodity in the true sense of the word. How does a piece of goods become a commodity? In describing this counterclockwise movement, to make the nomenclature quite exact, I ought really to write "goods" instead of "commodities," and in the opposite movement I ought to write "commodity"; for a commodity may be defined as a piece of goods in the hands of the merchant, the tradesperson who offers it for sale and does not use it personally.

Today my main purpose was that we should acquire concepts that point to the true relationships in the economic process. These true relationships are again and again being diverted, by falsified processes, into a mode of operation that introduces constant disturbances into the economic process. Continually to smooth out and compensate for the disturbances is one of the essential tasks of economics. People keep on saying that we ought to get rid of the damages in economic life. They are inclined to have at the back of their minds the notion that then everything would be all right and earthly paradise would begin. That is no different than saying, "I should like once and for all to eat so much that I need never eat any more." I cannot do that; I am a living organism wherein ascending and descending processes must constantly be taking place. Such ascending and descending processes must likewise be present in the economic life; there must be the tendency on the one hand to falsify prices by the formation of rent, and on the other hand the tendency to lower prices on the side of business capital. These tendencies are present at all times, and we must understand them in order to obtain, as far as possible, those prices that represent a minimum of falsification.

To this end it is necessary, by direct human experience, to take hold of the economic process, as it were, in the nascent state—to be within it at all times. The individual can never do this; nor can a society above a certain size. (such as the state, for example). It can be done only by associations, which grow out of the economic life itself and which are therefore able to work out of the immediate reality of the economic life. The greater the technical accuracy with which we study the economic process, the more are we led to acknowledge that the required institutions must grow out of the economic life itself. They will then be able to observe the kind of tendencies that are at work, and to understand how these tendencies can be counteracted.

Lecture 8

Supply and Demand

DORNACH, JULY 31, 1922

T ODAY we shall have to correct certain current misconceptions that hinder anyone who wishes to think objectively, in accordance with realities, on matters of economics or to enter with such thinking into the actual course of economic life. An economic science that cannot fructify our practical life is of no real value. The concepts derived from this merely contemplative economic science must always prove rather inadequate.

We have already seen that the most important question in economics is that of price. The point will now be to observe prices in the sense that I have indicated. The rise or fall, or stability, of prices—the fact that the prices of certain products are too high or too low (for one can have a feeling of these things)—indicates whether or not the economic organism is in good order. It must be for the associations to discover, from the barometer of prices, what is to be done in the economic life as a whole.

You are familiar with the point of view, still widely prevalent, according to which nothing can be done in practice with the price problem except to allow the so-called law of supply and demand to take its course. It is true that under the pressure, not so much of economic facts as of the increasingly urgent demands of the social movement, this theory has been shaken—the theory (maintained by many others besides Adam Smith) that prices regulate themselves of their own accord through the working of supply and demand. The theory simply states that if the supply is too great, this will of itself lead to supply reduction—the supply will not be maintained at that level. In this way a regulation of prices will automatically ensue. Similarly, if the demand is too great (or too small) it will inevitably follow that the producers will regulate matters so as not to produce too little (or too much). Under the influence of supply and demand, it is thus imagined that prices on the market will, automatically, as it were, approach a certain stable level.

It is important to know whether with such an idea as this, we are merely moving in a theoretical world—in a notional system—or whether we are truly entering into realities. And we are certainly not entering into realities. As soon as you really tackle these concepts of supply and demand you will see that it is quite impossible, economically speaking, even to establish them. As contemplative students of economics you can do so, no doubt—you can send people into the market to observe how supply and demand are working. With such observations, are you entering deeply enough into the working of the economic processes? Can you make any use of these concepts? In reality you cannot, because you are leaving out in every case what lies behind the processes that you are trying to grasp. You look at the market; you see the working of supply and what is called demand. But that does not include what lies behind the phenomenon of supply; nor will it comprise all that precedes the appearance of demand. Yet it is there that you will find the real economic processes; processes that are only summarized, so to speak, in the market itself. The best evidence of this is the extraordinary fragility of these concepts.

If we wish to form proper, useful concepts, our concepts can and must be mobile in relation to life. We must be able to carry such a concept around from one domain of reality to another, and as we do so the concept itself must change. It must not simply go up in smoke. But that is just what happens with the concepts of supply and demand. Take supply. It is supply when someone brings commodities into the market and offers them for a price. That is supply, you say. But I say no, it is demand. If someone brings commodities into the market and wants to sell them, in this case it is unquestionably a demand for money. In effect, if we do not enter further into the economic process, it makes no difference at all whether I have a supply of commodities and a demand for money, or whether I come forward with a demand in the cruder sense. If I wish to develop a demand, I must have a supply of money.

Supply of commodities is demand for money, and supply of money is demand for commodities. These are economic realities, since the economic process (in so far as it consists of trade or barter) cannot take place at all, unless there are both supply and demand in the case of both buyer and seller. For what the buyer has for supply (money), must also first have been evolved in the economic process somewhere behind the buyer's back, or behind the back of the demand, just as the commodity that appears as a supply must also first have been developed or produced.

Our concepts are quite unreal if we imagine that price arises from the interaction of what is ordinarily called supply and demand. In actual fact, price does not develop at all as it is defined by this line of thought. The development of price is undoubtedly influenced by the question of whether the demander can become a supplier of money, or whether perhaps, at a given time in the whole working of the economic process, the person cannot become a supplier of money with respect to a given product. The point is, not only that there must be a certain number of commodities available as supply, but also that there must be a certain number of people able to develop a supply of money for these particular commodities. This will show you at once that we cannot simply speak of an interaction of supply and demand.

If we look now not to the concepts (which may always be wrongly formed) but to the real facts—the facts of the market, or even of the pure, marketless exchange of commodities and money—it is unquestionable that prices evolve between supply and demand—only the supply and demand are always there on both sides. This is undoubtedly the case, as a pure matter of fact.

The important thing is that supply, demand, and price are three factors, every one of which is primary. We cannot merely write that price is a function of supply and demand, or—to speak mathematically—treat S and D as variables and P, the price, as a third magnitude resulting from the two, that is, $P = f(S, D)$. No; we must regard all of them, S and D (supply and demand) and P (price), as mutually independent variables, and by that means arrive at another magnitude, X. You see, we are coming to a formula. We must not merely suppose that S and D are the independent variables and that the price is a function of the two. No; we have three mutually independent variables that come into mutual interplay and give rise to something new: $X = f(S, D, P)$. The price is there between the supply and demand, but it is there in a particular way.

We must approach this whole line of thought from another angle. If we do see supply and demand, at any given point on the market, in the relationship in which Adam Smith saw them—if it really is so in any particular domain—then it is approximately so for the distribution of commodities as seen from the standpoint of the tradesperson or merchant. Even here, it is not entirely the case. It is absolutely not the case from the standpoint of the consumer, nor from that of the producer. For the consumer something quite different is true. The standpoint of consumers is conditioned by what they have. Between what consumers have and what they give, a relationship arises—similar to what arises for the merchant as between supply and demand. Consumers must consider the mutual interaction between price and demand. They demand less when for their pocket the price is too high; they demand more when for their pocket the price is sufficiently low. Altogether, consumers confine their gaze to price and demand.

We may say, therefore, that in the consumer's case we must observe the interaction of price and demand; in the merchant's case we must observe rather the interaction of supply and demand. In the producer's case we shall have to observe the interaction between supply and price.† For producers will in the first place arrange their supply of commodities according to the prices that are possible in the whole economic process. Thus we may call our first equation, $P = f(S, D)$, the merchant's equation. Adam Smith applied it to the economic system as a whole. Applied in that way, it is incorrect. For, we can also form the following equation: We can regard supply, S, as a function of price and demand. And third, we can indicate demand as a function of supply and price. In this last equation we shall have

$D = f(S, P)$—that is to say, demand is a function of supply and price. This is the producer's equation. In the equation where supply is a function of price and demand, $S = f(P, D)$, we have the consumer's equation. But please note, we shall still have made these equations qualitatively different, inasmuch as here (in the consumer's case) the supply is a supply of money, while in the producer's case it is a supply of commodities.[†] In the case of the merchant we deal with something that lies midway between "money" and "commodity"[price].

$$P = f(S, D)$$ Merchant's equation.
$$S = f(P, D)$$ Consumer's equation.
$$D = f(S, P)$$ Producer's equation.

You see how much more complicated our thoughts on the economic life must be. It is just because we try to get at the ideas so easily and quickly, that we have no proper science of economics today. If we wish to enter into the realities, we must ask ourselves what is in this economic life. What really lives in it? I may supposed that what I get for my own needs comes in the first place into my realm. (I will speak of "property" and "ownership" at a later stage; at present I will express myself as indefinitely as possible—even so, it will suffice to cover the facts). What I get for my needs passes— under the conditions that exist today—into my realm. I give money or something that I have produced instead of money. That is how things usually happen. In saying this, have we really exhausted the full reality of economic life? After all, I may acquire things otherwise than by giving a commodity for money or money for a commodity. I may acquire money and commodities in a different way. Suppose I steal them. Then, too, I shall have acquired something. If I should steal on a large enough scale, as the old robber barons sometimes did for decades at a time—then a very different economic theory would have to be developed to apply to such conditions. This would be different from the theory that has, generally speaking, to be developed for our own code of ethics! It may seem to you a crude example when I speaking of stealing. But what is stealing in reality? To steal is to take something away from someone else, without that person being able to prevent it; or again, when the stealer finds it convenient to not exchange the item for an adequate exchange or return. Compare, for example, this now disreputable concept of "stealing" with the concept that we (in the German language) signify with a foreign word, when we speak of "requisitioning" or "commandeering." Under certain circumstances one commandeers things—that is to say, one takes something away from people and gives them nothing in return.

In other cases, too, it happens in the economic process that something is taken away from people and they receive nothing in return. These are things that we need only mention, for if we were to dwell on them any longer, people would imagine that we were anxious to agitate, and I wish only to develop a science here; I do not wish to agitate. Now assume for a moment that somewhere or other, within a comparatively small region, I establish a social order wherein money is abolished. Instead, I organize a system of raids with the necessary armed forces. Those who possess anything are knocked down or killed and their possessions taken away from them. Well, what is there to prevent that from happening? There is this: that the others may perhaps defend themselves. In that case, they must have the means to do so. Or, again, it might not be worthwhile. If my territory is rather small, it would not be worthwhile.

All of this shows that something else has to play into the economic process at this point. I cannot, without more ado, take something away from someone else. Why not? First, because it must somehow be recognized by my fellow human beings that I should be allowed to keep it. It would by no means be recognized that I should be allowed to keep what I have acquired by killing my fellow human beings in the surrounding country. What is it then that plays into the economic life at this point? It is the life of rights; it is law and order. You cannot really consider the economic process without observing how law plays into it at every point. You cannot think out the economic life, nor can you bring to pass whatever it may be that you intend, without considering this interplay of legal rights and economics. The moment you pass from mere barter to trade assisted by money, you see directly how the principle of law plays into economics. How, otherwise, could it be possible in return for a pair of boots to get not a hat, say, but a dollar, or whatever else it may be? I have saved myself the trouble of giving the merchant, a hat; I have given him a dollar instead. I have my boots; he has the dollar. How otherwise could this be possible? If the dollar (even if it were a gold sovereign) were recognized by no one to be a real value—a value for which something could be received again in return—if it were not rightly integrated in the whole economic process, the shoemaker might have collected ever so many dollars, but it would be of no avail. The moment money makes its appearance in economic interactions, we see quite palpably the appearance of the element of law. It is extremely important to bear this in mind. We can look at the social organism as a whole only if we pass from purely economic events to events that take place under the influence of the life of rights.

Let us now assume that I have received my pair of boots from the shoemaker and have given him the dollar. Now it might happen that the shoemaker, just after having sold me the pair of boots, suddenly remembered that shoemakers have at times in the world's history been something else besides shoemakers (witness Hans Sachs and Jacob Boehme).† Having acquired the dollar, he might think of doing something quite different with it instead of making another pair of boots. He might do anything with it, into which he put his ingenuity, his genius. That dollar would then suddenly have quite a different value for him than the value of a pair of boots. Thus, the moment we have transformed the commodity into money, that is to say into a lawful right, the right can either be kept (I use the dollar to buy myself something equal in value to the pair of boots); or through my ingenuity I can do something with the money to produce an altogether new value in the economic process.

It is here that human faculties come in. Individual faculties, which develop quite freely among people, enter in and incorporate themselves in the rights that they acquire with money. In the same way money, which may be regarded—in this sense—as rights realized, incorporates itself outwardly in the commodity. Thus we have now placed into the organic process that we described provisionally when we spoke of nature, elaborated nature, and labor divided and organized by the Spirit—we have now placed into this whole process the principle of law or rights and individual faculties. We have found, within the economic process itself, a division that is in truth a three-fold order—a *Dreigliederung* (threefold membering, threefold articulation). It is necessary, however, that we think of this *Dreigliederung* in the right way.

If we observe the economic process, we perceive that just because the things I have now been describing are real facts—just because of this, certain impossibilities are actually realized in economic life. You see, one can also acquire a right by conquest or the like, by having the power to take it. One does not always acquire a right by mere exchange; one can also acquire it by having the opportunity or the power to take it for oneself. Here we have an element in rights that, in so far as it is present, is quite incapable of comparison with commodities. There is no point of contact between commodities and rights. Nevertheless, in the actual economic process, commodities (or the money values representing them) are perpetually being exchanged for rights. Precisely when we pay for land, even when we merely help with our rent to pay for the value of the land, we are paying for a right with a commodity or with the money that we have received for a commodity. At any rate, we pay for a rights value with a commodity value. When we hire a schoolteacher and give a certain salary, we are (sometimes, at least) paying for spiritual-cultural faculties with the value of a commodity or a corresponding money value. Thus, in the economic process there continuously occur exchanges between rights and commodities, between faculties and commodities, and also between faculties and rights.

Mutually incommensurable things are exchanged for each other in the economic process. Consider what happens when a man gets paid for an invention that he has patented. He accepts payment for a purely spiritual-cultural value that is being paid for in commodity values. There is absolutely nothing that could figure as a standard of comparison in such a case. Here we are touching on an element where life enters quite strongly into the economic process! The situation becomes still more complicated when we introduce the concept of labor.

I have already said that the wage laborers do not in reality receive what is generally understood by the idea of "wages," but they really sell the products of their labor for dollars and cents to the business person, and thus receive payment. It is only through their expert knowledge of the market that the business people give the proper value—or at any rate a higher value—to that which they buy from the laborers. Economically considered, the profit is not extracted from the labor as a surplus value. By thinking in terms of economics we cannot possibly arrive at such a judgment. We can arrive at it, at most, by a moral judgment. The business profit occurs because the laborers are in a less favorable social situation. The products the laborers sell have less value at the point where they sell them than at the point where the business person sells them, who are in a different position—they know the circumstances far better, and can sell at a greater advantage. The worker's relation to the business person resembles the case of a man who goes to the market and buys a commodity for a given price. He must buy it there, for the simple reason that his circumstances will not allow him, let us say, to buy it anywhere else. Another person may perhaps be able to buy it for less at another place. The two cases are exactly the same. Economically speaking, what exists between the business person and the wage laborer is simply a kind of market.

It does make a certain difference, undoubtedly, whether I am fully conscious that this is the case, or whether I imagine that I am paying the laborers for their labor. You may think the difference merely theoretical, but let such a view of things—or two such views, the one and the other—become real. Let them be realized, and you will see how the economic relationships change under the influence of the one view or the other. What happens between human beings is, among other things, the result of their mental outlook, of the ideas they entertain. As our mental outlook changes, it changes the course of events. Today the whole proletariat bases its agitation on the idea that labor must be properly paid for. But in fact labor is nowhere paid for, only the products of labor are paid for; and this, if it were truly understood, would also come to expression in the actuality of price. We cannot say that it makes no difference whether we call something a wage or the price of a commodity. The moment we speak of wages, we imagine that we are paying for labor. Then we go on to all the secondary concepts that confuse labor as such with other economic processes that are value creating. Then the social conflicts arise in a false way. The social conflicts arise in a true way, however, in so far as they arise out of sentiments and feelings. Sentiments and feelings are always in some way right, but we can never correct what ought to be corrected if we do not have the right concepts. This is the fatal situation in social life. Often the grievances arise in a way that is right, but the corrections are made under the influence of false concepts. People evolve these false ideas in every detail and carry them over into their whole conception of the economic process—and havoc results.

Take a very simple example. A gentleman (this is a true story) once said to me, "I am very fond of sending picture postcards to my friends. I send lots of them." I said, "I am not at all fond of sending picture postcards—and that is," I said, "for economic reasons." At that time I had not quite as much to do as I have now. "Why?" he asked. I said, "Every time I send a picture postcard, I cannot help thinking that perhaps a postman will have to run right up to the fourth floor with it. In short, I cause a change, a redistribution, in the economic process. It is not the labor of the postman that matters, but in the postman you cannot easily distinguish the service, the thing done, from the labor. It is the service that we must estimate. If I keep sending picture postcards to my friends, I increase in an uneconomic way the services to be rendered by postmen." "That is an economic fallacy," said the other man; "for on the assumption that one postman need do only a limited amount, an increase in the number of picture postcards will mean that additional postmen will have to be employed, and that they will get paid. So you see," he said, "I am really a benefactor to the people who get these jobs." I could only answer: "Yes, and do you also produce all that they eat? You do not increase the available means of consumption in the very least. You merely bring about a redistribution. To employ more postmen is not to increase the available means of consumption."

This very idea often brings about the most basic errors in individual cases. Suppose that there is a borough council consisting of people like my friend—as may well happen—indeed, such people may even become cabinet ministers, and then it will be a cabinet meeting. Then they will say: "There are a certain number of people unemployed. Let us put up new buildings or the like, then people will be provided for." Yes, for the next five steps ahead you have rid yourselves of the problem, but you have still produced nothing new. The workers as a whole have no more to eat than they had before. If I let one side of the scale sink, the other side must rise. Thus if you give such instructions, not as part of a whole coherent economic process but as a mere isolated measure, an economic calamity must necessarily arise on the other side. If we knew how to observe these things, we would be able to see that by making social reforms in this way (merely giving means of subsistence to the destitute or unemployed, by having new buildings erected), we will have increased the price of this or that article for a number of other people. In the economic sphere, above all, we must not think shortsightedly, but think all things in connection. We must think things in connection with one another, as a whole.

That kind of thinking, however, is not at all easy to do, for the simple reason that the economic process is very different from a scientific system. A scientific system in its totality can be contained in a single human being—perhaps only in outline, but still, it can be contained within a single human being. The economic process, in contrast, can never take place in its totality within a single human being. The economic process can find its reflection only where judgments, proceeding from those who stand in the most varied spheres, are working together.

The only possibility of arriving at a real judgment on these things—not a theoretical but a real judgment—is by way of association. In other words, take the three equations [see p. 95] once again. Those who are familiar only with the ways and customs of a merchant will always have the first equation in their heads. They will trade under the influence of this equation; they will thus be in a position to know the influence that this equation exerts. Likewise, the consumer who intelligently follows and observes the process of consumption will understand the influence of the second equation, and the producer will know all that is subject to the influence of the third. At this point you may say that, surely, people are not so unintelligent as not to be able to think beyond their own narrow horizon. Surely, those who are only consumers or only merchants can think beyond their own horizon? Yes, that is perfectly right, where one general world outlook is concerned. But in practical economic life there is no other effective way of knowing what is going on in trade, for example, except to be engaged in trade oneself. You must be in the midst of it, you must be trading. There is no other way. There are no theories about it. Theories may be interesting, but the point is not that you should know how trade goes on in general, but that you should know how the products circulate in the process of trade in Basel and its immediate neighborhood. If you know that, you do not thereby know how they circulate in the Lugano district. The point is not that we should know about things in general, but that we should know something in a particular region. If you can form an effective judgment, likewise, as to the higher or lower prices at which scythes or other agricultural implements can be manufactured, you do not thereby know the prices at which screws can be manufactured, or other such things.

The judgments that have to be formed in the economic life must be formed out of immediate, concrete situations. And that is possible only in this way. For definite domains or regions (whose magnitude, as we have seen, will be determined by the economic process itself), associations must be formed, in which all three types of representatives will be present alike. From the most varied branches of the economic life, there must be the representatives of the three things that occur in it—production, consumption, and distribution.

It is really tragic that no understanding is found in our time for what is, after all, so simple and so sensible. The moment there is a real understanding, the changes can be made—not even by the day after tomorrow, but by tomorrow. It is not a question of radical changes, but of seeking for the proper associative union and cooperation in each case. You need only summon the will and the understanding to do it. This is what touches one so painfully, for, after all, economic thinking does to some extent coincide with moral and religious thinking. To me, for instance, it is quite unintelligible how this way of tackling the economic problem could have been entirely missed by those who are officially in charge of the religious needs of the world. There can be no doubt that during recent times it has become clear that the economic facts are no longer being mastered. The facts have gone beyond the mastery of human beings. Today we stand before this question: How can the situation be mastered, how shall we grapple with it? It must be mastered by human beings, by human beings in association.

The science of economics has not kept pace in its concepts with the transition that has actually taken place from the economics of barter to the economics of money and the economics of human faculties. In its essential concepts, economic science still fumbles around within the economics of barter. It continues to regard money as though it were just a substitute for barter. This is not readily admitted. It is implicit, nonetheless, in the prevailing theories. So we have this situation. In the older economic systems (though these may no longer appeal to us today) people bartered or exchanged [German *tauschen* = to barter]. Then money came in. (I do not wish to make a pun at the end of a solemn line of thought, but the genius of language itself is working here.) *"Tauschen"* [barter] became *"täuschen"* [illusion or deceit], and everything became unclear. Today we deceive ourselves in almost all of our economic processes. The *"tauschen"* has become a *"täuschen"*—the exchange (or barter) an illusion. I do not mean that there is deliberate deceit, but that the whole process becomes confused and deceptive. We must first get to the root of things once more and see how the economic processes inwardly take place.

Lecture 9

Trade, Loan, and Industrial Capital

DORNACH, AUGUST 1, 1922

T HE equations I tried to give yesterday are not, of course, mathematical formulas; rather, like the ones of which I spoke before, they are formulas that must be verified in life itself. Not only that; they must also be conceived in such a way that they actually live within the economic process.

Today I must say a few things that may gradually lead us to understand the way in which these things do really live in the economic process. On one hand, everything that circulates within the total economic process must have a certain value. On the other hand, we must also realize that many things can occur in the economic organism, the value of which is not immediately expressed in the economic processes themselves.

Let me give you an example that will serve as an introduction to some further economic concepts. Unruh[†] has described very well, in his books on economics, such things that, reveal, as it were, the more hidden economic connections. I give here only what I myself have followed up, and what I can vouch for as being correct, purely as a matter of observation. Although Unruh is a man completely wrapped up in state economics, it is nonetheless true that, inasmuch as he thinks politically rather than economically, he is unable in the end to bring these things into their right relationship.

The price of rye in certain districts of Central Europe is a striking example of the complicated way in which things take their course in the economic process. If one hears big farmers or estate owners speaking of their work, one often hears them say, "We make nothing on the price of rye; on the contrary, we lose on it." What does this really mean? To begin with, it means that these people cannot sell their rye as other things are sold—in the main, at any rate, today—where the price is composed of the costs of raw materials, the costs of production, and a certain margin of profit. Taking the actual prices of rye in this way, we would find that they do not correspond to the costs of production plus a certain profit. On the contrary, they fall far short. If, in balancing their accounts, farmers were merely to include the actual market prices of rye, the values they would thus insert would undoubtedly influence the balance in a negative direction. As I said, we can follow the matter up and it is absolutely correct; the rye is sold, as we might say, "below cost price." It cannot be so in reality; it is impossible for this to go on in reality, yet apparently it does go on. What happens is this. Rye yields not only grain but also straw; and farmers who sell the grain below cost price sell scarcely any of the straw at all. They use it on their own farms; they use it for their cattle and strike a balance in that way. What they lose on the rye is made up for by the manure they get from the animals. For this is the very best manure; there is no better. It is extremely rich in bacteria; it is the best manure a farmer can have. Thus from the standpoint of their accounts they get the manure thrown in as a free gift and in this way, in the long run, a proper balance is struck.

We are thus obliged to posit an economic concept that, though it is most important, is comparatively hardly considered in the ordinary literature of economics. The concept I would here establish is that of "internal economies" within the general economic life. You have an "internal economy" whenever an economic organism, a business, does business within itself—exchanges products within itself. That is to say, it does not sell such products outwardly or buy them from outside, but lets them circulate within the business itself. This I would call an internal economy as contrasted with the general economy. Wherever such an internal economy is in force, it is quite possible for products to be delivered below the price that would otherwise be economically necessary. Needless to say, this implies that the forming of price within any economic domain is an extremely complicated chain of events.

Such connections, as I said, have been observed as matters of pure fact by our economists. There is another chain of events that I have touched upon from a certain point of view, and that must now be regarded also from a different aspect. I mentioned a few days ago that we do not take in at a glance all the links in the economic chain. I had us imagine the example, that a shoemaker falls ill and has an unskilled doctor attend to him. He remains ill and for three weeks cannot manufacture any boots. His products—the boots that he would have manufactured in the three weeks—are, therefore unavailable to economic distribution. Suppose, instead, that he gets a skillful doctor who makes him well within a week, so that he gets an extra two weeks during which to go on making boots as before. Economically speaking, we can now ask: Who manufactured the boots? Economically speaking, undoubtedly—at this moment of the economic process—the doctor did; there can be no doubt about it.

Here again we come to another point. For you may ask whether the doctor was paid for the boots. No, in reality he was not; for you can make the following calculation. Reckon it up, according to the market. What did the boots that the doctor manufactured amount to? And now if you draw up a rather full statement of account (it would have to be a very full one) you can set this off against what had to be spent on his training. And you will find, in all probability, that what was spent on his training was not so very different from the value of all the boots he manufactured and all the stags he shot. It is not regarded as universally characteristic of doctors that they withdraw from economic life, for one week only, patients who would otherwise be withdrawn for three. Be that as it may—however the final balance emerged, we would not make a true calculation in the wider economic sense if we did not strike the balance in this way, setting off against the cost of his training the boots he manufactures, the stags he shoots (assuming that he cures the hunter more quickly than would otherwise have been the case), the corn he gathers, and so forth. It is true, of course, that the economic process is very complicated, and so the payment also proves extremely complicated.

From all this you can see that it can by no means be said with certainty, at any given place, what the true source of payment for a given thing is, within the economic process. We must sometimes go far afield to discover what the real source of such payment is. People who look for mere simplicity in the economic process will never arrive at economic concepts coinciding with reality. They will not get far enough. They will not get to that aspect that is really there behind the formulas of price, supply, demand, and so forth. These are the very things we must get at. What makes it so difficult to estimate the economic process rightly? It is because outlay and return are often so widely separated. That is why it is difficult to see clearly, within the economic process as a whole, what is paid for, what is bought, what is lent and borrowed, and what is freely given. For example, assume for a moment that what I advocated a few days ago is realized. Assume that the masses of capital, arising in one way or another, are withdrawn from the tendency to become congested on the land and are given to the spiritual-cultural life—it may be in the form of foundations, scholarships, or other such things. These are free gifts. You will begin to see what happens on the one side of your gigantic account book, since it must be such that it comprises the real economic life in its totality. The boots that the doctor manufactures during the extra two weeks may actually contain an item that you must look for on the other side, under the heading of "free gifts." It may well be that he had a scholarship to help him in his training, or that he benefited by some foundation. In short, from this point of view you can raise a weighty question. What are the most productive transformations of capital in the economic process? What are the most productive of all? Follow out such connections as I have just described; follow especially those portions of available capital that go into foundations, scholarships, and other spiritual-cultural "goods," that in the course of time react to fertilize the whole process of spiritual-cultural production and enterprise of every kind. You will perceive that free gifts are the most fruitful thing of all in the whole economic process. We cannot arrive at a healthy economic process unless, in the first place, it is made possible for people to have something to give; and, in the second place, unless they have the goodwill to give what they have in a sensible manner. Here, then, we have something that enters into the economic process in a very particular way.

It is remarkable that this is something that we cannot extract from theoretical concepts. It can transpire only from a wide range of experience; and a wide range of experience will yield it to you—the more so, the more you follow the matter up. Indeed, I would recommend that you keep this question in mind when you are choosing subjects for dissertations. What becomes of the free gifts in the whole economic process? You will find that the free gifts are the most productive of all. Capital freely given, gift capital, is the most productive; loaned and borrowed capital is less productive in the economic process; and the least productive is what stands directly under purchase and sale. What is paid for immediately on a transaction of purchase and sale is the least fruitful in the economic process; what depends on lending and comes into the economic process through the functions of invested capital is of medium productivity; while what enters into the economic process through free gifts is of the very greatest productivity, for the reason that the work that would otherwise have to be done to earn what is here given freely, or rather the product of that work, is actually saved. We freely give the available proceeds of the economic process, which would only do harm if they were left to congest upon the land.

We see, therefore, that at a given moment of its evolution the economic process gives no real information of itself. The "before and after" must always be taken into account; but the "before and after" cannot be taken into account unless they are based on the judgment of people who join together in association and who are able to have a corresponding insight into the past and the future. We have to build the economic process on the insight of those whose feet are planted within the economic process. Once more, we come to the same conclusion. It is, generally speaking, a difficult and lengthy business to estimate how the several factors in the economic process play their part in the whole of human life—I mean the material life.

From a certain point of view we can speak of trade capital, loan capital, and industrial capital within the economic process. Circulating capital is more or less covered by these three categories. These three are contained in the economic process, moreover, in the most varied ways. You must remember that such "internal economies" as we exemplified at the beginning of today's lecture are scattered everywhere throughout the economic process. Where you have an economic process taking place within a larger whole, it is extremely difficult to say what the respective contributions, quantitatively speaking, of loan capital, industrial capital, and trade capital are to the general economic welfare. Yet it is possible to arrive at reliable concepts, if we extend our survey to a wide enough horizon.

Let us, to begin with, turn our attention to the economic life of entire nations, or state economies as we must call them, according to the economic life of recent times. Take France, for instance; I take it only as one example. The world economic connections of France, especially as they were before World War I, and as they revealed themselves in their effects during the war, are a good example of how loan capital works in the economic process on a larger scale. France always had a certain inclination to invest capital in loans—that is, in effect, to treat "loan capital" (investment capital) literally as loaned capital. You are probably aware of how these things penetrated into the political sphere—clearly illustrating the harmful effects of the coupling together of the economic life and the life of rights (that is, the political life)—when it came out in the extensive loans made by France to Russia and Turkey. France exported a very large amount of loan capital to Russia and to Turkey. Even in Germany, though Germany was not exactly in her good books, French capital found a home—for instance, when the construction of the Baghdad Railway was begun. England withdrew, but France did not withhold her capital from those who stood at the head of the undertaking—Siemens & Gwinner,[†] for example. France, therefore, was primarily a lending country. In France one could see how loan capital becomes involved in the whole economic process.

There is one historical phenomenon in which you can truly recognize what the interests of loan capital are. (I am not defending or attacking anything, but simply describing things objectively.) When we turn our attention, say, to private "economies" or businesses, we shall always find, as any bank will tell you, that the private business people are peace-loving people. They know very well that their interests and dividends will be upset if, just as their capital is nicely invested, a war begins to sweep through the economic connections of the world. Political economists always reckon with the fact that lenders are peace-loving people. That is the reason why it is always possible to say that France was innocent of the war. The moment we want to prove that the war was not desired in France, we need only point to the interests of the numerous small investors, not to the interests of those who urged on the war. In France you always have in the background those who decidedly did not want the war. This fact of history may show us on a large scale what is equally true on a small scale. Those who lend—those who are the happy possessors of capital available for investment—are essentially the people who would like to see the economic life protected, if possible, from disturbance either by events outside it or by catastrophic upheavals within it. The investors are all the more fond of tranquility because it saves them the trouble of having to form an independent judgment. They like to be able to rely on the assurance of someone else that a particular investment is "a good thing." In our age, although public opinion is very conceited, there is really very little public opinion in the sense of judgment. We may say that in our time the possession of capital available for investment is generally connected with a very strong faith in authority, both in the economic life and also in other respects. This, again, clouds the economic judgment to no small extent. Those, for example, who are in any way officially labeled, very easily get money lent to them. Personal credit is readily given to anyone with a title or some other official label. This is often the decisive factor. According to how this principle of authority is more or less cultivated, we see the consequences. In the one case, those who really have the stronger personal capabilities will be enabled to enter productively into the economic process. In the other case it will be simply those with a handle to their names—members of chambers of commerce and so forth—and often those have the name, not by reason of genuine ability but for some quite extraneous reason. It is one thing if such favored people are handed an opportunity to work into the economic life, and quite another if they have to depend on their genuine capabilities being recognized by an untainted public judgment. Here, once again, something elusive enters into the economic life. (In a certain community it has recently become far too common a practice to use a certain word whenever one fails to keep pace with things with one's clear thinking. In many places, recently, I have far too often heard this word, the "imponderables." I wish to emphasize that I want to avoid this word. All that I wish to point out is how these things, which we would like to take straightforwardly, become complicated, so that we may presently have to follow them up by somewhat curved and winding paths. It is unnecessary, as soon as this begins to happen, to have recourse to the convenient term "the imponderables," which we have heard *ad nauseam* in certain quarters.) So much, at the moment, for loan capital.

We will now go on to industrial capital. If we wish to study the essence and function of industrial capital, we shall be able to do so especially well by observing the quick rise of industry in Germany in the decades before World War I—though its history here is hardly an edifying one. We can study it here especially well, because, under the influence of the "enterprising" impulse, industrial capital arose by direct transformation out of loan capital to a greater extent in Germany in the last decades before the War than in any other part of the world. What I said in the first lecture is most decidedly true. In England, for example, trade capital was transformed gradually into industrial capital. In England industrialism evolved out of trade, and it evolved far more slowly than in Germany, where it sprang up with immense rapidity. Industrialism exists in its pure form where it transforms, not trade capital, but loan capital into industrial capital. It can therefore be best studied in its pure form in the life of Germany.

Now the point is that industrial capital, if I may put it so, is really placed between two buffers. The one buffer is raw materials; the other is markets. Industrial capital is obliged, on the one hand, to look around as far as possible for the sources of raw materials and, on the other, to arrange for markets. This is not quite so easy to study in the example of German industry. In German industrialism, you can, rather, study economically how industrial capital functions in itself. Still, the emergence of industrialism is evident in all countries during the nineteenth century and on into the twentieth, so you can observe this standing "between two buffers" everywhere. You need only search out the true facts. As I have said, it is a good thing to control the necessary direction—orientation—of our ideas, by taking things that can be surveyed as a whole; but you will find, if you are considering smaller economic territories, that extraordinarily difficult paths must sometimes be traced out. It is better to get your orientation and to derive your calculations from wide, comprehensive regions. The paths grow easier if you observe economic organisms on a very large scale. Then, for example, you will perceive how, usually, the concepts of force or might (which often appear masked under the guise of rights or justice) are realized most strongly where it is a question of opening up new sources of raw materials. We can study this on a large scale, for instance, in the Boer War, where it was mainly a question of opening up the sources of precious metals. The Boer War was a real war for raw materials. Of course it always showed itself in a kind of mask; nevertheless, it was a war for raw materials. Again, you have an example of how the economic life unfolds in a political way, playing over into the domain of political power. You have an example of this, for instance, in the military enterprises of Belgium, which had the ivory and rubber of the Congo as their object. From this, you can see how the opening up of sources of raw materials takes place in the economic life. Or again, take the case of North America, which annexed the Spanish possessions in the West Indies because it was looking for sources of raw material—sugar in this instance. In every case we can see how the search for raw materials very easily drives the purely economic life into the political, toward the development of might or force. This is the one side—the first buffer, if I may call it this.

With the search for markets it is different. It is easy to demonstrate from history that the search for markets does not lead into the political life in the same way. In this case, the plain fact is that human nature does not tend so much toward the use of force. We should have to go to the nineteenth century for a rather glaring example. I mean the so-called "Opium War," whereby England conquered for itself the Chinese opium market. Even there it did not go quite so easily by purely military means; even there, if I may put it so, peaceful persuasion, peaceful politics, had not a little to say. For when things began to grow uncomfortably hot, a hundred and forty-one doctors were found to pronounce an expert judgment to the effect that opium is no more harmful than tobacco or tea. Here, then, politics—peaceful politics—played a certain part. Politics, in any case, is always difficult to keep out. You know the saying of Clausewitz, "War is the continuation of politics by other means."† Such definitions are all very well, but by the same method we could establish the proposition: "Divorce is the continuation of marriage by other means." The relationships of life can always be represented in a particular light by using this kind of logic, and people admire it! Curiously enough, everyone sees through it at once if I say, "Divorce is the continuation of marriage by other means," but when it is everywhere proclaimed that war is the continuation of politics by other means, they do not notice the absurdity. On the contrary they admire it. In point of method, I should like to say that if we employ this sort of logic in economics, we shall not advance a step. Speaking of this second buffer, the hunt for markets, we must undoubtedly admit that a far greater part is played by human cleverness, which fluctuates between the extremes of slyness, astuteness, and wise economic guidance. In the arranging of markets a great deal could be seen at work of all three, particularly in the way they were arranged in those large economic domains that the states themselves had become as politics and economics coalesced. The states themselves did very much in this direction by way of wise guidance, and also by way of deceit, cleverness, slyness, and the like. The concepts we need to form with respect to smaller economic domains, concerning the relation, say, between the single industrial undertaking and its sources of raw materials and its markets, can be made clear and palpable only by considering these matters on a large scale.

If it is the functions of trade capital that we desire to study, we should take England as our example, especially in the period when England made its great economic progress. This it did by means of trade; consequently, its trade capital continued to increase in such a way that England entered quite gently and gradually into the new industrialism. At the time when industrialism was transforming the world, England already had her trade capital. In this early period, therefore, we can study trade capital most readily in England. In more recent times England has been chosen by Marx as a means of studying the economic functions of industrialism. In the earlier period—the period immediately preceding the creation of modern industrial-ism—going back, that is to say, to the last decades of the eighteenth century, it is the functions of trade capital, nevertheless, which we can best study in the light of England's economic destiny. Now it cannot be denied that here, either in the open or behind the scenes, the essential thing is always competition. Whether on the large scale, in the economic life of the nation as a whole, where it is mainly based on trade, or within trade or commerce itself, competition is the essential thing. Of course by the introduction of various ideas of what is decent and proper conduct, it may become very fair, but it is competition none the less. Productivity in trade—productivity that will enable trade capital to be treated in the economic process so that it eventually takes effect as industrial capital—such productivity depends, in the end, on the tendency of trade capital to accumulate. And that is impossible without competition. Thus we shall study the functions of trade capital most clearly by considering the function of competition in the economic life.

At the same time, these things are connected with historical changes. This is indeed the case. Right up to the first third of the nineteenth century, if we are considering the world economy that was gradually coming into being as a single whole (such as it was in a high degree before World War I)—up to the first third of the nineteenth century, the economic processes of trade and industry still played the most important part in the economic life. The heyday—the classical age, if I may put it so—of loan capital began only in the nineteenth century, indeed only towards the second third of the nineteenth century. And it is at this point that we notice the rise of those insti-tutions that more especially serve the process of lending—I mean the banking system. The classical age of loan capital, and with it the evolution of the banking system, falls into the last two thirds of the nineteenth century and the first decades of the twentieth. With the evolution of the banking system, borrowing and lending develops on an ever larger scale, enters more and more as a prime factor into the economic process. At the same time, precisely in connection with lending, a remarkable phenomenon appears. Through the instrumentality of lending on a large scale, and accompanying the expansion of the banking system, the control of the circulation of money is withdrawn from the individual. The circulation of money has gradually become a process taking place—I can find no other word to express it—impersonally. Thus, as I said in my first lecture, the time has actually come when money does business on its own account, and human beings fluctuate up and down according to how they are drawn into this whole stream of money economics, money business. They are drawn in far more than they imagine. Precisely during the last decades of the nineteenth century, the circulation of money became objectified—it became impersonal. This brings me to a peculiar phenomenon of the nineteenth century, particularly of the end of the nineteenth century. In economics, everything depends on an open-minded consideration of life as a whole; we must gain a clear vision—of the whole of life. The phenomenon to which I refer appears, to begin with, in the psychological sphere, but afterward plays a great part in the economic life. It is this. Conditions that were brought about in the first place by very real forces afterwards continue rolling on by a kind of social inertia, just as a ball will, when you have given it a certain momentum. These conditions go rolling on and on, even after the original impulses have ceased to be active in them. Down to the first third of the nineteenth century, there were true economic impulses present in the whole system of loan and investment. Then, through the instrumentality of the banking system, these economic impulses began to change into purely financial ones; and in this process the whole thing became not only impersonal but unnatural. Everything was drawn into the stream of money, as it moved itself along. Pure money business, without any natural or personal subject—that is the end toward which, as the nineteenth century drew to a close, everything that had originally been upheld by a personal and natural subject was gravitating.

Strangely enough, this "subjectless" economic life, this "subjectless" circulation of money, was accompanied by another phenomenon.

States themselves began to do business out of economic impulses; it was out of such impulses, for example, that they began to colonize. We shall see later what influence colonizing has; de-colonizing, too, will have to be considered in this connection. We can observe very well, as a real economic process, the significance of colonization in the case of England. Fundamentally speaking, England scarcely ever went beyond the kind of colonization that we may perhaps describe as "imperialism with an objective content." Such imperialism, I mean, as contains a real economic substance—economic meaning. On the other hand, if you take the case of Germany, you need only look at the colonial accounts and you will see that German colonization was burdened from the start with an adverse balance. There were at most tiny areas that showed a favorable balance. And in other countries too the tendency crept in, merely to enlarge themselves by acquiring colonies. Individual people—Hilferding,[†] for instance, in his book *Finanzkapital*, published in Vienna in 1910—actually called this process "objectless imperialism"—imperialism without an object.

These two modern phenomena are particularly instructive: on the one hand, the subjectless circulation of money, impersonal and unnatural; and, on the other hand, objectless imperialism. Characteristic as they both are of large scale economy, their appearance together suggests that the one depends upon the other.

Such a phenomenon is purely psychological, to begin with, though in the further course it becomes economic; for if we have unproductive colonies, we must pay for them—and that means that they at once affect the economic life.

So much for what we had to discuss today.

Lecture 10

Associations

DORNACH, AUGUST 2, 1922

W E must now consider something that I indicated yesterday to a few of you. I refer to the relation between labor, and what happens when nature is transformed and elaborated into an object of economic value. In the further course, as we saw, organized labor—divided labor—is caught up, in a certain sense, by capital; and capital eventually emancipates itself and passes over completely into free spiritual-cultural activity, so to speak. From all this you will observe that while there is no such thing as a direct economic value in labor (this has already been explained), it is labor, nevertheless, that sets economic value in motion. The product of nature, as such, comes into economic circulation by being worked upon; and the elaboration that gives it its value is the real reason why the object of economic value begins to move, at least within a certain sphere. Subsequently it is the human Spirit working in capital that keeps the movement going. To begin with, therefore, we have to do with movement. For as soon as we enter the sphere of capital, we have to take into account the movement that takes place through trade capital, loan capital, and eventually through production, capital proper—industrial capital.

Speaking of this movement, we must be aware above all that there must be something to bring the values into economic circulation. To get the right idea in this respect, we must today concern ourselves with a somewhat delicate question of economics. This question cannot be seen clearly unless we try again and again to discover from direct economic experience what can be said about it, and in a certain way, to verify things.

First, I refer to what we may call economic profit. The question of profit is extremely difficult. Let us imagine, for instance, that a purchase is taking place: *A* buys from *B*. In ordinary lay thinking, we generally apply the concept of profit to the seller only. The one who sells is supposed to make a profit. It is, of course, really an exchange between what the buyer gives and what the seller gives; but if you think the matter through exactly, you can by no means admit that the seller alone makes a profit in the case of purchase and also of barter. For if the seller alone were to profit, then in the total economic life, the buyer would always be placed at a disadvantage, whenever a simple exchange takes place. The buyer would always be at a disadvantage; and you will readily admit that this cannot be so; otherwise, every transaction of purchase would be an exploitation of the buyer, and that is obviously not the case. We are well aware that the one who buys wants to buy advantageously, not at a disadvantage; there can be no doubt about that. Thus, the buyer too can buy in such a way as to make a profit. We have therefore this peculiar phenomenon. Two people make an exchange, and—at any rate in the normal process of purchase and sale—each one of them must make a profit. For practical economics it is far more important to consider this than is generally realized.

Let us suppose that I sell something and receive money for it. I must gain by giving my commodity away and getting money for it. I must desire the money more than I do the commodity. The buyer on the other hand, must desire the commodity more than the money. This, then, is what takes place in the reciprocity of exchange. Both objects passing in exchange—the one in one direction and the other in the other—increase in value. By the bare process of exchange, the things exchanged on both sides increase in value. How can this be?

Only in the following way. When I sell something and receive money for it, I am enabled to do more with the money than the one who gives it can do. Conversely, the other person who receives the commodity, must be able to do more with it than I can. This therefore is the position: the two of us, the buyer and the seller, must stand in different economic situations. The increase of value can only come about through what lies behind the actual process of purchase and sale. Thus, when I sell something, I must be in such a position, economically speaking, that the money has a greater value in my hands than it has in the other person's; while the commodity has greater value in the other person's hands than it has in mine, by virtue of this person's particular connection with the economic system as a whole.

In economics, you will perceive, we cannot merely consider the actual fact of buying or selling in the abstract. The essential question is what are the respective economic relationships in which the buyer and the seller stand. If we look at things precisely, we are led, as is so often the case, from what takes place immediately before our eyes at any given place to the whole interconnected economic system. This can also be seen by taking another illustration.

We can observe the real facts if we take our start from barter. Fundamentally speaking, the line of thought I have just laid out can tell you that barter is not entirely transcended even by the introduction of money into an economic community. In effect, we still barter commodities for money. Precisely inasmuch as both parties make a profit in the transaction, we shall see that the important point is not the mere fact that the one possesses a commodity while the other possesses money. The real point is what each party can make of what is received. What can they each do with it by virtue of their particular economic situation?

To understand it more exactly, let us turn back to the most primitive form of barter. That will throw light on what occurs in circumstances that are economically more complicated. Suppose that I buy peas. I can do many different things with these peas. I can eat them. And so, assuming that barter is the order of the day and that I have exchanged some other thing that I have manufactured—that is, some commodity—for peas, I get the peas by means of barter and I can, if I like, eat them. But suppose I have acquired a very, very large number of peas, so many that I cannot eat them all—not even if I have a large family—then I shall find someone who may be needing peas, and I shall exchange them for something that I in turn require. I give that person peas in return for something I can use. Substantially, the peas have remained the same; but economically they have not remained the same at all. Economically they have changed through the very fact that I, instead of consuming them myself, have passed them into circulation—I myself merely effecting a transfer of them in the economic process. Economically speaking, what have the peas become through this process? Given the necessary conditions— including a statute enacting that everything shall be exchangeable for peas (a sufficient number of peas would have to be produced, and it would have to be the law that everything can be exchanged for peas)—it would follow that the peas would be money. In such a case, peas would have become money in the economic process. I mean it literally, in the true sense of the word "money." A thing does not become money by being essentially different from other things existing in the economic process. It becomes money by undergoing—at a particular point in this process—a transformation from commodity to money. This has been the case with all money; all money has at one time or another been turned from a commodity into money.

From this you will see once more that with the economic process we always come to the human being; we can do nothing other than place the living human being into the process. The human being is there in the economic process in any case as a consumer. As consumers, human beings stand within it from the very outset. But if they play an active part in some respect that does not lie within the sphere of consumption, they enter into quite another relationship with the economic life than as a pure consumer. Such things must be taken into account if we would work toward the formation of true economic judgments—the kind of judgments, in fact, that must above all be formed in what I have called the "associations." Within the associations there must be people who by their practical experience can form their judgments on the basis of such points of view.

Now the point is that if we have any kind of elaborated nature or divided labor in the economic process, we must investigate what it is that brings these economic elements into movement, into circulation. Yesterday, in another place, [see seminar 2] I said that we ought to bring into our economic thinking the work or labor that is active in the economic process—in precisely the same way that physicists, for example, bring the concept of "work" into their thinking about physics. Physicists do this by developing a formula, wherein mass and velocity occur. Mass is a phenomenon that we determine with a scale. It is with the help of the scale that we are able to determine it. Apart from such quantitatively determinable mass, there would be nothing to move forward in the process of "work" in the sense of physics. Is there anything similar in the economic process, so that here, too, labor or work gives value to the objects, and then at a later stage the active entry of the Spirit or mind gives them value? Is there anything in the economic process comparable, as it were, to the weight of an object in the process of "work" in the sense of physics? If I describe diagrammatically the progression of the several economic processes, I see at once that something must be there to bring the whole system into movement— to push or press the economic element, so to speak, from here to here [see below]. Moreover, the system would be still more pronounced if there were a pressure working not only from here to here, but also a suction from the other side, so that the whole system is driven forward by a real force present in the economic process. The economic process would, in fact, have to contain something that drives it forward.

What is it then, that drives economic process forward? I showed you a little while ago how certain forces constantly arise, in the case of both the buyer and the seller. With everyone who has something to do with any other human being in the economic process—not at all in the moral but in the purely economic sense—advantage or profit arises. There is no place within the economic process where we cannot speak of advantage or profit. Nor is this profit anything merely abstract; our immediate economic desire attaches to it, and it must necessarily be so. Whether one is a buyer or a seller, one's economic craving attaches to the profit, to the advantage of the transaction. It is really this attachment to profit that generates the economic process and is the force within it. It is the thing that corresponds to mass in the process of "work," in the sense of physics.

You will observe that we have thus revealed something very weighty in the economic process—literally weighty, I would say. Weight, you will admit, is a most prominent thing in purely material products—those products that the stomach desires. It is the stomach that tells the purchaser that the fruit is more advantageous than the money, in the moment of the exchange. Here, then, we have within the human being himself the driving motor. And in other cases too—not only in the case of material goods—there must be such a driving force. You need but consider that the mood or feeling of making an advantageous deal is also present in me when I sell a thing and receive money for it. I know that I, by my faculties or opportunities, will be able to do more with the money than with the commodities that I possess. At this point, I am already entering with my faculties into the process.

Transfer this idea to the total of loan capital in any economic organism, and you will soon see: Those who desire to undertake or to do anything, and who need loan capital for this purpose, have precisely the same motive force in their need for capital as is inherent in the striving for profit; only, the loan capital works as a kind of suction. If we regard advantage or profit as an impelling, pushing force, the effect of loan capital is one of suction. Moreover, it sucks in the same direction in which advantage or profit pushes. Thus, in profit and in loan capital respectively, we have the forces of pressure and of suction in the economic process.

We thus gain a clear picture of the following fact. Inasmuch as the economic process consists in movement and everything must be brought about in it by movement, we must place the human being in it everywhere. For an objective science of economics this may be uncomfortable; the human being is a kind of incommensurable magnitude and is changeable; we have to reckon with the human being in so many different ways. But there is no getting away from it, this is the fact; and we must reckon with the human being in many different ways.

Now we have seen that, in the process of lending, a kind of suction takes place in the economic process. You know that there were times when it was considered immoral to take interest on loans; it was considered moral only to lend free of interest. Under these conditions there would be no profit in lending. This is indeed the fact. Originally, lending did not arise from the profit one derives from it—that is to say, from the interest; but it arose from the following presumption. If I lend someone something, this person can do something with it that I cannot do. Take the simplest instance. Suppose that a man is in dire need and that he can alleviate his need if I am in the position to lend him something. Under conditions more primitive than those of today, he would not pay me interest, but the presumption would be that if I, too, am ever in need, he in his turn will help me out. Wherever you trace the matter back in history, you will see that the presupposition of lending is that the other will lend to me in turn when need arises. It even applies to more complicated social conditions, for the same thing happens when someone borrows money from a money-lending firm and requires guarantors. It has always been the experience of money lenders that mutual aid plays a great part even in this service. *A* comes to a money lender and brings *B* and *C* along to stand as sureties; they enter their names as guarantors. In such a case, money-lending firms always count on the probability that if *B* ever comes to borrow money, he or she will bring *A* and *C* as guarantors; or again, when *B* has paid the debt, *C* will arrive one day and will bring *A* and *B* as guarantors. In certain circles this is taken as a matter of course. Economists declare that such a law can be assessed just as well as any that can be clothed in a mathematical formula. Of course, these things are to be taken with the well known "grain of salt" that we must always take into account. Our power to do so is part of the mobility of the economic process.

To summarize, therefore, we say that originally, there was no return for the service of lending, except the presumption that the borrower will lend to us again; or if not that, at least will help us in borrowing, as we had helped. Notably where it is a question of lending and borrowing, human mutuality or "give and take" enters the economic process in a striking way.

If this is true, what is interest? Interest—as has already been stated by some economists—is what I receive if I renounce this "mutuality"; that is to say, if I lend someone something and we agree that this person shall be under no obligation to lend to me. If I renounce this mutual right, the person pays me interest for it. Interest therefore resolves something that takes place between two human beings; it is a compensation for the human mutuality that plays in the economic process.

This is, however, something that we must set in its right place in the whole economic process. In doing so we must of course remember that there is no sense these days in studying economic processes other than those that stand entirely under the sign of the division of labor; for it is these with which we are in fact concerned. When labor is divided and distributed, human beings grow dependent on the principle of mutuality to a far greater extent than is the case when one not only grows one's own cabbages but also makes one's own hats and boots. It is with the division of labor that the dependence on mutuality comes. In the division of labor we have a process working in such a way that the several currents diverge. Yet in the economic process as a whole, we see it come about that all of these different streams tend to unite again, though in a different way, through the exchange that, in the case of a more complicated economic process, takes place with the help of money. Thus at a certain stage the division of labor makes mutuality a necessity. In other words, it involves the same element in human dealings that we find in the case of lending and borrowing. Where much is lent, this principle of mutuality is inherently involved, but in this case it can be redeemed by interest. For interest is mutuality realized. It has been transformed into an abstract form as money. The forces of mutuality are the interest, which has undergone a metamorphosis. And what we see quite plainly here in the payment of interest takes place throughout the economic process.

This is the great difficulty that besets the formation of economic ideas. You cannot form them in any other way than by conceiving things pictorially. No abstract concept can enable you to grasp the economic process; you must grasp it in pictures. Nonetheless, it is just this that makes the intellectual world so uneasy today—this demand, no matter in what sphere of thought, that we should pass from the mere abstract concepts to ideation of an imaginative kind. Yet we can never found a real science of economics without developing pictorial ideas; we must be able to conceive all the details of our economic science in imaginative pictures. And these pictures must contain a dynamic quality; we must become aware of how such a process works under each new form that it assumes.

You will understand me correctly if you will acknowledge to yourselves that there are actually human beings in the economic process—no doubt at its more primitive stages—who are quite unable to think in the way you have learned—or are supposed to have learned—to think in the course of your studies. Nevertheless, they are often excellent farmers and excellent economists. They feel precisely whether a given item can be bought or not be bought at a certain price—whether or not it will be advantageous to buy it. Sometimes farmers, for example, who do not have the remotest notion of economic concepts—yet who have attained a certain age and have simply observed the conditions of the market in their district—know with precision, without relying on any theoretical concepts, what the picture signifies when they give a certain sum of money for a horse or plough. Of course they may make a mistake, but you may do that even if you have studied the logic of economics! But the mistakes will not be the most important thing. The picture that is composed in their minds—the picture of a certain sum of money and a plough—calls forth in them the immediate feeling that they can still afford to give a little more money, or else that they cannot. They see this directly out of their feeling-experience. Now even in the most complicated economic process, this feeling-experience must not be eliminated. That is thinking in pictures.

To form abstract ideas would be fruitful only if we could say definitely that one thing is a commodity and another thing is money, and we are trading the commodity for money and the money for the commodity. If that were all, it would be simple. As I have shown you just now, however, even peas may become money. It is simply not true that we can grasp anything of the economic process by working abstract concepts into it. Only by working imaginative perceptions into it can we grasp anything of it. For instance, we may have the imaginative perception of peas on their way from the market stall to the mouths of the people. That is one definite picture. Or we may have the imaginative perception of peas being used as money. That is another picture. Even in economic science we must work toward such pictures, taken from what is immediate perception. This means, in other words, that to act rightly in the economic sense, we must make up our minds to enter into the events of production, trade, and consumption with picture-thinking. We must be ready to enter into the real process; then we shall get approximate conceptions—only approximate ones, it is true—but conceptions that will be of real use to us when we wish to take an actual part in the economic life. Above all, such conceptions will be of use to us when what we do not know by our own sensibility (supposing we ourselves have not arrived through sensibility at the corresponding pictures) is supplemented or corrected by others who are connected with us in associations. There is no other possibility. Economic judgments cannot be built on theory; they must be built on living association, where the sensitive judgments of people are real and effective; for it will then be possible to determine out of the association—out of the immediate experiences of those concerned—what the value of any given thing can be.

Strange as it may sound, it is not possible to determine theoretically wherein the value of a product may consist. We can only say that a product enters into the economic life as a whole through the several parts of the economic process; and its value at a given place must be judged and estimated by the association.

How can it be done? How is it that such judgments can be formed—judgments that, if they arise in the true way in the economic process, do actually arrive at the truth? You can understand it best by analogy with any human or animal organism. The human or animal organism assimilates the food that comes into it. For example, the human being absorbs food, permeates it with ptyalin and pepsin, passes it through the stomach, through the intestines. No matter whether the food is animal or vegetable, the first thing necessary is for the food to be killed as it passes through the organism; its life must be quelled. All life must be eliminated from the food we have in our intestines. Thereupon, what we have in our intestinal organs is sucked up by the lymph glands and called to life again within us. What passes from the lymph glands through the lymph vessels into the blood consists of nature-products (plant or animal) that have died and have been called to life again. Now if you wanted to determine theoretically how much a certain lymph gland should receive and call to life again, you simply could not do so, since in one person a lymph gland must absorb more, and in another less. Not only that; in one person a lymph gland at one place must absorb more, and a lymph gland at another place must absorb less. Digestion is a most complicated process; no human science could keep pace with this wisdom of the lymph glands, with all their beautiful division of labor.

In such a case we are not dealing with judgments propounded, but judgments working in reality. In truth, between our intestinal organs and our arteries, such a total of intelligence is working that nothing comparable to it is to be found in all our human science.

So it is with the economic process. The economic process can be sound only when such a wise self-active intelligence is working within it. This can happen only if human beings are united together—human beings who have the economic process within them as pictures, piece by piece; and, being united in the associations, they complement and correct one another, so that the right circulation can take place in the whole economic process.

Of course, the right attitude is needed for such an activity as this, but the attitude alone is not enough. You may even found associations whose members have a great deal of economic insight; yet, if something else is not contained within the associations, all their insight will be of little avail. Something else must be contained in the associations, and will be contained in them once the necessity of such associations is recognized. There must be in them the community spirit—the sense of community, the sense for the economic process as a whole. Those individuals who immediately use what they buy can do nothing other than satisfy their own egotistic sense. Indeed, they would live very poorly if they did not satisfy their own egotistic sense. As an individual in the economic life, one cannot say, if someone offers a coat for 40 francs, "Oh, no, that price does not suit me; I will give you 60 francs for it!" That will not do; at this point the individual within the economic process can do absolutely nothing. But the moment the life of associations enters the economic process, it is no longer a question of immediate personal interest. The wide outlook over the economic process will be active; the interest of the other person will actually be there in the economic judgment that is formed. In no other way can a true economic judgment come about. Thus we are impelled to rise from the economic processes to mutuality, the give-and-take between one person and another, and furthermore to what will arise from this, the objective community spirit working in the associations. This will be a community spirit, not proceeding from any "moralic acid" but from a realization of the necessities inherent in the economic process itself.

Observe this in relation to all the discussions that are opened up, for instance, by my book *Towards Social Renewal*. There is no lack of people nowadays who say, "Our economic life will be good—ever so good—if only we are good human beings; we must become good." Think of the people like Professor Förster and his kind,[†] who go about preaching that if human beings will only become selfless, if they will only fulfill the categorical imperative of selflessness, the economic life will become good. Such judgments are really of no more worth than to say that if my mother-in-law had four wheels and a steering wheel in front, she would be a bus! Truly the premise and the conclusion stand in no better connection than this, except that I have expressed it more radically.

What underlies *Towards Social Renewal* is none of this moralic acid, which can, no doubt, play a great role in another field. Rather, the purpose is to show, simply out of the economic facts, how selflessness cannot help being inherent in the very circulation of the elements of economic life. This is the case, even in the details. Take, for instance, the case where a man is in a position to receive loan capital on credit, and is thus enabled to establish an undertaking or an institution and to produce something by means of it. He goes on producing so long as his own personal faculties are united with the institution. Afterwards, the thing he has built up will be handed on in the most sensible way to some other individual who has the necessary faculties. It will be transferred as a gift—a gift, not just from one person to another, but one that takes place through the whole course of economic life. We need consider only how such gifts will be enabled in a reasonable way by the threefold social organism. Here the domain of economics borders on the social element in the human being in the most comprehensive meaning of the term. It touches on what needs to be conceived for the social organism as a whole.

See it also from the other side. I pointed out how in the simple case of exchange, where money becomes more and more important, or indeed where exchange is recognized at all, the economic life enters directly into the domain of law and rights. Moreover the moment intelligence or reason is to enter the economic life, we must allow what prevails in the free spiritual-cultural life to flow into the economic domain. The three members of the social organism must stand in the right relation to one another, so that they may work on one another in the right way.

This is the real meaning of the threefold nature of the social organism—not the splitting apart of the three members; the splitting apart is always there. The point is rather to find how the three members can be brought together, so that they can really work in the social organism with inherent intelligence, just as the nerves and senses system, the heart and lungs system, and the metabolic system, for example, work together in our physical organism. That is the point, and of this we shall have more to say tomorrow.

Lecture 11

World Economy

DORNACH, AUGUST 3, 1922

In the opinion of a number of economists, as you are probably aware, it was quite impossible for World War I to last as long as it actually did. From their knowledge of economic relationships, these economists declared that the economic life as existed at the time would not permit such an extensive war to last more than a few months. Yet, as you know, the facts of life refuted this idea. If people thought objectively, this in itself would convince them of the need to revise their theory of economics. If you took the trouble at this moment to follow up the reasons that some economists, at any rate, adduced for their assertion, you would by no means be able to conclude that they were mere fools. Quite the contrary. You would see that their arguments were not at all bad and carried some conviction. Nevertheless, the reality of life refuted them. The war went on far longer than was theoretically possible. Obviously, therefore, economic science did not encompass the whole reality; the reality turned out quite differently from what the economic theory had supposed.

We can understand such a thing as this only if we see clearly the nature of the evolution of economic life upon the earth. It consists of a series of successive stages, but one in which the earlier stages continue to exist side by side with the later. Similarly we may say that the lowest organic forms now living are somewhat like the earliest living creatures of earthly evolution. Thus, in a sense, the most primitive creatures are still here, existing side by side with the highest creatures that have evolved up to this time. There is a difference, but there is also a marked resemblance in the forms. So it is in the economic life. The phenomena of primitive phases of economic life are still here today, side by side with those that have attained a higher stage. But in the economic life there is another peculiarity. While in the animal kingdom, for example, the more primitive forms can live literally side by side in space with the more highly evolved, in the economic life the more primitive processes are constantly penetrating into the more highly evolved ones. We might very well compare it with those cases where bacteria penetrate into higher organisms, except that in the economic life it is infinitely more complicated. Nevertheless, we can detect certain underlying structures, and from these we can take useful examples that will help us to bring our line of thought to its conclusion.

The more primitive forms of economic life must be conceived as private agricultural economies on a large scale. Their magnitude is relative, of course; but we must understand that if the private agricultural economy is self-contained, then it includes within it the other members of the social organism. It has its own administration, possibly even its own defense force, its own police, and moreover its own spiritual-cultural life. Such a private economy—grown to gigantic proportions, it is true, but still preserving in all essentials the character of a primitive agricultural concern, a large estate—was the so-called kingdom of the Merovingians.† It was a "kingdom" in a quite external sense, but it was certainly no state. It was in fact no more that an immense farming estate, comprising a huge area. Economic life underlay everything in the entire social structure of the Merovingian kingdom. On it was built an administrative system that accorded with the prevailing ideas of rights and justice; and into this was placed a spiritual-cultural life—an extraordinarily free one for that time. It is only in more modern times (and notably under the influence of "liberalism") that we have seen the rise of the maximum of lack of freedom in the spiritual-cultural life. Not until "liberalism" came did the spiritual-cultural life begin to grow more and more unfree; and it reached the zenith of lack of freedom in that embodiment of all political bliss, the Soviet Republic of Russia. Only books approved by the Soviet government can be sold at all. The Pope does at least content himself with proscribing books; but under the Soviet government proscription is automatic, inasmuch as no books are printed and published except those that the government permits.

Now if we trace the further course of evolution, we see how private economies gradually passed over into national economies,† which again at a certain time—at the beginning of the modern period—tended to become state economies.† The way it happens is characteristic. Private economy—initiative in private business—gradually passes over into the hands of government departments, and thus the fiscal administration grows increasingly into industrial organization. We see the economies passing over into the life of the state, absorbing cultural life in the process. So then we witness the rise of the modern economic and cultural organism of the state. The state, as such, has grown increasingly powerful. We, as you know, are aware that it will have to be, so to speak, articulated once more in distinct members if economic life is to progress.

At the moment, however, we are not concerned with "threefolding." We observe, as I said, how private economies were gradually joined together. It generally happened on a rather large scale. Private economies grew into something that could be called economy on a larger scale—national economy; and in this way a new social structure was created. Yet, within the new, the element of private economy was still preserved. The more primitive phase of evolution was still there as an insertion into the new. What is it that arises at this stage in the true sense of national economy? It is a mutual exchange between the several private economies. The exchange is regulated in many different ways. The regulation hovers like a kind of cloud over it all. The exchange, the trade or commerce between so many private economies, is the essential thing that arises with this welding of private economies into a national economy. What is the outcome? We saw yesterday that in the process of economic exchange each of the parties has an advantage, or can have an advantage. The result is, therefore, that the single economies that join together for the sake of mutual exchange (the essential thing in all economic life) profit by so doing. Once more, then, the single economies, the single businesses, gain an advantage by joining together. They profit by this connection simply because they can now exchange with one another. We can draw up a statement. We can calculate how much the one private economy or business will gain by means of the other private economies with which it is now connected. Each party gains an advantage, and the gain of each and all becomes significant for the entire economy.

At the time when the modern science of economics was founded, that particular stage had been reached. National economies had taken shape out of the private economies. This must be borne in mind if we wish to understand the economic ideas of Ricardo or Adam Smith.[†] Only on this foundation can we understand the thoughts that they evolved about "political economy," as they called it. It was this working together of private economies that they actually saw and upon which they based their views. In Adam Smith you can see it again and again—how he thinks from the point of view of private economy or private business, and from that draws his conclusions. At the same time he has before him the picture of their joining together into a national economy. Yet even in their ideas about this latter process, the elder economists retained to a large extent a way of thinking based on private business. Such were the views at which they commonly arrived; they treated national economy on the analogy of private economy. Thus the fertility, the prosperity of a national economy, as they conceived it, lay in the fact that one national economy would exchange with another, would come into mutual interchange with another, and would thus derive profit and advantage. Mercantilism, for example, was based on the advantages arising from such exchange between national economies.[†]

Now already at this early stage, where the single private economies or businesses come together into a large national economy, there is sure to arise a kind of leadership. In effect, the most powerful of the private economies that have merged into a larger complex will naturally assume the leadership; and this would undoubtedly have happened at the transition from the stage of private economy into that of national economy. But it was masked and hidden; it did not come fully to expression, inasmuch as the state undertook the leadership.

If this had not happened, one private economy—namely, the most powerful of them all—would naturally have been the leader. So in effect it happened that the single private economies passed imperceptibly into the state economy.

But it was different at the next stage, when in the further course of modern history the mutual exchange between national economies—world trade, in other words—became more and more comprehensive. Then, indeed, such a leadership emerged quite evidently. It happened, as an absolute matter of course in the further progress of economic life, that England's national economy became the dominating one. From another point of view, I have already drawn your attention to the fact that England evolved directly from trade into industrialism. Let us think what happened while England was acquiring colonies— England set the standard for currencies. Its colonies, in the manner of private economies, joined together into a larger complex. In the first place this gave rise to those internal advantages that are always the result of mutual exchange. Not only this; it also gave rise to a powerful economic hegemony that, with the further evolution of world trade, subsequently exerted a dominant influence on the economic life of the world. While England was gaining its colonies, it set the standard for currencies, because it was precisely through England that gold was forced on those countries that adopted it throughout the world. You may easily compute that in economic dealings with a rich country having a gold currency, any country that did not possess the gold currency would be at a disadvantage. In a word, we may say that under the influence of world trade, England became the leading economic power.

While this was going on, moreover, it was still possible to develop concepts of national economy continuing in a straight line—with whatever modifications and improvements—from Hume,† Adam Smith and Ricardo, and, we may add, Karl Marx. Fundamentally, though he effectively turned their ideas upside down, Karl Marx only continued along the same lines. The ideas of these economists are to be understood only if we have before us the picture of the economic life that arose under the dominating influence of England's economic power.

Now, with the last third of the nineteenth century, there was a transition from world trade to world economy. It is a very remarkable process, this passage from world trade into world economy. Definitions are of course inexact, for these transitions tend to take place in successive stages; but if we want a definition we must say that at the stage of world trade the economic life of the world is characterized by single national economies exchanging with one another. This traffic quickens the whole process of exchange and thus essentially alters prices—alters the whole structure of economic life. In all other respects, the economic life is carried on within the several territories. In contrast it may be called "world economy" when the single economic units not only exchange their products with one another, but when they actually work together industrially. For example, partially manufactured products may be sent from one country to another for their manufacture to be continued there. That is a radical example of what I mean by their working together industrially. So long as it is merely a question of raw products, the account will continue to show a condition of pure trade. This cannot yet be described as an actual working together in the industrial life. But when all factors in human life (in so far as they are affected by economics), that is to say, when all production, all distribution, all consumption—not merely production alone or consumption alone—are fed from the entire world; when all things are intricately interwoven and fed from the entire world—then we have world economy. And through the rise of this world economy, certain advantages that existed formerly for the national economies are lost.

Let us look back once more. When private economies join into a national economy, they gain on the whole; they derive advantages. Every single one derives advantages. But, apart from this, what is it that impels them? It is, of course, not always conscious insight that impels them thus to join together. Their joining together is, usually, not brought about by conscious economic insight, since in most cases the feeling for liberty is too great; the private business person is not as concerned with the piling up of the profits that arise in this way. Economically, these profits certainly arise; but the process is more complicated than that. The fact is that the single private economies or businesses have the same characteristic as every living organism; their life tends in the course of time to become weaker and weaker. It is a universal law, and it applies equally to economic life. An economic life that is not being constantly improved always deteriorates. Usually, therefore, the merging into larger "wholes" did not take place with the object of making private businesses profitable beyond their original level, but with the object of protecting them from imminent decline.

When once the businesses join together, they gain the corresponding advantage, though of course it varies from one case to another. And we may say that whatever the single economies have lost in the course of time is amply compensated by their joining into national economies. Indeed, it is usually more than compensated. Moreover, whatever the national economies have lost in the course of time is amply made up by world trade and the transition into world economy. But when world economy is once achieved, what then? With whom can it exchange? This, in effect, is what has happened. We have seen the economic life of the entire earth gradually merging into world economy. And at this point the possibility of reaping further advantages by merger is at an end.

The economists who declared that World War I could not last as long as in fact it did were thinking in terms of national economies, and not of world economy. If world economy had been national economy, their declarations would have been quite true. But from the very beginning the war had the tendency to spread and spread, and by this very fact it had a longer life. If in the state of world economy we continue to think in the spirit of national economies, world economy itself will at a certain point break up. Even if the break-up had not already been precipitated by various dark forces, this would be the inevitable outcome of our continuing to think in terms of national economy.

You see there how circumstances that are quite clearly perceptible play into the economic domain, but cannot, in the nature of things, be easily grasped with figures and statistics. This will show you that it is quite impossible to prolong the old economic ideas in a straight line. We are obliged to admit the need for a science of economics that will express the realities of the immediate present. The economic categories formed about a century ago no longer hold good today. What we need is an economic science capable of thinking in the spirit of world economy. Herein you see one of our greatest historical problems.

Observe the political leaders of today coming together at Versailles, Genoa, or the Hague. Science has provided them with a way of thinking only in terms of national economy. Whatever results they arrive at, unless and until they are permeated with world economic thinking, must lead downhill. Can they deny that they are tearing the economic life still more to pieces, erecting fresh artificial barriers, and thus hindering the transition into a pure world economy? We see this tendency in the immediate past—the tendency to break the world asunder as far as possible even in the economic life, and at the same time to conceal the tendency under the cloak of political and national pleas. Yet, we shall have to pass into a real world economy and a corresponding economic science, or we shall create an economically impossible state of affairs across the earth. Such a condition of affairs can continue to exist for a time only through one part of the earth that steals advantages at the expense of another by means of differences in currency or the rates of exchange. This is precisely what is happening in economic life at the present moment.

To conceive what world economics really means, we must see clearly, to begin with, that at the frontiers of the domain of world economy (if we may use the expression) the conditions will be quite different from those of economic domains bordering on one another. Relatively speaking, a world economy exists today; and therefore, relatively speaking, a science of world economy will have to follow. The domain of world economy borders on *nothing* else, and this makes it necessary for us to observe still more precisely those economic processes that emerge within a closed economic domain, independent of its external frontiers. The cardinal problem for modern economics to solve is the problem of the closed economic domain—a self-contained domain of one giant economy. Today the very smallest question—even the price of breakfast coffee—is influenced by the economic life of the entire earth. If it is not so, it means that progress is only partial. This state of affairs is actually on the way, and our thinking will have to follow.

To understand the economic conditions in a closed economic domain, we must see clearly that within the economic domain—in the mutual interplay of production, consumption and commerce (that is, in effect, circulation)—we have on the one hand consumable commodities, some of them relatively lasting, no doubt; while on the other hand we have the thing we call "money." Regarding the form of economy to which these things are subject, it makes an essential difference whether we envision the class of food products for example (consumable products) or of clothing (more durable) or, let us say, of furniture or houses (still more durable). With respect to their use and consumption we have these important differences of durability between different kinds of economic products. As an instance of a very long-lasting economic product, we might point once more to the diamond in the Crown of England, or any other crown. Or, again, we might think of the Sistine Madonna. Such things may be to some extent regarded as a kind of product that will endure; we find them especially among works of art. Now in a social organism subject to division of labor, having therefore an extensive process of circulation, there must be some equivalent of every product. There must be the money value, representing the price. But a very cursory observation of the economic realm will convince you that this equivalent between the commodity value and the money value is fluctuating. A product is worth so much at one place and so much at another. A product can be worth more if it is processed in one way, or less if it is processed in another. Be that as it may, however, in the total economic life you will perceive that apart from a few exceptional goods of great durability we always deal with goods that pass away in time. They lose their value, and after a certain amount of time are no longer there.

The one exception, strange to say, in our whole economic life is money. Although it occupies a position of perfect equivalence to the other elements of economic life, money does not wear out. You can get to the root of the matter in this way. If I have $20 worth of potatoes, I must see to it that I get rid of them. I must do something to get rid of them. After a time they are no longer there; they are used up, they are gone. Now if it were in a true relation of equivalence to the goods that are produced, then money, too, would have to wear out, like other goods. That is to say, if the body economic contains money that is incapable of being used up—money that does not wear out—we may well be giving money the advantage over goods, which do wear out. This is a most important point, and it becomes all the more so when we take the following into account. Think of all that I must do if, let us say, through my activity and labor I want to thrive so well that as a result of having a certain amount of potatoes today I shall have double the amount in fifteen years. And think, on the other hand, how little I would have to do if I possessed $20 in money today and wished to possess double the amount in fifteen years. I would need to do nothing at all; I could withdraw my entire labor power from the social organism and let other people work. All I would need to do is lend my money and let other people do the work. Unless I myself in the meantime would see to it that the money is spent, the money need not be used up.

This is the very situation that brings into the social organism so much of what is afterwards felt as a social incorrectness, as an injustice. Indeed, gigantic changes are brought about in the social organism, even economically speaking, by this reshuffling. I will not say reshuffling of the relationships of property (I will not speak of these), but of the relationships of work and activity. And we may ask how these changes are related to another factor, by which it is perhaps easier to comprehend them. For there is still something rather vague about it if I merely describe empirically, as I did just now, this existing discrepancy between money and the real objects in the economic organism. How can we get a picture-thought of some particular instance?

We can get a picture of it if we consider, to begin with, how absolutely fundamental for the whole economy in a closed domain is the consumption by all the human beings contained in it. This is the very first premise: the total consumption by all the human beings who live in the economic domain. That is something that is simply there; the consumption by all the human beings contained in any economic domain is presupposed.

There is also another factor that is of fundamental significance; and that is the land as such. Though this was badly misunderstood by the Physiocrats,[†] for example, it is nevertheless true that land is of fundamental significance, in spite of the fact, which has emerged from these lectures, that it must be constantly devalued. Indeed, it is just because of its fundamental significance that it must again and again be devalued. The Physiocrats made the following mistake. They lived in a time when land (as is of course still the case) had capital value. They conceived their ideas under the influence of this fact. They traced the economic relationships, indeed, in a very clear and graphic way. Of all the economists, they were the most rational. From their standpoint they came to the conclusion that the intrinsic worth of an economic realm lies in the cultivation of the land; that is, in the production of those goods that actually serve human nourishment. So long as we remain within this paradigm, we must in fact regard the land as the more or less fixed and given foundation of what constitutes the intrinsic worth of an economic realm. You need only reflect on how the workers who work upon the land, who unite their labor with the nature-products that subsequently serve for human nourishment, do in effect—so far as food is concerned—feed all the others along with themselves. All the others are dependent on them; all the others must be nourished by them. The others, it is true, can somehow get the means to pay for food, and pay more or less. But we may think it out in simple terms in order to grasp the essential point. Let us suppose that there is a certain number, A, of eaters. This number A will include all the farm workers, all the industrial workers, all the investors, all the merchants, all the spiritual-cultural workers—in effect, everyone. All require feeding. There will be another number, B, of those who have nourishment to offer. That is to say, B is the number of those who by their work really provide whatever passes over directly into human nourishment—into that part of the sum of economic consumption that represents the food consumed. Now if A is increased to A^1 while B remains constant, B's product will have to be further divided; and unless B can also be increased in its value somehow, people will have to be brought into the country and the yield of the land increased.

In other words, you cannot arbitrarily increase the number of spiritual-cultural workers, for example, within a given economic domain, without increasing on the other side the number of those who are responsible for the production of food. Alternatively, you can increase the fertility or yields of the soil. Increasing the yields may, of course, be the achievement of spiritual-cultural workers, but in that case it follows that those who so contribute during a period when the yield is higher must be wiser; they must have higher faculties than those who went before them. Thus the increased yield of farm labor is in a certain sense equivalent to the enhancement of the insight with which we elaborate the products we receive from nature. This enhancement may be done in various ways. Someone may, for example, enhance the forestry of a whole country by improving the bird life of the country. It may be done in countless ways; we are only concerned with the principle.

As long as we are thinking only in terms of national economy, it is clear enough that such things can happen. Into a country whose people have little insight, cleverer people may immigrate from another country, and then they may improve the cultivation of the land. On the other hand, if more people move up into the classes that are not actually producing food, fresh workers may be called into the country. All these things actually happen within and across the frontiers of national economies that border upon other national economies.

All that we can think about this matter may now be expressed in the question of what is to be done if on the side of *A*, consumption is in excess of what *B* can produce. Whatever we may think at this point in terms of purely national economy, it ceases to be thinkable when world economy arises, and when the conditions of the world are already in a certain sense disposed as for world economy. What we have to do is to form an idea of the changes entailed by the existence of a self-contained economic domain.

We can study a self-contained domain empirically by observing some small economy wherein exports and imports can be more or less disregarded. After all, there have been such economies, and we find it to be true that the foundation is the land. What the land yields is subjected to labor—elaborated—and thus receives an economic value. Thereafter labor itself is organized. We come to the class of people who are no longer actual producers of food, who are consumers, but not producers as far as food is concerned. Above all, when we come to the spiritual-cultural workers, we have consumers and not producers, so far as food is concerned. In a self-contained economic realm we must therefore distinguish, with respect to food, a certain number of producers who indeed (if I may say so) are very much aware of the fact that they are the producers; and over against them the consumers.

These things, of course, are relative; the transition is gradual. But if we consider the whole of human life within a self-contained economic realm of this kind, we must bring about what I explained a few days ago. The capital must not be allowed to become congested. At the place where the spiritual-cultural life is most highly evolved in the forming of capital (this "place" is of course spread out throughout the entire economic realm), the excess of capital that has been acquired must not be allowed to flow into the land, where it would become dammed up. Provision must be made for the elimination of the excess capital. The capital must not be allowed to become congested in the land. That is to say, at an earlier stage in the process, the congestion must be prevented by the free gift, to spiritual-cultural institutions, of the excess that has been acquired. The only exception is that what I described as a "seed" must be allowed to pass on to the land. It is here that the concept of "free gift" confronts us inevitably; there *must* be free gifts.

Study any of the self-contained economic realms that have arisen in the course of history, and you will see that the free gift is always there. In all essentials, spiritual-cultural life is dependent on what, in the economic sense of the word, are free gifts, pure and simple.

From the simple case in which Charles the Bald,† out of what he had available to give away, maintained Scotus Erigena† as his court philosopher (whom some have regarded as a rather superfluous piece of furniture!) to the case of Peter's Pence, whereby the Roman Catholics all over the world give their free gifts to the Church in small doses—such gifts are always there. Wherever an economic life, no matter how gigantic it may become, represents an economic domain more or less self-contained, you have the transformation of accumulated capital into gift capital for the maintenance of spiritual-cultural institutions.

In other words, now that we have inevitably come to a closed economic realm, namely that of the entire world, we should reflect upon the fact that one thing is inevitable in a truly economic sense: what would otherwise become dammed up in the land must vanish into spiritual-cultural institutions. I say once more, it must somehow vanish into the spiritual-cultural institutions. It must take effect as a free gift.

For a truly modern economic science, we must seek an answer to the question of how (in the sense of economics) must we buy and sell in such a way that the values, primarily created as food values within the purely material realm, may vanish within the spiritual-cultural domain. That is the great question. I will formulate it once more. What form of payment must we strive for in our economic interactions, so that what is created by the elaboration of nature, where the productive process primarily works for the nutrition of humanity, eventually vanishes in spiritual-cultural institutions? This is the great economic question to which we will find the answer in the next lecture.

Lecture 12

Money

DORNACH, AUGUST 4, 1922

Y ESTERDAY we formulated a very important question which came
to the fore with the transition from national economy to world
economy. With this transition the question of price begins to acquire
a very different significance in the economic life from what it had
before. But there are other things to consider before we can gain a
concep of the factors that really determine price. For the price—the
public price, so to speak—that eventually emerges in the market, or
in the circulation of goods, is really of far less economic importance
than what lies behind the forming of prices and of which price formation and price fluctuation are merely the final results.

Now these factors that precede the forming of price, both on the
buying and on the selling side, are connected with the social relationships in the middle of which the buyer and seller stand. It is these
relationships that determine whether the buyer will attach a greater or
lesser value to a certain sum of money. I mean value not only in the
subjective sense. Economically speaking, the subjective is important
only to the extent that it is properly grounded in the objective—that
is, to the extent that it rests on a true judgment of objective processes.
The value of money is very important even in an objective sense.
The economic question these days cannot be isolated from the social
question. One can reach a valid judgment only by observing the
interplay of the two. Thus we must recognize that the social discontent underlying the present social disturbances is connected above all

with what precedes the forming of prices and of which the forming of prices is merely the final result. As I have shown already, even in the payment of wages—that is, in that price formation that, under the existing economic system, ultimately finds expression in the rate of wages—we really have an instance of purchase and sale. Everything that leads to wage disputes really depends on social relationships in which both the worker and the entrepreneur are involved, relationships of which the result is the kind of price formation that constitutes the payment of wages. Accordingly, the first thing to investigate is how the money itself influences setting a price. Money itself plays the chief part nowadays both in ordinary purchase and sale; in the payment of wages; and in all the rest of economic life as well. We must distinguish between what eventually emerges as price in terms of money, and what constitutes the essential value of the money in the hand of one person or another—in the hand of the seller or of the buyer. Today, therefore, we must pause for a moment to consider money as such.

In contemporary treatises on economics you will find various elegant statements on the nature of money. For instance, you will find a list of the qualities that money must have in order to permit its use as money. Let us consider critically some of the qualities that are thus enumerated, for this will show you how necessary it is to get away from many of these current ideas of economics into a rather different way of thinking. For instance, it is said that in the first place money must have a universally recognized value. But the question is who the "recognizer" will be. When you have said that money must have universally recognized value you have said nothing. You have simply asserted that it ought to have a certain property, but you have not said how it is to get it. The second property enumerated is still more remarkable. It is said, for instance, that money must be small in volume and yet, being rare, in spite of its small volume it must be possible for it to have a high value. For this, property makes money especially easy to store up and, if only for this reason, will constitute a fairly strong inducement to the amassing of wealth. If gold sovereigns were as big as tables, it would be far more difficult to hoard them. Lycurgus† saw this long ago and introduced a rather more bulky currency as a preventive against excessive enrichment. If gold sovereigns were as big as tables it would indeed be less comfortable to get rich than it is now. People would notice it more. The reason, therefore, appears to be a rather superficial one. The next thing they say is that money must be divisible at will. (I have found this statement, too, in one of the textbooks on national economy). But this again can be brought about only by some act of recognition. Something must first be done to make it so. It is therefore once more a rather empty statement. Then they say that money must be easy to preserve. Well, this property of being "easy to preserve" will be brought home to us in its full significance in the course of today's lecture.

You see, we must be clear not only on this, that nature as such receives an economic value only when it enters into the general economic circulation—when it is taken up by labor—and again, that labor receives an economic value only through the way it is organized or divided; and finally, that capital receives a value only through the fact that it is taken over by the human Spirit and thus worked into the economic process. We must also be clear that money as such receives its value by the free process of circulation. Now we must consider the changes that money undergoes in the course of circulation. The premises are given to us by what we have said already in these lectures.

Speaking of money, the first thing we have to deal with is ordinary purchase money—the money we use to buy anything that serves us for consumption. But we must also consider what we may call loan money. This we have seen in a former lecture. Bearing in mind its connection with the whole economic process, is loan money quite the same as purchase money? If you are considering purchase money you will have to ask how purchase money comes into existence among all the other elements of buying and selling. It comes about because those who make use of money, in giving their money, have given something that not only effects an immediate exchange, but have given something that also mediates an exchange. They give something that inserts itself into the exchange. As I have shown already in these lectures, everything that enters as a mediator into the process of exchange is money. Suppose I am not content with acquiring as many peas as I can eat myself. Suppose I acquire peas with the object of using them—trading them—in order to obtain some other things that I require. In that case, simply through this mediating function, I am already transforming what would otherwise be an article of consumption into money. Spengler[†] makes a very shrewd observation on this point. Spengler develops his ideas along a general line of thought that is unfruitful, but he often makes very sound observations. He says that at a certain period of Roman history human beings, economically speaking, became money. The slaves became money. So long as I used the slaves for myself—that is to say, if as an Ancient Roman I acquired only as many slaves as I could use in my own household—the slave was, of course, a means of production. But it is different the moment a slave is hired out or lent. At a certain period of the Roman Empire this lending and hiring was the case. People had so many slaves that they were able to lend them out. They could apply slaves to all manner of profitable purposes by trading them. When this took place the slaves became money, and for that time, we may say, human beings became money. This is a perfectly correct observation of Spengler's, from which you can see once more how what acts as purchase money gradually emerges out of what is at first only an article of exchange. It follows from this that whatever we use as money, to be a really useful form of money, must not merely oscillate, like peas, between the function of being consumed and the function of being passed from hand to hand. This change would involve constant fluctuations of value in the process of circulation. We want something that is used for no other purpose than for mediating an exchange; and to this end there must be a certain (albeit only a tacit) agreement among those who use the money. This, then, is an essential point. The money must be used only for an exchange, as a medium; it must not be used for consumption.

Loan money, however, is something essentially different from this purchase money. In the case of purchase money you have no other foundation on which to estimate its value. No, you have no other need to estimate its value than how much you will get for it. Time makes no essential difference. Whether you buy a pound of meat today or after a certain lapse of time, you must estimate the pound of meat according to its consumption value. Your money may in the meanwhile have acquired a different value in relation to the pound of meat. But for the human being who eats it, the value of the pound of meat cannot, properly speaking, change in course of time. The duration factor, however, is essential. The given pound of meat can only be eaten during a certain period of time. That is to say, it can have a value only for a certain period of time, since it will go bad. This is a very pertinent economic fact. Everything that is a genuine object of use or consumption is subject to decay.

When for the purposes of pure exchange we use money as an equivalent, we must admit that, as opposed to articles that decay, money is an unfair competitor. In normal circumstances, nowadays, money does not seem to decay. I say expressly, it does not *seem* to decay. Here you can see what an unhealthy element is introduced into the economic life when we bring into it relationships that are different from those in reality. By our established institutions money has a fixed numerical value under all conditions. No matter how it may otherwise be placed in relation to the social life, money has its face value and is supposed to keep it permanently. But in reality it does not do so. Everything else is honest. Meat after a period, which varies with its quality, begins to smell. Money does not do this, no matter what its quality may be. Money does not openly "smell." Yet, when we see circumstances bring it about that an article grows less or more expensive after a certain time, we are obliged to admit the following. While the article itself, by virtue of its qualities for human life, must retain the same value (for general conditions will ensure its being consumed at the right moment and its replacement with a new one), the same thing is not true of money. Consequently money, as such, as a pure medium of exchange, is an unfair competitor because it does not reveal in any way the fact that it is also really subject to changes. If I have to pay a certain sum of money for a pound of meat today and a different sum of money for a pound of the same meat two weeks later, the difference (the increase, for example) in the money I must pay cannot be because of the pound of meat. It must therefore be because of the money. If the money still bears the same face value, then the money is beginning to tell a lie, for its real value has decreased. If I must give more in exchange for a pound of meat, then the value of the money has decreased. That is quite obvious. In this way, by the act of circulating the money, I bring into the process something that is not really there economically. Economically the facts are otherwise. Economically the situation is that money itself, simply through the economic process, undergoes changes.

We must now investigate the occasions upon which money undergoes changes. In addition to exchange money or purchase money we have loan money. Take for instance the loan money that a man obtains in order to begin some enterprise. For him it is not purchase money; for him it becomes working capital.† Now you must see that this working capital, this loan money, has an essentially different value—an essentially different property. Loan money is fundamentally different from purchase money. Except for the fact that it still consists of gold, silver, and paper, not many of its original properties are left when purchase money is transferred to the sphere of loan money. It acquires its value in quite a different way. The moment loan money comes into circulation, the human Spirit seizes it. Human thinking sets to work, and it is through this entry of human thinking into the process that loan money receives its actual value. When a banknote is lent to a man who is about to undertake some business—at the moment he begins to use it—it would be far more important to write on the note whether the man is a genius or a fool in business. For the value of the loaned money in the whole economic process will henceforth depend upon the way he acts with it.

We must pass from loan money to the third kind of money that I mentioned a few days ago. These days, as a general rule it is not taken into account, and yet it plays the greatest imaginable part in the economic process. In fact, we must now pass from loaned money to gift money. Gift money, fundamentally speaking, is all that is spent on education. This plays an enormous part in the economic life. Gift money, again, is all that is spent on endowments and the like—all that has the effect of preventing the evil damming up of capital in the land by capital investment, which is so ruinous for the economic life. At this point we must say that for the person whose livelihood depends on purchase money, gift money simply becomes valueless. It loses its value. Gift money is the opposite of purchase money, as we can see from the simple fact that only one who has received the gift can purchase with it; one who has not received the gift cannot purchase with this particular money!

We have therefore three kinds of money, qualitatively different from one another: purchase money, loan money and gift money. To comprehend the relation between these three, we must consider economic systems such as, for instance, the private economies that we assumed hypothetically in the last lecture—economies representing a kind of closed domain. There we shall find that after a certain time all that is loan money passes over into gift money. Nor can it be any different in the case of that closed economic domain that is "World Economy." Loaned money must gradually pass over entirely into gift money. Loan money must not be allowed to be dammed up into purchase money, so as to disturb the latter.

Loan money, therefore, passes over into gift money. So it must be in a self-contained economic system. And what does it do in the domain where gift money is working? It loses its value. We may say of the domain of purchase money that the money will here represent a certain value. In the domain of "gift," on the other hand, the money has, with respect to all that obtains in the domain of purchase, a negative value. It lets the purchase value vanish into nothing. Finally, between the two, the transition is brought about through loan money. The loan money itself gradually vanishes into gift money.

Perhaps you will say that this is hard to follow. It is. I am sorry that we cannot go on for months detailing instances where we can see that the facts are as I have stated, with regard to the valuation and devaluation of money. This, however, should really be our task; all that can be said in the present lectures should be taken as a basis for further research in economics. In the brief period of two weeks, only hints and suggestions can be given; but you will find that all the economic statements that have been made here will be transformed by detailed investigation into valuable economic truths—valuable both in science and in practice.

It does actually take place in the economic process that money undergoes metamorphoses; it acquires different qualities as it becomes loan money or gift money. But we mask this fact if we simply let money be money, and use the number inscribed on it as the unit of measurement, and so forth. We mask it and the reality takes its revenge—a revenge that reveals itself in fluctuations of price, with which (though they are actual enough in the economic process) our reasoning faculty cannot keep pace. We ought to be able to follow them. We ought not to let money merely flow into circulation and give it freedom to do what it likes. For we thereby do something very peculiar in the economic life. If we require animals for some kind of labor, the first thing we do is to tame them. Think how long it takes to train a riding horse. Think what would happen if we did not tame our animals, but used them wild, taking no pains train them. But we let money circulate quite wildly in the economic process. If and when it chooses to do so, so to speak, we let it acquire the value it has as loan money or as gift money. And we do not foresee that, when an industrialist has money, from whatever source, which has been wrongly transformed from loan money into gift money, and he pays his workers with it, the result is quite different from what it would have been if he had paid them, say, out of pure purchase money.

In effect, the more a man is obliged to pay his workers with pure purchase money, the less he will be able to give them—that is to say, the cheaper they will have to deliver their products. On the other hand, the more he is able to pay them with money that has already been transformed (that is, that has already passed into the sphere of loan or gift), the higher the wages that he will be able to give them. That is to say, more can be charged for their products in the market. The point is to grasp the matter with our reason.

You see, as things are today, the function of money has constantly had to be corrected. Take the case, for example, of a national economy bordering on other national economies. By letting money function in this wild unguided way, without bringing any intelligence into the process, a national economy may easily find itself in a disastrous position with regard to the price of some piece of goods, or something else that is required. So long as the national economy is one among others (and no repressive measures are adopted), people will simply import the article in question. Their imports will be increased. Things are constantly being corrected in this way. For world economy, on the other hand, no such correction is possible. We cannot import things from the Moon. If we could import from, or export to, the Moon and Venus and the rest, world economy would also be like a mere national economy. This is precisely the great question. What becomes of our science of economics—through the fact that the world is now a single, closed economic domain?

And now let us suppose that we really make up our minds to allow money to grow old. Suppose you have a certain piece of money, no matter what substance it is made of, or what date is inscribed on it. Say it is "1910." And now you take another piece of money with the date "1915." The money marked "1915" begins to exist, as money, economically, in that year. And now suppose that by some reasoned treatment it undergoes the process that is undergone by all other exchangeable products; it loses its value after a certain time. The precise figures I mention are not important; they are merely illustrations. The actual figures required would have to be the subject of infinitely numerous—but perfectly possible—calculations, as we shall presently see. Suppose, therefore, for the sake of example, that the piece of money would have lost its value for economic activity by the year 1940. It would have a definite value only between 1915 and 1940. For that period it would have, as we shall see directly, a determinable value. If money loses its value in the economic process after twenty five years, a piece of money bearing the date "1910" will have lost its value in the year 1935. Thus I would assign a particular property to the money that I carry around with me; I would assign to it a kind of age. This 1910 money is older; it will die earlier than the 1915 money. Now you may say that is just a scheme. No, what I have just explained to you is the actual reality. That is how the economic process actually wills it. The economic process of its own accord makes the money grow old. The fact that it does not appear to grow old—the fact that we will still buy things with 1910 money in the year 1940—is only a mask. In doing so we do not really buy with this money; we buy with a fictitious money value.

If therefore the money in my purse grows old in this way, if its date of origin has a real meaning (and by "growing old" I mean getting nearer and nearer to its death), then money, like a human being and every other living thing, has a certain value impressed upon it by the fact that it is growing older. The money comes to life and a value is impressed upon it. Why? Suppose you have young money, money of the present year—1922 money. This 1922 money will be good purchase money, needless to say. But now suppose that I am an entrepreneur and I ask myself how I can supply myself with money for my undertaking. Suppose, according to my calculations, my undertaking must be planned for a period of twenty years. Shall I provide myself with old money or with young money? Then I will think that if I take old money, it will have lost its value in five years, or in two. Therefore it will not do for me to use old money. If, according to my calculations, I must provide for a long period, I must have young money. Thus, under the influence of long-term undertakings, young money receives its particular economic value—a value far greater than that of old money. This economic value really exists—and it is there now. On the other hand, suppose I have to embark on an undertaking that involves calculations covering a period of only three years; in that case I should be a poor economist if I used very young money. The young money, by virtue of its youth, is the most valuable and, accordingly, the most expensive. If I require the money for a shorter period, I shall provide myself with less valuable money. For those who have to apply their spirit—their intelligence—to money, the age of the money can begin to play a part, of which they are quite conscious.

Please note that this is not something that does not exist already. It exists, but in a wild, untamed way, which results in mutual disturbance and unhealthy economic conditions. On the other hand, if you *tame* money, if you really assign to it a certain age, letting young money—as loan money—be more valuable than old, then you will be impressing the money with its real effective value, the value it possesses through its position in the economic process. This value really inheres in the money only while it is loan money, for even if money is loan money, as purchase money it still retains its former value. You do not need to consider too carefully whether you ought to provide yourself with still other money, for what you as entrepreneur are going to consume. These things will correct themselves of their own accord.

Remember that free gifts also play a part in the process, in which they have a very real significance—those gifts of which I have already spoken in various connections. All that we put into the educational system is a gift—notably when it is a question of a truly free spiritual-cultural life. This, too, is happening already, though people fail to notice it. When you give directly, your intelligence is in the process. As things are now, you do give, but the gift is absorbed into the general pool of taxation. It vanishes into a vague economic fog, and you do not observe what happens. So the situation runs wild. In the other case, conscious intelligence comes into it. Consider, for a moment, what kind of money you will use where it is a question of free gifts. If you are thinking in a true economic sense, then, where it is a question of free gifts, you will use old money—money that loses its value as soon as possible after the gift is made; provided that the person who takes the benefit of the gift has just enough time to make purchases with it.

At this point, needless to say, there must be some rejuvenating process in the economic process. Money, in fact, must have a successor. The important thing is, as you will readily perceive, that things must not be allowed to happen arbitrarily through the general chaos that the economic state spreads everywhere. The economic state brings about a hopeless confusion of values by failing to distinguish purchase money, loan money, and gift money, though in reality these three are separated all the time. You will readily see that if you do not wish to leave the process to chance—if you wish to bring reason into it—you simply must interpose the necessary associative bodies at the transition points between purchase money, loan money, gift money, and the renewal of money. Take the case of those who have money to lend. You would not let them lend it in a senseless way. You would bring them into connection with their association. The association would act as a mediator. The association would provide them with the most sensible way in which to lend—or again, with the most sensible way in which to give. When a gift takes place (and every individual is free to give or not to give), the money, if it has a year value as explained above, will not undergo the same process. But the important thing is to bring about sensibly and in accordance with reason the things that happen in any case in the economic process, but behind a mask. The money, when it has served its purpose, must be collected. And then once more, at the beginning of the process of purchase and sale, it must receive its original value. That is to say, it receives its new year number and passes into the hands of those who are dealing once more with nature-products, products of nature that are just beginning to pass into the sphere of labor. For here it is pure purchase and sale that are going on. This is the associative method of managing things.

The three kinds of money must be treated in different ways. In the first place, gift money, which is the oldest, must be handed over to an association that will bring the valueless money back again into the whole economic process, by uniting it with labor at the point where the nature process begins. There can be no economic difficulty in this. What then will be the essential difference from the existing practice? It will be that in a self-contained economic system (which, as we saw, is not like a national economy bordering on others, where exports and imports can be carried on) three distinct domains arise, as far as money is concerned: the domain of purchase money, the domain of loan money, and the domain of gift money. When anything occurs that would otherwise have had to be corrected by export and import from another country, it will be corrected by the three domains. If purchase money sets up a disturbance, there will be a corresponding flow between the spheres of purchase money, loan money, or gift money. These things will adjust themselves of their own accord. Irregularities will undoubtedly arise, and having arisen they must correct themselves. Life cannot go on without irregularities coming in. It is an irregularity when the stomach is full. Accordingly, digestion has to follow. In the same way, circumstances must continually arise under which, for certain commodities, purchase money is too cheap or expensive—and then the cheap money will flow into the other domain, so that on the other side it becomes more expensive again as purchase money. What would otherwise have been corrected by export and import will now correct itself within the self-contained economy. All that is required is actual human reason; this will be brought into the process through the associations, which will be there observing things with their collective experience and taking the proper corresponding measures.

It is necessary above all to understand the essential nature of money. People fail to understand it precisely because it is always there before them without their being able to see what it really is. In the social organism there is no such thing as "money as such"; there are only these three kinds of money. Moreover, each kind of money becomes what it is only at the moment when it is actually entering into the economic process or passing over from one form of economic process to another. In the very process, it is constantly being changed. The point is that we must learn to know money properly, before we can pronounce what part it plays when it becomes an expression of the price of something else. To penetrate the economic process clearly, we must not remain at the surface, merely observing how things appear on the surface. Seen on the surface a 10 franc piece is of course a 10 franc piece today, no matter whether 1910 or 1915 or 1920 is inscribed on it. Outwardly considered, it is always the same 10 francs, and, of course, in ordinary sale and purchase it behaves accordingly. I do not observe that a difference has taken place, until I have less of it—or things have become more expensive. But in this very "having less" or "becoming more expensive," there lies inherently what I expounded to you today as the greater or lesser age of the money. To perceive the economic process clearly, we cannot merely speak of cheap or expensive money, of cheap or expensive commodities. We must find out what money is in its real essence; this must first be recognized and known. For it is with money that we master the economic process nowadays. (We shall show tomorrow how substitutes for money have to be treated in a similar way).

This is the important thing. We must not shy away from penetrating beneath the surface, into the depths, to see the real underlying facts. In economics, we must not speak of cheap or expensive money in relation to commodities; we must realize that in the living economic process, we must speak of money as being "old" and "young."

Lecture 13

Spiritual-Cultural Needs

DORNACH, AUGUST 5, 1922

To understand how the sort of thing we discussed last time can be maintained, we must now turn our attention to certain features in the economic process that also take a part in the determination of economic values and that at the same time show how very difficult it is to value in the economic sense what comes into the process through the human mind and spirit. I will give you an example, not exactly fictitious, but put in such a way that its value as an example does not depend on the specific facts on which it is based.

Suppose that at a given time there lived a great poet, recognized as such during his lifetime, and increasingly so after his death. Now a man who is interested in this poet, being perhaps particularly fond of his poetry, may hit upon the following idea. "In the near future," he says to himself, "people will make more and more of this poet. I know for certain—at any rate I can afford to take the risk—that in the near future, say within twenty years, he will grow even more popular than now. Furthermore, following the thinking habits of our time, within twenty years an archive is sure to be set up to collect his manuscripts." From various information he has picked up and turned over in his astute head, this man says to himself, "These things are quite sure to happen. Very well, I will begin at once to purchase autographed manuscripts of this poet. For they are still very inexpensive." And then one day, when he is sitting in the company of others, one of them says, "Personally I am not very keen on speculation; all I desire is to have a reasonable interest on my savings." Another says, "That is not good enough for me. I am buying shares in a certain mining concern." He is more of a speculator; he is buying "paper" (industrial shares). But the third, our man, says, "I am buying up the best paper on the market. It is very cheap indeed. But I shall not tell you fellows what it is" (for it is part of the venture that he does not give his game away). "The paper I am buying will rise in value more than any other in the near future." So he buys nothing but autographs of the said poet. And after twenty years he sells them to the archives, or to others who will sell them to the archives in their turn. He sells them for many times the amount he gave, so that he turns out to be the biggest speculator of the three.

It is a perfectly real case, though I will not give any further details now. It did in fact occur. As you can perceive, it brought about a very significant reshuffling of economic values. Now what were the factors that contributed to this reshuffling of values? In the first place, simply the prudent exploitation of the fact that the poet's reputation was growing—a growth that in the end found expression in the establishment of archives. To the reshuffling of values, the bringing of it all into the hands of a single man, you must add the fact that he kept his own counsel about it, did not draw the attention of others to it; nor did they think of the idea themselves. Therefore, he was able to make an enormous profit.

This case is mentioned to illustrate how complicated the question can become, how many factors converge in the nature of value, and how difficult it is to grasp them all. Is it quite impossible to grasp all the factors in one way or another? You may say that for a considerable part of life it will be perfectly possible for men and women of sound intelligence, in the right associations, to estimate the factors, even to the extent of giving them numerical expression. But there will still be many things—things of decisive importance for a true estimate of values—which it will not be possible to grasp with ordinary common sense, unless we look for some fresh aids to understanding.

We saw how nature, to acquire an economic value, must be transformed by human labor—must be combined with human labor. There is the product of nature, which in an economic organization

based on division of labor, has, properly speaking, no value to begin
with. Now let us try to find our way into this picture. Values arise
by the joining together of the material of nature, if we may call it so,
with human labor. Thus, if only in a kind of algebraic formula, we
may begin to approach the real "function" of value formation. For
instance, we can see at once that it cannot be a question of simply
superimposing labor upon the nature-element. For the labor changes
the nature-element; it cannot be a merely additive function. It will be
more complicated than this. But we can hold to what we have already
said; we see the economic value arise where the product of nature is
first taken over by human labor.

Obviously the first stage in the process—in the taking over of
the nature-product by human labor—is direct work on the land.
Therefore, when all is said, we must always look upon the cultivation
of the land—in the widest sense of the term—as the starting point of
economic life. This is the condition preceding the whole of economic
life. But how is it when we go over to the other side of the economic
process? I need not enlarge on it any more at this stage; it is quite
evident from the preceding lectures that even such a thing as the
redistribution of values plays a considerable part in the movement of
economic values. How shall we find anything comparable in all these
different factors? If we regard "nature times labor" as the value that
comes up from the one side (or, as I said, whatever the right function is), then we must look for something comparable on the other
side. We cannot simply compare nature with the Spirit or mind, for
we shall find no point of comparison—least of all by way of purely
economic considerations—if only for the reason that a highly subjective element enters in here.

Think of a simple village economy—a self-contained one, if you
will. There have actually been such economies, self-contained to
some extent at least. It will consist, to begin with, of the things
produced; we can imagine even the market and the town from this
picture. This economy will consist of the farmers, the workers on
the land, the workers in the different trades (those who clothe the
people, for instance, and a few others) but no special proletarians.
Such a thing will not yet exist, nor need we, in our present line of

thought, turn our attention in that direction. Whatever is relevant to the proletariat will appear in due course. But our village economy will also include the schoolmaster and the parson, or two schoolmasters and two parsons. They will have to live on what the others give them, if it is a purely village economy. Whatever develops there of the free spiritual-cultural life will in the main have to develop among the teachers and the parsons; or possibly a parish clerk will be added. Now we must ask ourselves how a proper valuation comes about in this simple economic circuit.

There will be very little else of a "free spiritual-cultural life." We can scarcely imagine the schoolmasters or the parsons blossoming into novelists, because if the village economy is a closed one, they would not be able to sell very much. Novelists would be able to earn, in this community, only if they were able to instill into the farmers, tailors, and shoemakers a passion for their novels. In that case no doubt they might be able to call into being a small industry. But it would cost a great deal to do that. We cannot, in the ordinary way, imagine such a thing existing in our little village community. In fact, the free spiritual-cultural life must await certain conditions. But from the simple fact that there are the parsons and the teachers and a parish clerk, we can conceive how the achievements of these spiritual-cultural workers (for they are such, in the economic sense) will come to be valued economically.

What is the requisite condition for these spiritual-cultural workers to be able to live in the village at all? It is that the people send their children to school and that they have religious needs. Spiritual-cultural needs, therefore, are the fundamental premise. Failing such needs, even these few spiritual-cultural workers could not be there. And we shall have to ask ourselves how will these spiritual-cultural workers economically imbue their products with value—their sermons, for example (even these must be conceived in an economic sense), and their school lessons. How will these things be valued in the whole of economic circulation?

This is a fundamental question. We shall gain an answer to this question only if we begin by imagining quite vividly what the others must be doing. They must be doing physical work. Through bodily labor they call forth economic values. If there were no need for sermons and school lessons, the parsons and teachers would have to do physical work. Everyone would be working with their hands and the spiritual-cultural life would drop out of the picture. We would no longer be concerned with the economic valuation of spiritual-cultural products. Thus we arrive at the required valuation precisely by observing that parsons and teachers are spared physical labor. If they are to do their spiritual-cultural work, which is desired, they must be relieved from the physical work. Here you can introduce into the line of thought something amenable to, at least, a more general treatment. Suppose, for example, that there is need for only half as many sermons and school lessons. What will then have to happen? You cannot appoint half a parson and half a teacher. Therefore the parson and the teacher will have to spend part of their time in physical labor. Therefore the valuation on their side will depend on the amount of physical labor of which they are relieved. This is the measure for the valuation of their work. One person contributes physical labor; another saves it and this person's spiritual-cultural achievement has a value corresponding to the amount of physical labor that he or she saves by virtue of it. Take these two economic aspects and think the process through economically, and you will see that even a sermon must have an economic value; and moreover think of how it acquires this economic value. It acquires it inasmuch as labor is saved or spared, whereas on the other side labor has to be applied.

The same principle runs through the entire spiritual-cultural life. What does it signify, in the economic sense, if a man paints a picture—painting it, shall we say, for ten whole years? It signifies that the picture acquires a value for him inasmuch as it will enable him once more to spend ten years painting another picture. He can do so only if he can save himself physical labor for a period of ten years. Therefore, the picture will have to become worth as much as would be made from other products by physical labor during ten years. Even if you take such a complex case as I explained at the beginning of this lecture, the same result will emerge. In all cases of spiritual-cultural production, if you try to find the concept of value you will arrive at this other concept—the concept of labor that is saved or spared.

It was the cardinal error of the Marxists that they looked at all economics exclusively from the physical side. They said that capital is to be looked upon as crystallized labor—as a product with which labor has been combined. Now if an artist paints a picture, the Spirit painted into it during ten years is certainly combined with it; but this could at most be computed by those who believe that Spirit is the inner "work" of the human organism transmuted, which is sheer nonsense. The spiritual-cultural cannot be compared to the natural in that facile way. If I complete a spiritual-cultural product, the point is not that labor is in some way stored up in the product. The work stored up in it is economically irrelevant. As physical work it may be very little. Moreover, what little there was, in any case, falls under the other concept of physical work. What gives value to the product is in truth the labor that it will save me. On the one side of the economic process the actual doing of work, the bringing of labor to the product, is the value-creating factor; the product absorbs labor—attracts it. On the other side the product rays out labor, begets labor; the value is the original thing that calls the labor into being.

We now have, therefore, a means of comparison—namely, labor on the one side and labor on the other side—and we are therefore in a position to relate them, for we may say: if the value in the one case equals "nature *times* labor," in the other we must call it "Spirit *minus* labor."

$$V = N \times L$$
$$V = S - L$$

The direction is exactly opposite. Physical labor has meaning only inasmuch as the one who wants to contribute it to the economic process actually does it himself or herself; while what is related to the product on the spiritual-cultural side is the labor that one person does for another. It must therefore be entered as a negative in the economic process.

It is a remarkable thing. Study the history of economics, and you will always find that what is said is right, but only in a limited sphere. There are economists who believe that it is labor that gives things value—the school of Adam Smith and the school of Marx, for example. But other schools give another definition, which again is correct in a certain sphere. According to them, a thing becomes capital, that is, a source of value, inasmuch as it saves labor. Both points of view are true. The one is true of all that is in any way related to nature, to the soil, the land; while the other is related to Spirit or mind. Between these two there is a third. In effect, neither of the two extremes is ever there in its pure form; they are only there in an approximately absolute sense. After all, even in picking blackberries (which acquires economic value only inasmuch as the workers actually go there and do it)—even here there is some Spirit or mind at work. If, of two blackberry pickers, one lacks insight and has extra work by picking where the berries are scarce, while the other finds a place where there are plenty and obtains a better yield for the labor, the blackberries of the former worker are of less value, relatively speaking. The first blackberry picker will get less money for the same amount of berries. In effect, then, neither extreme is ever realized absolutely. Even the gathering of blackberries entails Spirit or mind at work (although we might not call it so). The work of using one's wits creates values, just as it did with the collector of autographs; at least it creates values through re-distribution.

Once more, then, we have labor in the one direction and in the other, and this alone enables us to compare the economic values. But this comparing is done by the economic process of its own accord. We can at most raise it, in a certain way, into the sphere of conscious reason. Indeed, all that I have given in these lectures amounts to this; we lift certain instinctive processes into consciousness.

As I said just now, we have neither of the two extremes in any absolute sense. For on the other side ($V = S - L$), no matter how much painters use their intelligence, they must still do some physical labor if they wish to create anything of economic value. Even if they exercise clairvoyant power (a thing that one cannot grasp at all in terms of economics), even then they must still do some physical labor. Relying on their genius, it may be that they can afford to be lazy; still, now and then they must take up the brush. Some physical work has to be done even in this case, just as some little effort of thought must go even into the picking of blackberries. (Things that take place in real life cannot be grasped merely quantitatively. They have to be grasped while they are actually happening. Therefore we can grasp them with our concepts only if we realize that the concepts themselves need to be kept in constant movement).

It is between these two extremes that we can perceive more clearly how in real economic life physical and spiritual-cultural work play into one another, moving back and forth. Just as in some machine there is a regulated backward and forward movement, so in industry physical work from the one side and spiritual-cultural work from the other are passing back and forth. It is in this mutual interplay from two directions that we have, as a third, what plays into the economic process between the other two. We have the case where people have to do physical labor, yet by their spiritual or mental power (using their wits) they are relieved from some of it. This is always actually the case, except that it sometimes approximates more to the formula I wrote above ($V = N \times L$), and sometimes more to the formula I wrote below ($V = S - L$). The latter, in effect, would be fulfilled in its entirety only if there could be among the consumers someone who did nothing but save labor by means of his or her spiritual-cultural faculties; and it could only be someone who was born already fully mature.

In this way we can look into the economic process from this aspect of valuation, valuing what comes from nature on the one hand and from Spirit on the other. At this point we can say that where positive and negative work into one another, somehow an intermediate condition will emerge. Either the positive or the negative can predominate. Let us assume for a moment that the positive dominates. In the village economy it certainly will do so, for in such a community there will be no widespread interest in spiritual-cultural work, beyond what is absolutely necessary. But the more life grows complicated (or, as we are apt to say sentimentally, the more "civilization advances") the more highly, as may be seen even empirically, spiritual-cultural work is valued. That is to say, the more labor is saved, the more a negative element comes in as against the positive. I beg you to consider well, that by characterizing it in this way we are taking hold of a real process. It is not that physical labor is done on the one side and then negated on the other. That would be no real progress in the economic sense; it would at most be a process of nature. All that is done out of physical labor helps to create values. None of the value is destroyed. What counteracts the saving of labor from the other side, counteracts it only in a numerical sense. In a purely numerical sense, it affects the value of physical labor. For this very reason, we are enabled to express in a real way what actually happens. Physical workers are active; spiritual-cultural workers are active—but the achievement in the one case is work that is positively done, while in the other it is a work that in reality signifies a saving of work. Only by this means is an effective valuation brought about.

The aspects are divested of their particularity and it becomes possible to grasp the process in terms of numbers, inasmuch as it is the same factor that emerges on either side and only the valuation is altered. With the advance of civilization, then, spiritual-cultural work increases in importance, and this implies that bodily work has a less powerful effect on the valuing process. Physical strength is of course applied, and it must be so more and more as we go forward. Even the cultivation of the soil must be made more fruitful as civilization advances. More work must be done, in a positive sense. The point is that the physical labor is divested, to some extent, of its value-creating power. Yet this again can be so only if those who perform the physical labor evince a growing need for what has to be achieved from the spiritual-cultural side. Here, once again, a human factor comes into the economic process. You cannot get around it; indeed, with the advance of spiritual-cultural life, this particular human factor makes itself felt as an objective necessity.

It is quite true that, to begin with, when there are only the parson and the teacher, there is not much spiritual-cultural life in our village. But suppose there are two villages. In one village the parson and the teacher are average people; things will go on as they are. In the other village the parson or the teacher, or both of them, are above average people. They will be able to stimulate all manner of spiritual-cultural interests in the next generation and, in all probability, by the time the next generation arises, some other spiritual-cultural worker is brought into the village. Now there are three of them. In this regard the spiritual-cultural has a very fertile power, which in its turn works back into economic life.

What, in the last resort, does the process signify? It signifies that precisely labor, or rather the value-creating power of labor, which in the purely material phase of economic life has an infinitely great value, is more and more reduced in course of time by what comes to meet it from the other side. I cannot exactly say it is "devalued"; it is reduced numerically. In the working together between all that is represented by working the land (the tilling of the soil, and so forth), and what is done from the spiritual-cultural side, we have a kind of mutual compensation. And a certain compensation is the only right thing.

Complex conditions arise again here. It may well turn out that in a given place there are too many spiritual-cultural producers; that is, the counteracting labor-saving power may be too strong. The resultant value is then negative, and the people cannot all live together except by consuming one another. Thus there is a limit somewhere to this compensation process. For every economic realm there is a certain balance, in the very nature of the case, between production from the land on the one side and spiritual-cultural production on the other. Until this is understood in economics—how production from the soil, taken in the widest sense, of course, is related to spiritual-cultural production—until this problem, which has hitherto hardly been considered, is very seriously dealt with, we shall never have an economics able to cope with our present needs.

The first thing necessary is that we should begin working on definite data from which we may convince ourselves in an atmosphere unclouded by prejudice and agitation how some particular area gets into an unhealthy economic condition because it contains too many spiritual-cultural workers. We may also perceive what power of the further development of culture and civilization an area has, where that limit, of which I have just spoken, has not been reached. Progress is possible only within a given area so long as this limit, determined by the necessary compensation, of which I spoke, has not yet been reached. The task then will be to investigate those elements that still survive today of closed economies—such survivals are to be found everywhere, because we are passing only slowly into a world economy. We must investigate those elements where the economy of some area is still closed; we must study the aggregate welfare of those areas in which there are comparatively few poets, painters, shrewd business people, and so forth, and where there is still much agriculture or other activity connected immediately with the land. Then we shall have to study other areas where the opposite is the case.

From the available data, we must work out empirically the general laws that will emerge, for a true theory of balance between agriculture (or the working of the land in the widest sense) on the one hand and spiritual-cultural work on the other. It will be necessary that, for any region, we take what we might call the average spiritual-cultural workers (not choosing examples that would falsify the whole balance); and on the other hand, the average manual workers. Balance the one against the other, and you will perceive how the one works compensatingly upon the other.

This is a point of cardinal importance for anyone who wishes to contribute to the further progress of economics today. The fact is that this problem, which should really underlie our thinking about price and value, is scarcely seen correctly anywhere, as yet. As I said yesterday to a few of those present,[†] in economics, people are always allowing themselves to be misled into a partial, instead of a comprehensive, way of thinking. There is no doubt that Spengler makes some very shrewd economic observations at the close of the second volume of his *Decline of the West*, but he ruins these brilliant observations because he does not succeed in translating what he perceives historically into terms of present-day economic realities. He points out very justly how, in the ancient economies, the economic life that comes directly from the soil was predominant; whereas today the economic life that predominates thinks in money—and consists, therefore, properly speaking, in spiritual-cultural work. But he fails to see that these two stages of economic life, which he records historically, continue side by side to this day. The one has not replaced the other in history; they stand side by side to this day, just as the most primitive abides within the most advanced. We find the amoeba crawling about free in external nature, and we find the same thing in our own blood, in the white blood cells. The different historical stages even in nature live side by side to this day. And so it is in economic life;

the most varied conditions co exist. Sometimes, indeed, in the most highly cultivated economic life (if we may call it so) it is precisely the most highly cultivated elements that return to the most primitive. Values created by our living in a most elaborated culture harken back, in a certain sense, to the state of primitive barter. Those who create their labor savings, as it were, will sometimes barter one of these for another, to satisfy certain needs among themselves. Such things occur. We often find the most primitive functions applied once again to the most highly elaborated products.

I wanted to add this remark to the present lecture so that tomorrow I may be able to give you, as best I can, some sort of conclusion to these lectures.

Lecture 14

World Economics: Living Concepts

DORNACH, AUGUST 6, 1922

Y ou will have seen that the main object of our present studies was to find concepts, or rather pictures, of the economic life, such as would help us actually to get inside it. In none of the activities that are now being pursued in the Anthroposophical Movement, and in which I have myself been taking part, is it my opinion that all the existing scientific information should be simply flouted. On the contrary, I am convinced that there is a wide range of very useful conclusions in the existing sciences. The method of treatment, however, both in natural science and in the other branches of knowledge, needs to be developed in some essential respects. Thus, I have tried mainly to give you pictorial concepts, ideal pictures, to aid you in making proper use of the wide range of valuable material that is already there in economic science. For this reason I have given you pictures that could really live. A living phenomenon, you may be sure, is always many-sided and contains many meanings. Many of you may therefore go away from these lectures with the feeling that various objections can be made to what has been said. In a sense I shall be rather glad if you do have this feeling, provided it is combined with real earnestness and with a genuine scientific spirit. Faced by a living phenomenon, this feeling is indeed inevitable. Life will not endure dogmatic theories; and it is in this sense that you must conceive the ideal pictures I have given to you.

The thought-picture of money growing old or getting used up is a particularly suggestive one. You must relate yourself to such an ideal picture as you would to, let us say, a growing human being. You have a general feeling that a particular person will prove to be very capable in one direction or another. You may have fairly definite ideas of what this person will accomplish. But these ideas could well turn out to have been mistaken. This person may accomplish what is destined in quite other ways. So, too, for the concept of money's being used up in course of time, you may find various ways in which this can be brought about. The way I have tried to present the situation is as one conceived as little as possible along bureaucratic lines; it results naturally from the economic life itself.

Many objections may no doubt be made. Here is a very easy one. How will it be settled that an entrepreneur puts young money and no other into business? After a short time it may no longer be recognizable whether the money was young or not, for business will be going on. In answer to this, you must bear in mind that we do not simply get the money from the sky; we borrow it from someone. Moreover, you can see from my book *Towards Social Renewal* that I do not think interest on money should be abolished, provided the money has real value (on the contrary, I believe that up to a point interest is actually necessary in the economic life). You may wonder how you, as an entrepreneur, can get money from those who might lend it to you if you are going to pay them interest for an extremely short time? They will wish to give you money only on the assumption that they will get interest out of your business for as long a time as possible. Thus, you may find that it is not enough simply to let money grow old in the way described. This may lead you to think out the method in greater detail. For instance, money issued today might be date-stamped, not with the present year but with a future year, in such a way that the value increases up to that year, and after that it decreases.

In short, a living thing may realize itself in a variety of ways. By the act of grasping it livingly, you give it the possibility to realize itself in the most varied ways, just as living human beings can use their capacities in various ways. This is the essence of a non-dogmatic concept. To make such concepts your own, especially in economics, is to see how well these things enter into real life. Only on this foundation will you be able to make proper use of what is given in the so-called economic science of today out of quite good, but only partial, observations.

Take, for example, what is said of price. You will be told that the conditions determining price levels are the following, so far as the sellers are concerned: their relative need for money, the value of the money, the costs of production that they have to meet, and the competition among buyers. But if you analyze these concepts you will always find that, though you can think about them rightly enough, you cannot enter with them into the realities of economic life. You would first have to ask yourself if it is an economically healthy state of affairs if prices rise and fall, when it happens that a particular entrepreneur is in need of money at a particular time. Thereby, in accordance with the private need for money, should prices rise or fall in a particular direction? Can the utility value [*Gebrauchswert*] of money, if we may call it so, work in a healthy way at all? Both prices and utility value can work in a healthy and in an unhealthy way. Or again, speaking of costs of production, it can be desirable for the attainment of a healthy price not to think how the price will come out if costs of production are looked upon as something absolute, but on the contrary, to think how the costs of production for a given article might have to be reduced so that it has a healthy price when it comes into the market. In other words, you need to have concepts that really begin at the beginning. You cannot let a living human being begin life at the age of twenty-five; nor should you let your concepts, which are to enter into real life, begin at any arbitrary point. You should not let your economic concepts begin, for example, with the competition of buyers or sellers. May it not be, under certain conditions, the fundamental error of our economic life that an excessive competition exists between sellers or between buyers? These are matters of principle that must be taken very much in earnest.

Quite apart from whether one or other of you may agree with particular parts of our exposition, the endeavor has been throughout to make our concepts living. If they are living, then, in a given case, they will show of their own accord how they need to be modified. What matters is that we should be brought onto the path of these living concepts. If we have money that is used up (that is, grows old) then, inasmuch as money comes into circulation and figures as purchase money, loan money, and gift money, the peculiar qualities of money will bring it about in the natural course—if they are allowed to function in a purely economic and unhampered way— that the demand for young money will arise at one place and the demand for old money at another.

If I could go on elaborating these things for many weeks, you would see how well they fit in with a sound economy. Wherever an illness arises in the economic system, you would see that it is just by observing these things and acting accordingly that it can be healed.

What is it that really emerges when we think in this way? In money in circulation we have a kind of reflection of the element of use and wear that is present throughout the whole range of consumable goods—and even spiritual-cultural services are consumable goods for the economic life. In a money that wears out, we have a parallel process to goods, commodities, and real values, which also wear out. What do we have, in effect, if we perceive this parallelism between the real value and the token value? (We can extend it over the entire world economy.) Truly we may describe it essentially as a kind of bookkeeping system for the whole world economy. It is the world's bookkeeping. When some item is transferred or delivered, this simply signifies the entry of an item in another place. In actual practice the transfer is done by passing money and commodities from hand to hand. The principle is fundamentally the same, whether we contrive to record the items in their proper places in an immense bookkeeping system embracing the whole world economy, and so direct things simply by transferring credits; or whether we write out a check and give it to the person concerned, so that the thing is done in external action. In the circulation of money we have, in effect, the world's bookkeeping. This is, as everyone can really see for themselves, what should be aimed at. In this way we give back to money the only quality that it can properly have—that of being the external medium of exchange. Look into the depths of economic life, and you will see that money can be nothing else than this. It is the medium of exchange of services or things done. In reality human beings live by the things actually done, not by the tokens thereof.

It is quite true that money can create a false impression of things done; and with the rise of a kind of intermediate trade in money, the whole economic life can thus be falsified. This kind of falsification is possible when we do not give money its true character.

It is important for us to see, as I emphasized in the last lecture, that different kinds of services must be judged in different ways with respect to the values circulating through the economic life. As we saw yesterday, what is gained from nature to begin with, and on which labor is expended, corresponds to the picture of "labor-united-with-an-object-of-nature." In a certain sense, we can begin the economic process at this point. Here, we may say that the value is created by the labor that I unite with a particular product of nature. But in the economic process there is also the contrary stream, which comes into play the moment there are spiritual-cultural services or products. As soon as these come into play, another formula of valuation, if I may call it so, has to be introduced: "A spiritual-cultural product is worth the amount of labor that it saves to the person who contributes it." Take, for example, the artist who paints a picture and thereby provides a value—a value for which real interest is felt (otherwise it would not be a value). If the production of the picture and the existence of the artist are to be economically healthy, the artist must value it in this way. It must save the artist the amount of labor required to satisfy the artist's needs during the time that it will take to produce a new picture in like manner. Thus, in the economic process spiritual-cultural services or products come to meet those that are mainly based on the elaboration of nature (that is, on manual labor, on means of production). On the one side we must have labor uniting itself with the means of production, while on the other side labor must be saved or spared. Thus there arises the economic circuit with its two opposing streams, which must compensate each other in a healthy way.

The great question is how the two opposing streams will compensate each other? In the first place, we need only bear in mind the universal bookkeeping of our world economy. It is here that we should find the items on either side that must somehow be mutually balanced. This would be the source of price. But the point is that the items in this universal bookkeeping must mean something. Item

A that I insert, will correspond to what we may describe as "labor-united-with-nature"; or item *B* will correspond to "so-much-labor-is-saved-by-this-service." Every such item must have concrete meaning. It can have a meaning only if it represents something that is comparable, or which is at least made comparable by the economic system. We cannot simply ask how many nuts a potato is worth. We cannot ask a question like that without more information. First we must say that the "nut" signifies a nature-product united with human labor; the "potato" signifies a nature-product united with human labor. Then we can ask how the two values are to be compared. The problem is to find something that will enable us to assess economic values one against the other. It becomes still more difficult if you take, say, a literary essay. The essay, too, must be, economically, worth the amount of physical labor upon some means of production that is saved by it, minus the very small amount of physical work spent on the actual writing. At any rate you can see that it is not altogether easy to work out how these things are to be compared or assessed against each other.

By taking hold of the economic process from another angle, we shall find means of reaching such an assessment, nevertheless. We have the physical labor spent on the means of production, including nature itself. At a given time, it is quite a definite amount of labor. I mean that at a given time a definite amount of labor is needed, shall we say, to produce wheat over a given area—say *x* square meters of land—taking "production" as ending in the moment when the wheat is in the merchant's hands, or at some other given point. Once more then, a definite amount of labor is needed to produce wheat. It is a given magnitude, which under certain conditions can actually be ascertained. Properly regarded, all human economic service or achievement—of whatever kind—eventually takes us back to nature. There is no other possibility. The farmer works upon nature directly. Those who provide, shall we say, clothing, do not work directly upon nature, but ultimately their work goes back to nature. Their labor will contain an element of "labor saved" to the extent that they apply Spirit or mind to it. Nevertheless even their work has its connection with nature. Everything, right up to the most complicated of spiritual-cultural services, eventually goes back to nature—to labor that is expended upon the means of production. Think it through clearly and you will see that everything in economic life can be traced back, in the long run, to bodily work upon nature. The process begins from nature; values are created there by the application of labor; and it is these values—taken to some definite point still as close to nature as possible—which have to be distributed over the whole of a "closed" economic domain.

Go back to the hypothetical case I gave yesterday—the closed village economy. In such a self-contained village economy you have the manual workers, and I assumed that the only spiritual-cultural workers were the parson and the schoolmaster and possibly the village clerk. It is a very simple economy! Most of the people are doing physical labor, physical work upon the soil; in addition, they have to do enough physical work to provide for the needs (food, clothing, and so forth), of the schoolmaster, parson, and clerk. It will be additional, because the schoolmaster, the parson, and the village clerk do not do their work upon nature themselves. Say that the village economy consists of thirty farmers plus the three—what shall we call them?—"receivers of honoraria." These three supply their spiritual-cultural services. They need the spared labor of the rest. Suppose that each of the thirty farmers gives to these three, or to each one of them, a token, a ticket, on which is written an amount, say *x*, of wheat—that is, wheat elaborated to a certain point. Another member of the community might give a ticket on which something else was entered, something comparable to wheat for purposes of consumption. These things can be ascertained. The schoolmaster, the parson and the clerk will collect these tickets. Instead of going out into the fields to procure their wheat and rye and beef for themselves, they will hand over their tickets to those concerned, who in their turn will do the necessary labor in addition to their own and will give them the product in exchange. That is a process that cannot help developing of its own accord. It cannot possibly be otherwise, nor does it make any difference if it occurs to some bright individual to introduce metallic coins instead of tickets. Some kind of tokens must be devised, based on the stored-up material labor—labor expended on means of production, labor invested in economic values. And these tickets must be handed over to those who need them, so that they can save themselves the labor.

You will see, therefore, that no kind of money can in reality be anything other than an expression of the sum of means of production available in a given region, means of production including in the very first place the land itself, reduced to the form in which it can be most suitably expressed. This will relate the economic process to something that we can at least grasp. It is not possible to bring about an economic paradise anywhere on earth. Let those believe it, who invent utopias without reference to reality. It is easy to say that an economy should be set up in a particular way. But an economy, including that economy of the entire earth that we can call "world economy," cannot be absolutely determined, but only relatively so. Suppose that in a closed economic region we have an area, say Ar, of land. Now suppose all the people in this area are doing everything that is possible for human beings to do; then a different amount will be available for consumption if B million people live in this area of land, than will be the case if the population is B^1 million.

In effect, the economy thus depends on the ratio of population to the area of land, and on how much a given population can get out of the given area, for it is from the land that everything ultimately comes. Take now the hypothetical case of an economic area that has a population of, say, thirty-five million—the number does not matter. What holds true, here, of a self-contained economic territory, is true also of the world economy. Assume there to be thirty-five million inhabitants at a given time; and that the problem is to bring these thirty-five million people into an economically just relation. (I may not be putting it quite clearly and precisely, but you will soon see what I mean). What would you have to do if you wished such a condition to prevail among these thirty-five million that would bring about feasible prices? The moment you begin to lead over the economic life of the region into a healthy condition, you would have to give each one of them an amount of land corresponding to one thirty-five millionth of the entire area available for production, adjusted according to fertility and ease of cultivation. Suppose that every child were to receive such an area of land at birth, to be worked by him or her perpetually. The prices that would thus arise would be feasible prices for such an area, for things would then have their natural exchange values.

Now the curious hypothesis that I have here put forward is nothing other than the reality. The economic process actually does this of its own accord. Of course you will not believe that I mean what I am now saying in any other than a figurative sense. Yet these are the actual conditions. You can imagine the entire area distributed among the people concerned, remembering that they will also have to elaborate, in the proper way, such products as become detached from the soil. You can imagine the entire area divided up among the population, and it is in fact this which gives to each individual thing its exchange value. Indeed it might well be that, if in some place you were to write down the actual exchange values, you would find a very close approximation. But if you now compare this with ordinary present-day conditions, you will find the price of one thing far above, and the price of another far below, that level. Still, if you like to suppose a utopia somewhere, populated solely by newborn children (looked after by angels to begin with), to each of whom you have given a piece of land, then, when they are able to begin work, you will have produced conditions under which the natural exchange values will arise. If prices are different after a time, it can only mean that one has taken something away from another. It is this kind of thing that produces the various social discontents; people dimly feel that here something works into the process that does not correspond to the real prices at all.

If the economic life becomes permeated with a way of thinking such as we have here adopted, the actual measures we take would bring about the result I have stated. It all depends on that. We would find that our currency, representing the day-to-day bookkeeping of world economy, would have to be inscribed, "Wheat producible over a given number of acres." This amount would then be equated to other things. The various products of the soil are the easiest things to compare. You see where it is we must start—our figures must mean something. It simply leads away from reality if money has inscribed on it, "So much gold." It leads towards reality if it has inscribed on it, "This represents so much labor upon x product of nature." We would then have this result. Say there is written on the money "x wheat," all money will be stamped "x of wheat, y of wheat, z of wheat." The real origin of the whole economic life would then be made evident. Our currency would be referred to the usable means of production upon which bodily work is done; that is, the means of production of the given economic region. The only sound basis of currency is the total of the usable means of production.

Those who can look into the realities of life with an open mind will see, as they perceive the situation, that this is so. It may be objected that no one value can be precisely equated to another. But to a great extent this can be done. In this method of valuation everything is ultimately valued through consumption; therefore, the values of different kinds of services do not differ so very much from one another. However much spiritual-cultural a worker I may be, I need so much saved labor every year—as much as I require to maintain myself as a human being. Moreover, by this means it will be evident how and to what extent a spiritual-cultural worker needs something in addition—beyond what a manual laborer needs. When the issue has become as transparent as this it will be acknowledged, because it is transparent. Even today, conditions do exist (though they become increasingly rare) in self-contained economies under which such workers receive all that they need. The others give to the spiritual-cultural workers gladly, without even writing it down on slips of paper beforehand. In saying this, I do not wish to reduce an economic argument to a sentimental one. I say it simply because this, too, is part of the realities of economics and because in an economic system you are, after all, always dealing with human beings.

Above all, you will attain in this way a relationship between the members of an economic whole that will be really visible to all. Everyone in every moment will then have their connection with nature, even in the money. It is just this which makes our present-day relations so unhealthy; they have become so far remote from nature— the connection with nature is no longer there. If we can bring it about (and it is only a question of evolving the necessary technique in the associative life) that we really have the nature-value recorded on our paper money in place of the indefinable gold value, then we shall see directly—in everyday business and interaction—how much a given spiritual-cultural service is worth. I shall know, when I paint a picture, that for me to have painted this picture, so many workers on the land, for example, have to work for so many months or years on wheat or oats, and so forth. Think of how transparent the economic process would become. The ordinary way of phrasing it today would be to call it the substitution of a nature currency for a gold currency. Yes, and that is just what we need. For by this means, true economic conditions will be brought about.

Once again I have placed a picture before you. I have to speak in these pictures, as they give the reality. What people generally have in their heads in economic activity today is not reality. Those alone have the reality who, in receiving a piece of money of a certain magnitude in exchange for something, know that it signifies so much work upon the land. We must, of course, include in our calculations the work that is done on other means of production. These will, however, be equivalent to nature. For the moment they are finished, and thus leave the realm of commodities altogether, they are devalued inasmuch as it is no longer possible to buy or sell them. They thus become equivalent to the means of production that we have in nature directly. It is therefore only a continuation of the part that nature already plays in the economic process, when we say that means of production should be dealt with in this way. Moreover, it is only in this way that we can have a clear idea of nature itself as means of production. The concepts of land that you will generally find in economics are always open to objection, unless you conceive of "means of production" in the way I attempted in my book *Towards Social Renewal*. You need only consider that even a given region of nature may have to be worked upon to some extent before it is available as "land"—before it is fit for cultivation. Up to the moment when nature, or a given part of nature, has been cleared and can be handed over for use, during this period also, some labor must be expended on it. In other words, by the time this labor has been done, even a piece of land may justly be considered a commodity, an economic value, in the sense that it is a part of nature combined with human labor.

Only by formulating the ideas in the way we have done will you make the concept "means of production" clear and transparent, and you will then be able to work it out in the most varied spheres. You will perceive, when for example an author writes an article, that the main value of it, economically speaking, consists in the labor saved; from this you would have to deduct only the minute amount of bodily work that the actual writing entails. Your concepts will be capable of differentiation in manifold directions so that you stand with them in actual life, inasmuch as you are forming them out of life itself. For example, if you are concerned with some question of prices, you will no longer be content merely to trace the question back to the immediate costs of production; you will have to trace it back to the primal phase of all production. You will have to see what the conditions are of price formation right from the primal phases of all production. It is only then that you will be able to trace conditions rightly to any given point in the economic process.

In this way perhaps I may have been able to give you an idea that will at least guide you on your way toward the cardinal question of economics—that of prices. To engage in economic activity at all is to bring about the exchange of products among human beings, and this exchange lives itself out in the forming of prices. It is the forming of prices that matters, and in this respect you do not have to go back to anything vague or indefinite. You can always follow things back to the fundamental relationship of value that is brought about by the very fact of work upon the land, the proportion of the population to the available area of cultivation. In this relation you will find what originally underlies the formation of values. In effect, all the labor that can be done must come from the given population and, on the other hand, all that this labor can unite with must come from the given land. Everyone needs what this labor brings about and, as to those who can save themselves the labor on account of their spiritual-cultural services, the others must perform it for them in addition to their own. Thus we arrive at the actual basis of economic life.

Looking at things in this way, we shall admit that even in our present highly complicated economic life, what was universal in the most primitive conditions (where the simple exchange of goods, shall we say, was the essential thing) still plays its part. The difference is that we are no longer able to see the connection clearly everywhere. But we shall have it before us always, when the connection with nature is expressed in our currency notes. Whatever we may do, the connection with nature is always there. Do not let us forget it! It is reality. Once more, speaking pictorially, let me say that while I am giving my dollar quite thoughtlessly for some product, there is always a little demon who writes on it how much labor, actually done upon nature, it corresponds to; for this alone is the reality. Here, too, if we would get at the reality, we cannot stop short at the outer surface.

It has not been possible in these two weeks to give you more than a few stimulating suggestions to guide you on your way. Nevertheless, as I well know, these are the suggestions that need to be developed in every possible direction. The most important thing of all is that you perceive how, compared with the usual ideas, the ideal pictures we have here evolved do represent something living.

If you have absorbed what is living in these picture-concepts, you will not have spent these fourteen days here in vain. It is this that weighs on one so heavily. Great issues are impending. Human beings are in need of free and clear insight into the essentials, for the healing of so many ills of our civilization. There is much talk of what should be done, but there is little will, ultimately, to dive down into realities and to draw forth from there what should be done. We have gradually departed from the sphere of truth, and from the real life of rights (rights that spring forth from the very nature of the human being) and from what must unfold in us if we are to be of value to our fellows—the genuine practice of life. From words of truth we have slid into the empty phrase; out of the sense of right into mere conventions; out of a practical hold on life into dead routine. We shall not escape from the threefold untruth of phrase, convention, and routine until we develop the will to go down into the facts and to see how things are shaped in their own real nature. But if we do so, then, precisely as those who approach the matter as students, we shall be met with understanding. There are so many inflammatory sayings in the world today, doing appalling harm, just because there are so few people with an earnest will to go into realities.

For this very reason it gave me deep satisfaction to see you here, prepared to work with me during these two weeks, thinking through the realm of economic science. I thank you sincerely. I may express this thanks, because I believe I see how significant it is that those who stand in life today as academics can contribute to the healing of our civilization and to the reconstruction of our human life.

We must endeavor to make economic science more than a mere theory; it must be our aim that it should prove itself of real economic value, so that the labor we are being saved can be put to good use by those who relieve us of it for the benefit and progress of humanity. I believe that in resolving to come here you were thus mindful of the task of the economist; and I hope that this has been confirmed in you by what we have attained, however inadequately, through our united work. We can hope that we will have an opportunity to work with these ideas again another time.

PART II

Six Seminars Held in Dornach, Switzerland

July 31–August 5, 1922

First Seminar

DORNACH, JULY 31, 1922

QUESTION: The internal logic of "The Social Question" appears to be sound in itself, but the criterion "in accord with reality" is not to be found in "The Social Question."

RUDOLF STEINER: It would really be good if our friends would express themselves a little more clearly on this point. You must consider that the teachings of economics as such are really very recent—scarcely a few hundred years old—and that until the great Utopians came along everything in the field of economic life took place more or less instinctively. Nevertheless, these instinctive impulses people had were something that developed into reality. In order to gain a better understanding, just consider the following: what we can think about economic matters really arises from the contradictions of class distinctions, but also from the economic ways of working, and so on. I will not even look at here what is most extreme, in the way it is represented by Marx and his followers. But even teachers of economics who relate strongly to the middle classes say that everything really arises from economic fundamentals as if out of automatic necessity. However, when people discuss particular concrete aspects, then it is as if the concrete arrangements that were brought into action in order to bring about today's economic life were nothing else than the results of medieval thinking itself, but in relation to various realities.

Think what the Roman concept of ownership, a purely legal cate-gory, brought about as a system, and what was then created through this concept. One can see that these things were not handled in a scientific way; but one can also see that those legal categories, and those thought of as legal economic categories, have worked in a formative way. And then came those mercantilists, etc., who were not creative, but were theorists.

One can say, for example, that the advisors of the Emperor Justinian, who created the Codex of Corpus Juris, were far more creative people than the later teachers of economics. They not only created in our present sense a Justinian Codex, but also in the further course of medieval development, we see the contradictory impulses developing themselves on the basis of what was set down in those laws established by Justinian.

So we have arrived at the present time where people no longer think creatively in economics, but only as observers. This has its real beginning with Ricardo.[†] Take, for example, the law of diminishing returns from crop yield. This is a law that is really correct, but is abso-lutely not in accord with reality—because in practice it will always be apparent that when one takes all the factors into account that Ricardo did, and when one correctly follows what he called the law of diminishing returns (when, on the other hand, a technically more intensive management takes place), this law is found to be incorrect. It does not establish its truth in the real world.

Let us take something else that is more trivial. Let us take the "iron-clad wage law" of Lassalle.[†] I must admit it seems to me like a kind of scientific frivolity that one still finds this law described as having been "overcome," because the facts do not prove to be true. This is because the situation is as follows. From Lassalle's kind of thinking and from the view that work can be paid for, the only correct result is this ironclad wage law. It is logically so strong that one can say it is absolutely correct, when one thinks as Lassalle must have thought, that no one is interested in giving workers more wages than are needed to just make their subsistence possible. They will, of course, not be given anymore. But if they are given less, then the workers will waste away, which must be atoned for by the one paying the wages.

There is basically no other way than to admit that the ironclad wage law is theoretically correct. Already within the proletariat itself the people say the ironclad wage law is wrong, because it is not right that within the last decades the wage has been held at a certain minimum that at the same time is its maximum. Yes, but why is the ironclad wage law of Lassalle wrong? If the same conditions had continued in which he had formulated it (I would say the conditions from 1860 to 1870), and if one had continued to operate within a purely liberal philosophy, then the ironclad wage law would have conformed with reality with absolute justification. There was a turning away from the liberal economy, and now the ironclad wage law is continually being improved in that state laws are being enacted that are correcting the reality that would have arisen from that law.

So you see that a law can be correct, but not in accord with reality. I know of no one who was a greater thinker than Lassalle, except that he was very one-sided; but he was a very consequential thinker.

When one is confronted by a natural law, then one substantiates it. When one is confronted by a social law one can also substantiate it, but it is valid only as a trend, and one can correct it. Insofar as our economy is based on free competition—and there is still much there that is based only on free competition—the ironclad wage law is valid. But because under these suppositions it would be valid, one must make the corrections with the enactment of social laws, with definite hours of work, and so on. If you give business people a completely free hand, then the ironclad wage law is valid. Therefore in economics you cannot use the purely deductive method. The inductive method doesn't help at all. This is what "Lujo Brentano" followed.

We can merely observe the economic facts—it says—and then we gradually come up with a law. Yes, here we do not arrive at any creative thinking whatsoever. This is the so-called newer economics that claims to be the scientific one. This really wants to be just inductive, but with it we don't get any further.

In economics you need a method of characterizing whereby one seeks to find the concepts by coming from various starting points, holding them together, and letting them culminate as concepts. In that way one arrives at a definite concept. In a certain sense this will probably be one-sided since one can never survey the whole range of the facts, but only have a certain sum of experiences. Now go over the phenomena once again with the concept and try to verify it. Then you will see that this is really a modification. So through characterizing you arrive at a concept that you modify as you verify it, and then you arrive at a perception of it according to economics. You have to work to arrive at perceptions.

I would like now to work out such a perception in the lectures of this course on economics, in my showing you all the things that always enter into the setting of prices. The method of economics is a very inconvenient method because in reality it involves having to put together the concepts from infinitely many factors. You have to work toward economic imaginations! Only with those can you make any progress. If you have them and they approach something, then they modify themselves on their own, whereas with a fixed concept it is not so easy to modify it.

You are familiar with the so-called Gresham's law: Bad money drives away good money. If bad, cheaply coined money is circulating somewhere, it supplants the real money that then travels to other countries. This law is also an inductive law, it is a purely experiential law. But this law again is such that one also has to say it is valid only so long as one is not in a position to guarantee the value of the money. In the moment one had the enterprising spirit to be in that position, then the law would be modified. It would not quite die out. There is no economic law that is not valid up to a certain point, but they all become modified. Therefore we need a characterizing method. In natural science we have the inductive method, which at most leads to deductions. But generally the deductions have much less significance in natural science than one thinks. There, only the inductions have any real significance.

Then you have pure deductions, which one perhaps finds in jurisprudence. If one proceeds inductively there, then one brings something into jurisprudence that destroys it. If you bring the psychological method into jurisprudence, then you dissolve it. Then you have to declare every person innocent. Perhaps these methods could actually be introduced, but that would lead to the undermining of the juridical approach as it exists. It may very well be justified, but then it is jurisprudence no longer.

So in economics you cannot make sense of it with deduction and induction. You could manage with deduction only if it were possible to give general rules from which reality itself would uncover the cases. I will refer only to those who want to proceed in a purely deductive way, however, with a principal induction that they place at the very top. Oppenheimer,† for example, puts at the very top the story of his land settlement association and deduces from it a whole social order. Well, it was many years ago, and Oppenheimer was also already a settler and said, "Now I have got the capital, now we will found the modern cultural colony!" I replied to him, "Doctor, we will talk about it when it has failed." It had to fail because it is impossible to establish a small region within the general economic sphere that wants to enjoy its advantages through something else, so that it would be a parasite within the whole economic body. Such enterprises are always parasites. They survive until they have devoured enough from the others, then they fail!

Therefore in economics you can characterize only by entering into the phenomena with your thinking. That is also due to the reason that in economics one must constantly work into the future on the basis of the past. And in working toward the future one comes across human individualities with their abilities, so that in economics one can basically do nothing else then to stand on the *"qui vive."*

If one is to take hold of the practical sphere, one must be prepared to constantly modify one's concepts. One is not dealing with pliant material that can be shaped, but with living people. And that is what makes the theory of economics a science of a special kind, because it must be permeated with reality.

Theoretically, you will easily be able to understand that. You will think it is very inconvenient to work in the science of economics. But even that I do not want to admit to be true. In certain circumstances you can gain a great deal when you study the pertinent literature of some field and you compare the various opinions. This is also helpful if you are at the point of wanting to write dissertations, for example. In the theory of economics there are the most unbelievable definitions. Try once to put together all the definitions of capital from the various textbooks on economics or from the great treatises! Try to put them—eight, ten—one behind the other!

Just now I recall one of them: "Capital is the sum of the produced means of production." I must confess I don't understand what the adjective is doing there. The opposite: "unproduced" means of production—one could also even imagine what that means, for example nature, that is, the soil, and that is presumably what is meant by that. But of course one is then incapable of justifying how the soil can ever capitalize itself. It does indeed capitalize itself. So one can really not make sense of it, and that is because one has such concepts that one must search for, and must then just try to enrich somehow. These things are all too narrow.

I say that the people who are within associations will find the right way. I want to count on people, and that is what is relevant to reality. A discussion about the "concept of work" would have to be set up in a way so that you would now really discover the concept of work in the sense of economics. This concept must be freed from everything that does not create value in work, and indeed in economic values. This has first to be eliminated. In that way, of course, one comes only to a characteristic. And it is this characterizing method that is the important thing. Of course one must now say this in a methodical way.

If you find it difficult to see what conforms to reality in these considerations, then I would like to say that what conforms to reality could really be quite easy! You say "the esoteric aspects of the social question" are logically sound in themselves. They are not at all—neither they nor any of the other things! By this I am emphasizing that I did not want to speak purely from the economics point of view, but also from the social point of view. The whole style and position taken by these writings is of course determined by that, so that they cannot be evaluated at all from the pure economics aspect. At the most, that could be done with certain essays on threefolding. But I don't find them logically grounded in themselves at all, because, carefully enough, I gave only guidelines or examples, or really only illustrations. I wanted people to realize what can be accomplished if a man is allowed to manage a production facility only as long as he can himself be there with it; after which it must be handed over to whoever will again manage it in person. I can well imagine that what is to be accomplished by this could also be accomplished in another way. I only wanted to give guidelines. I wanted to show that one will find a way to go if one carries out this threefolding in a way that is relevant; if one actually frees the spiritual-cultural life as such; if one puts the rights life on a democratic basis and the economic life on a real professional basis that can be taken on by the associations. I am convinced that then the right things will happen in the economic sphere.

I say: The people who are within the associations will find the right way. I want to count on people, and that is what is relevant to reality. A discussion about the concept of work would have to be set up in a way so that you would now really discover the concept of work in the sense of economics. This concept must be freed from everything that does not create value in work, and indeed in economic values. That has first to be eliminated. In that way, of course, one comes only to a characteristic. And it is this characterizing method that is the important thing. Of course, one must now say this is a methodical way.

QUESTION: To what extent is inspiration necessary for understanding economics?

RUDOLF STEINER: That is how it is meant: that when one takes the matter seriously, this inspiration is not so extraordinarily difficult. It is not a matter of finding suprasensible facts, but of actually making the inspiration effective in the field of economics, so that it cannot become particularly difficult.

The way in which one defines work would stipulate that I proceed by showing the following: A person can do work without its having any economic value. That is a half-truth. One can strain every nerve through talking without creating any real economic value. I would then demonstrate how work, even when it begins to have economic importance, becomes modified according to its value. Let us assume there is a woodcutter who, in performing his work, actually creates value; and there is a cotton merchant who has nothing to do with cutting wood, but whose work makes him nervous, so that every summer he goes up into the mountains where he cuts wood. Now the thing becomes complicated, because this merchant could also get plenty of value from the cut wood, he could receive something for it. But you cannot place a value on it in the same way as you can with the woodcutter. Under certain circumstances you have to assume that if the man does not cut wood in the summer for fourteen days he will be able to work much less as a cotton merchant in the winter. Then, in view of the decreased work, you have also to take his decreased benefit into consideration. The economic value of the wood cut by the cotton merchant is quite equal to the value of the wood cut by the woodcutter; but the effect on the economy of the work that results from his activity is now considerably different.

If the woodcutting has its value for the cotton merchant, in that it affects his activity as a merchant, then I must find out if it is also true that when a man goes on an exercise machine and steps from one step to the next, he thereby makes himself thinner. This is an effort for him, but here there is no effect on the economy. That is true, but here I must distinguish whether this person is an entrepreneur or has private means. The former will be more able to create value for the economy.

One must gradually work out this matter by way of characterizations and then, when you go ever further and further, you get the direct value of the work and an indirect, reflecting value of the work. In this way you arrive at a characteristic of the concept of work. With this you can again go back to the ordinary woodcutter and see what the woodcutting of the cotton merchant signifies in the economic process compared to that of the professional wood cutter. In this way one can let oneself drift along from one step to the next and must everywhere observe how the matter is working. That is what I call being in accord with reality. You must show how work functions in the most varied areas of life. Just like Goethe with the concept of the archetypal plant: of course he had outlined a scheme, but he meant something that is constantly changing. In life, economic concepts must be constantly subject to metamorphoses. That is what I mean.

Of course you will not have much luck with such concepts. The university professors do not consider them valid today; they want to have a definition. But I have not found the concept of work to have been rigorously taken hold of in the teachings of economy. One should characterize, not constantly speak in a negative way. For example, I have found in economic analyses that work cannot be the decisive factor in the price, for the reason that the personal effort of the particular people concerned is different. You certainly find negative instances recorded. But the positive aspect is missing, so that one goes on to characterize work in such a way that it really loses its original substantial character and gets its value from other aspects from which it is considered. When one begins to characterize in this way, then the substance is lost; in the end you get something that in every way is part and parcel of the economic structure.

Work is that element of economics that originally comes from real human effort, but that overflows into the economic process and thereby achieves economic value in the greatest variety of directions. One should speak of processes that lead in the most various directions in the evaluation of work. Inspiration depends on finding out how to advance from one thing to the next. To find just the right examples depends a little bit on the *spiritus*.

QUESTION: But is a primary concept not necessary? Even with the descriptive method one must surely give weight to the causes that give rise to the observed effects?

RUDOLF STEINER: As far as what concerns the effects, I agree that one must go back to the causes. But as is the case already in certain areas of nature (that one cannot find the causes in a way other than by starting from the effects), so it is even more the case in the area of economics, that knowing the causes is of no help if one has not obtained them from the effects. For example, the tremendous effects of the war industry, they are there! If one did not know them as effects, then one could not confirm their cause at all. It is a matter therefore of acquiring a certain sense for the quality of the effects, in order to be able to determine the causes. Of course in actual practice one will have to determine the causes directly. But that depends on what economic theory requires in actual practice. One learns to evaluate the effect, and in seeing the sidetracks of the effects one comes to recognize the causes and then to change them for the better. It does not do much good to learn to know only the causes. One must determine the causes in such a way that one can say, "I know them because I started out from their effects." Knowledge of tremendous importance such as that the speech center is in the left brain was gained entirely from its effect—lost speech-paralysis. You first know the effect; only then are you led to investigate the matter. So therefore this recurrent method is necessary.

QUESTION: I cannot see everything having to do with art, religion, and also sport, from an economic point of view. Some part of these one can see from that point of view, but surely not the whole of them?

RUDOLF STEINER: I am visiting a place and find there extraordinarily artistic buildings—this, of course, is a utopia. This is to be seen not only as something artistic. These artistic buildings are possible only on the basis of a certain economic situation. If I visit a place full of artistic buildings, I will immediately have a picture of how things are managed there. If, on the other hand, I visit a place where even so-called beautiful buildings are lacking in taste, then from that I will get an idea of the economic situation of that particular place. And even if I find only utilitarian kinds of buildings, I will get an idea of the economic situation in that particular place. Where I find artistic buildings I can conclude that there higher wages are paid than where I do not find any. So I cannot imagine there is anything that cannot be considered economically.

Everything, including even the highest spheres, must be considered in its economic aspects. If today an angel came down to the earth, it would either appear merely as a dream (then it would not change anything); or as soon as it appeared to people who are awake, then it would certainly affect the economic life—it could not do otherwise.

OBJECTION: I admit that one can consider these matters from an economic point of view—but only just able! But one can surely also consider them from other points of view.

RUDOLF STEINER: You are going round in circles. All one can say is this: it is necessary for our consideration to first take the economic point of view as a basis. This has only a heuristic value, a value for research, for investigation. But if you want to find an exhaustive economic theory in accord with reality, you will not be able to avoid characterizing the economic effects from every angle. You will have to characterize what influence it has on the economic life of a region, whether it has a hundred excellent painters or only ten. It is otherwise hardly imaginable that the economic life could be fully grasped. Otherwise I would not have insisted so much on stressing this. Just through stressing it one always arrives at definitions that in some area are basically not valid, or which are extremely forced. It is actually impossible to define the income a man should have by pointing out that he has a claim on what "he himself produces." This definition exists: a person has a claim on what he himself produces. It seems to be quite nice when one makes such definitions. In certain circumstances it is correct. But a sewer cleaner could not do much with it. The point is that in economics one should not stress one thing out of the whole range of manifestations, but should go through the whole range. One needs to realize that we begin to think in terms of economics because we can then help those who cannot do so. But one must also realize that economic thinking must give rise to the demand that it be quite total in nature, a thinking that is very inclusive. It is much easier to think juristically. Most economists think very juristically.

COMMENT: The opinions diverge so far as to what is "normal" in economics that one does not know at all what is normal.

RUDOLF STEINER: I do not think it is worthwhile to debate about what is understood as "normal" and "abnormal." There is a saying that there is only one state of health and innumerable illnesses. I do not agree with that. Each person is healthy in his or her own way.

People come and say, "Here is someone with heart problems, he has these little defects, he ought to be cured." I have often said, "Let people have their little defects." A doctor brought to me a man who was sick. The man had injured the bridge of his nose so badly that one nasal passage was so constricted that he did not get enough air. The doctor said, "That has to be operated on, that is an extremely simple operation." I said, "Forget about the operation! He has a lung that is so constituted that he should not get more air; he is fortunate to have a constricted nasal passage. This way he can live for another ten years. If he had a normal nose he would quite certainly be dead in three years." I do not therefore make much of "normal" and "not normal." To me that is most trivial. I often say, "A normal citizen, a normal citizeness." People will readily understand what I mean by that.

QUESTION: About the value of statistics.

RUDOLF STEINER: It is true that statistics can help a great deal. But today the statistical method is applied in an external way. Someone produces statistics about the increase in value of houses in a certain district and about the increase in another district, and then puts them alongside each other. But that is not good. The only safe way is to investigate the conditions as such. Then one will know how to evaluate such numbers. For sometimes a row of numbers can indicate something special simply because an extraordinary event has inserted itself into that row....

QUESTION: In putting together numbers is inspiration also involved?

RUDOLF STEINER: Inspiration is also involved in that when you have one row, a second row and a third one, and you then find out—once again by inspiration—which facts, when you consider them qualitatively, become modified in the first row because of corresponding facts, let us say, in the third row. In that way certain number values are perhaps retained. In the historical method I call that the symptomatic way of looking at it. One must have the possibility of evaluating matters and eventually correctly weighing the contradictory things against one another.

In economic theory, things are sometimes dealt with in a highly objectionable way. One has the feeling that statistics are handled in a way such that, for example, the finance ministers of the various countries establish balances according to party-political points of view in one way or another. And where someone wants to support a particular direction in the party, the numbers can actually support another point of view just as well. There we are really dealing with something of a basic, elemental nature. In every science that has to do with human nature (yes, even if you want to name a science that enables you to learn how to treat and to tame animals), your concepts must be capable of modification. And especially so in economics. That is where inspiration comes in—that is what one has to have. Do not be offended, if I say it just like that.

I am convinced that many of those who are students today would have this inspiration (because it is not something so terrible, not floating in nebulous mystical heights), if it had not really been entirely driven out of them at school, already in the prep school and in the public school. As university students today it is your task to recall what was driven out of you in prep school, to have a living connection with science, which today is pursued in a terribly dead way.

Once I happened to speak with a number of professors of economics in another country. They said, when we want to visit our professional colleagues in Germany they say, "Yes, do come, but not to my lectures, come visit me at home!" Today one really needs an unprejudiced insight into things. This theory of economics has really lost ground, especially in recent times. It is really all connected with the fact that people have lost the creative element of the spirit. Today people really have to have their nose rubbed into something before they believe in it.

One can now read articles in the newspapers about the spiritual blockade in Germany. This has of course been developing for some time. If today we want to deliver the periodical *Das Goetheanum* to Germany, then because of its prime cost we have to get eighteen marks per copy for it. Think of the technical, medical journals! It is impossible to get them. Think of the cultural consequences! That is also a question of economics. Germany has a spiritual blockade. The withdrawal of these periodicals led directly to the result of making people stupid. In Germany this has an economic character; in Russia it has already taken on a state character; there you can no longer read anything that is not supplied by the Soviet government itself. The people develop into a pure stereotype of the Soviet system. At the most one can smuggle in a book now and then.

QUESTION: Would it be more useful, in observing the effects of economics, not to consider the statistics in the first place, but to observe the facts with which we are confronted?

RUDOLF STEINER: One needs to do this, even when one goes to statistics for advice. One can prove these things only numerically with statistics. Clearly, if one now goes to Vienna one needs only to walk through the streets to gather experiences.

You need only to consider in which apartments your acquaintances lived ten years ago, and where they live now. And so it goes piece by piece. You can make such observations of the most awful kind. You can go and see for yourself that a whole middle layer has been wiped out, which basically only still survives, yes, because it has not yet died. It does not live in an economic sense, because one can see from what it lives on—and that is terrible. You can start out from that, but you may still feel the numbers needed for proof to be extraordinarily important.

You must have a "good nose" for these things because when you can prove things numerically, then the numbers get you a little bit further again. For example the devaluation of the krone in Austria; it is really ridiculous how little it means today, but something cannot decrease in value without something being taken away from something else. If you now look for the victims of the exchange rate of the currency, then they are to be found among those whose incomes have declined in value. Here one can do the calculations, and the remarkable thing is that the calculation may no longer be correct for Austria, let alone for Russia. Austria should have the right, since all other efforts are exhausted, to devalue the krone even more, and yet it still does not declare the state to be bankrupt. Of course, this can be achieved only through the sanctions that have somehow been brought about. As soon as these sanctions are lifted, people will have to adopt quite different measures....

QUESTION: As long as there is wealth, can the state forcibly take this wealth by issuing more money?

RUDOLF STEINER: Certainly the state can exist by issuing more money, but when the point has been reached where the income has been used up if it is not artificially maintained, then the state could really not exist any more in an economic sense, even if it produces more bank notes. Because further fabrication of bank notes must lead to where every redoubling would lead to an increase into infinity. The state must step back ever more and more.

QUESTION: Does the state not itself live off the economic capital that is invested in the businesses?

RUDOLF STEINER: Yes, but from what is income in them.

QUESTION: Yes, I presume that it sucks up the capital. The capital is diminished?

RUDOLF STEINER: Insofar as it has the character of income. Because if the state sucks it up, then it has this character. The state certainly can remain alive, but can no longer do business. That is no longer a business. It can live only from what has already been done; it lives only off the past. The income is totally used up. In Austria the point must have been reached long ago when the income dried up. In Germany things have not yet gone so far, by a long way. It is quite certain that things could not continue in Austria if it were not for certain mandatory laws concerning rents, for example. There you really pay nothing—about twenty-five centimes for a three-room apartment, I believe. Only in that way can the situation be maintained, that certain things are free. In Germany it is also the case that one pays perhaps only one tenth of one's income for an apartment. In a certain class of society that can generally pay up to a point, things can be maintained. In Austria a certain class of society has fallen so far that they can not pay even the twenty-five centimes any more. People who used to have an income of, say, three thousand kroner could under certain circumstances live from that; today that is a little more than an English shilling. One cannot live on that!

Today economic developments are actually so awful that people now ought to realize that one should really study the laws of economics, and in such a way that it would be of practical help. This attempt failed in 1919; at that time, the currency crisis was not yet as great as it is today.

We could address the question of what economic thinking means. And then, how does one arrive at a concept of work in an economic sense? And then it would be good if some people would also continue to work with the concepts that I have already used, quite freely and in their own way. It would also be good if someone would try to work out the concept of business capital. What is pure business capital? If one wants to characterize business capital according to its concept, one must accurately contrast it with mere income capital.

Second Seminar

DORNACH, AUGUST 1, 1922

WALTER BIRKIGT: Work in the sense of economics is human activity directed toward its profitability. In the field of physics one knows precisely that physical work is determined by its mechanical effect. Is every effort that is economically profitable already work? No—in the end, value can be created only by the consumer. If through work something is achieved that produces real value in connection with economics, then it can be called economic work.

RUDOLF STEINER: I would like to provide a little stimulus by asking Herr Birkigt what his position would be if we were now to discuss these statements and, let us say, this question came up. If in some way I were to compare work within the economic organism or process with the physical meaning of work, where does one stand then, if one now considers the concept of physical work more precisely?

Certainly what you have said is all correct, but physicists will then introduce the concept of mass when they set up a formula for their work—because physical work, energy, is a function of mass and velocity. You will easily find an analogy for the latter in the economic process. But that is just the peculiarity of the physics formula for physical work: that the concept of mass is introduced, that is physically determinable through weight. Therefore we have "weight" in the physical concept of work that we merely replace with "mass" and "velocity." Now the question is, if we keep to your analogy, whether it is necessary to introduce something like the concept of mass or weight into the way we look at economics. If we did that, then we would just have to try to find what corresponds to mass in the economic process. Therefore I believe this question could be brought up in the discussion.

OBJECTION: Acknowledgment on the part of the buyer is part of the character of work. The business person presumes this thought of acknowledgment. The fact that the purchase of a product takes place is in itself acknowledgment.

RUDOLF STEINER: Since your concept of acknowledgment is not primarily an economic one, but more in the area of philosophy, it is necessary, in order for you to somehow justify that this concept has economic value, that you give it economic significance. Because in acknowledgment as such—for example when the housewife sees that she can well use something—there is scarcely more than a judgment. The element of economics enters in only when she can buy the item. It could well be that it is an excellent thing, but for economic reasons it cannot be bought because it is too expensive. So mere acknowledgment can no doubt be a category in philosophy. But it would be an economic category only if it were able to enter into the economic life. And thereby the concept of economic activity would be clarified.

QUESTION: What is now the connection between the verification of an economic activity and acknowledgment?

RUDOLF STEINER: "Acknowledgment" as such can hardly be a category of economics. That may be because acknowledgment has to be something subjective. Of course something subjective does enter into economics categories. But then one must show how it can become objective. Let us assume two housewives acknowledge something quite differently, and as far as I am concerned the "yes" can lead to an economic success and the "no" to an economic failure. The economic aspect would be found where the reasons lead in one case to success, in the other to failure, because the acknowledgment can only be a philosophical concept. To be sure, the acknowledgment can "slip down" into the private economic area, but surely it must then "slip back up" into the economic one.

COMMENT: I understand an economic activity to be an anticipation representing itself as an initiative of the physical statement of a verification.

RUDOLF STEINER: Perhaps we are here really dealing with something quite different than what could arise in the discussion. Here we surely want to stay in the realm of economic thinking. This formula has not given me any proof that you have entered into economic thinking in this matter. The formula is of course worthy of every acknowledgment, but it is really more the formula of an economic philosophy that attempts, even in a rather scholastic way, to discover the concept of economic activity, in order to justify economic activity metaphysically before the whole world. If that is your intention, then you may take this route; then it would be most interesting to have a conversation about it. But unless you ask yourself the question if, for example, it is the point today—and it is the point!—that a number of people, who are in fact the people of today, bring something out of their thinking into economics that could help lift up the economic life, then it is hard to see right away what could really be particularly gained by such a formulation.

Of course what could be gained is that people learn to think better, but we are also faced by the necessity to make economics as such really fruitful. In natural science and in medicine it does not matter very much in the end whether one has a methodology. There it is really more a technique in using the methods, the research instruments, and so on, but the methodology itself has no extraordinarily great value. In the theory of economics it does have such a great value, because what we think about things has to become practical in economics. Otherwise it is just what Brentano does in his own way: just empirical. It does not become practical. Today we need an economics that can become practical. And therefore it would be really interesting now to go through the definition word for word. But it really lies more in the realm of the philosophy of economics than than to economics itself.

Herr Birkigt's explanations were intended to develop the concepts of work so that someone in a union who wanted to become clear about how to value various kinds of work would be helped by those explanations. That was your intention, and that would have to be our intention today if we were stuck in a union, perhaps as some kind of workers, so that we would somehow have a basis on which to value these things in their economic process.

REMARK: Economic work is every human activity that indirectly or directly results in creating value.

RUDOLF STEINER: I believe something else must be considered, particularly when one wants to achieve a practical economic thinking. In order to be clear about it, we will make an analogy from natural science. The whole process in the human organism is totally incomprehensible if one considers only the up-building processes; those, therefore, that go in a certain direction. You get a real understanding of the whole process only if you also consider the disintegrating processes. So throughout the bones and nerves, for example, we have disintegrating processes; in the blood, besides definite up-building processes we also have disintegrating ones. We can even say, starting with the formation of chyle through lymph formation up to the creation of venous blood, that we have up-building processes throughout. Then we have the processes that represent a kind of labile equilibrium between up-building and disintegrating processes. And those going on in the nerves and bones are distinctly disintegrating processes. Devolution in contrast to evolution! We attain a real understanding only when, for example, we arrange our concepts in such a way that we understand the liver process as a combination of building up and disintegration. Others can come along and can have a merely theoretical interest; then they will also distribute the disintegrating processes among the up-building ones. They will say that the human being develops physically with the up-building processes up to a certain point.

Then the human being starts to build up spiritually, therefore, differently. Well, then we go from one sphere into the other, only retaining the abstract web of concepts, and thereby do not learn to understand anything. We learn to understand the effect of Spirit in the human organism only when we know that the Spirit begins to work when no up-building processes are present; when we know there is no up-building in the brain, but disintegration, and it is only in disintegration that the Spirit puts itself to work. Then I have a way of understanding through which I enter into reality.

When I cling on to a conceptual direction step by step with a purely dialectic logic, then I do not arrive at any practical understanding.

In economics it is necessary that one take into consideration not only the creation of value, but also of devaluation; that up to a certain point one also speaks of actual destruction. I have really done that. It already begins with consumption, but there is also a spiritual-cultural process involved, where devaluation also takes place.

You would think that when I tear down a house, then that also has a value, because at that place the removal of the house means that something productive is created for someone. Certainly one can look at it that way if one stays within abstract conceptual development. But in practice it is significant where I put together the economic process out of value creation and devaluation. And then it must of course be clear that work is of significance, not only in the creation of value but also in its destruction. Without considering that, I do not reach an adequate concept of work. If work did not also exist for destruction, one could not do business at all. This you must bring into your concept.

I believe it to be really of the greatest importance for the immediate future to recognize what should happen economically in the area of value creation and value destruction. For when values are created that are not destroyed in an appropriate way, although they are there to be destroyed, then a disturbance of the economic process also occurs. The process is disturbed by too much production. The process is disturbed simply because, put picturesquely, there is too much in the stomach of the economic life.

QUESTION: Should we not conceive of work as an activity that comes into consideration for a closed economic organism?

RUDOLF STEINER: There it must be considered that things must be accepted as realities. Undoubtedly making too many umbrellas can be a process of retrenchment; but as far as the work performed is concerned, it is in any event an up-building process, so long as we are just considering the work. This is not the opposite of the retrenching process of destroying umbrellas. Under certain circumstances the destruction will not be accomplished with what you would define as work. But in any case, you cannot call the making of too many umbrellas a down-building process, if you think the matter through in relation to work.

We must be aware that in regard to economic considerations we should characterize, that is, should try to arrive at a concept so that we look at it from various points of view, to arrive at a really clear judgment. We get nothing from an abstract definition. This concept of work has been put forward: work is a human activity with regard to its economic value; in short, it is the economic activity of the human being. But how is such a definition of work in the sense of economics differentiated from the definition of work in the physical sense? For there is no reality in such an economic definition. When physicists defines work through a formula, through a function, and it has mass and velocity in it, then there is a reality in it, because mass can be weighed. When physicists want to define velocity, they set up a definition. This definition serves only to provide understanding. The physicists are entirely aware of the fact that with it they are only pointing out what should be understood. For one only has a concept of velocity who knows it from experience. What they will define is the measure of velocity. And so the physicists will never think they have given any real explanation when this is the one they give. But they are probably of the opinion—whether rightly or wrongly, that I will not investigate—that they are giving a real explanation when they state work to be a function of mass and velocity. With that they start off on a real explanation.

If I do that in the economic life then it is a matter of grasping the history from the right angle. If, for example, I give my explanation of value from that angle in such a way that value is created, that value is a function of work, of a natural object, of a natural being, or of Spirit and nature; then the work consists of the change that is taking place.

This, however, is a qualitative change, whereas for the physicist the moving body undergoes a change of place. What the physicist has as a measurement is the real natural substance. But I come up with a definition that in fact very well meets the requirements of such a real definition in physics. I do nothing special for the economy when I try to define work for itself. Above all, I must myself be clear about the fact that work as such becomes an economic category only when I bring it to function with a product of nature. When one makes such definitions one comes into a way of understanding things that later on one actually finds astonishing. You know, for example, that during the era of classical physics the physicist always defined work as a function of mass and velocity. Compared with the modern perceptions of ion and electron processes, this definition of work completely loses its meaning, because there the concept of mass disappears; we deal only with acceleration. There the physical process emancipates itself from what is in it as ponderable mass, just as with myself capital emancipates itself from nature that has been worked upon and enters into a function of its own.

So one comes into an area that actually justifies itself in every way. This is the characteristic of thinking that is in accord with reality; that one's thinking goes beyond what is contained in definitions. I want to draw your attention to the fact that when I speak of economic matters, I never try to take hold of a concept where it cannot be taken hold of. I also cannot take hold of "mass" in physics, only its function. "Mass is the quantity of matter," that is also only a word definition! Just as little do I want to regard it as significant in economics that one defines the concepts of nature, labor, and capital, one after the other, but one has to take hold where the realities are: not nature, but processed nature; not labor, but organized labor; not capital, but capital directed by the human Spirit or mind, brought into movement, capital brought into economic movement. To take hold of things there where they are: that, I believe, is necessary today in economics!

QUESTION: Not recorded.

RUDOLF STEINER: I want only to point out that the distinction between mental work and physical work is not really justified. If one wanted to define the one mental work and the other physical work, then one could not really find anything other than a slow transition from one pole to the other, but no real opposite. That these things were wrongly looked upon you can see from the fact that people were always mistaken about the recuperative effect of gymnastics. Today one knows that gymnastics does not represent that recuperation that was formerly ascribed to it. The student will not work more doing so-called mental work than doing gymnastics for the same length of time. Of course it is always a matter of thinking about economic things in a fruitful way.

QUESTION: About the relationship between economic and biological thinking.

RUDOLF STEINER: Economic activities in their reality, such as they are, are very strongly analogous to biological entities. You can very well verify this when you try to establish the economic value of work, for example the work of a printer. Let us suppose a lyric poet imagines himself to be an extraordinarily great poet, and also brings it about that his poems are printed, be it through patronage, through financial support, or something of that sort. And for the realization of this volume of poems the papermakers, typesetters, a whole number of people, are now at work who, according to Marxist ideas, are definitely doing productive work. But let us assume not a single copy is sold, and they are all turned to pulp. Then you would have the same result as if the books had never been made at all. In that case the work that was performed was basically completely futile.

But now you must first again investigate whether what the Marxists say is seven-eighths nonsense or whether it does really have some significance. And there you will observe that the biological way of looking at it offers a certain analogy. You can say however: In biology I can observe a whole being from beginning to end and have it before me, whereas in economics I deal only with tendencies and the like. But now I ask you whether you have more than tendencies in all the nature around you when you consider that not all of the herring eggs become herrings, but that in comparison with those that do become herrings, innumerable herring eggs are simply destroyed? It is a question, however, whether those destroyed have no significance whatever for the entire process of nature, or whether they merely go in a different direction in the whole biological process. Because that is the case. There would not be any herrings and many other sea creatures if so and so many herring eggs were simply not destroyed. Now you are still not on firm ground if you say, well, so eggs are being destroyed and so on. Here you are duty-bound to say, I have an evolution before me here. The egg is created and perishes because of something. The whole herring is also created and perishes because of something. The processes go in different directions, and the herring merely follows the tendency indicated by the egg. In no way can you say that the herring has a greater right to cease to exist than the egg. And now you have an analogy between work that perishes and economic entities that perish.

One comes across innumerable things when there are analogies between economic thinking and that of biology. It is not noticed because we have an orderly thinking neither in biology nor in economics. If biology would begin to develop correct thinking, it would become very similar to that of economics. In order to pursue biology in a real sense one needs the same capacities as one needs to pursue economics.

QUESTION: Wherein lies the justification for the printed but later destroyed poems, as compared with that for the herring eggs?

RUDOLF STEINER: The situation can be as follows. If people who are employed were not kept occupied, then of course they would have to find work somewhere else. And if they had to work elsewhere, then possibly not enough would be derived from their human activity. For under certain circumstances something must be "wasted" from human work, just as with the herring eggs, and this wastage also has an economic effect. One must absolutely say—what one says so easily—sleep is rest, life is activity. But from a certain point of view sleep is far more necessary for life than being awake. It is the same with this activity. Of course, you can say you will employ it in a more useful way, but one could ask whether it is more useful if it is umbrellas that are being produced in too great a number.

To begin with, these are stop-gap measures—in a quite incorrect economic process which is done in order to eliminate ork that would have troublesome consequences.

The matter would turn out differently if one had sound thinking in economics. If there were sound thinking in economics, then one would have to be tremendously smart—but here we are going beyond the usual economic considerations—in order to evaluate the surplus work time created by those people who are not able to be self-employed. Well, it actually is so: If one were able to be a sound thinker in economics, then something would immediately come about which you would probably welcome with joy. But people cannot imagine that it would be necessary to teach those people who cannot employ themselves, who do not know how to spend their time. But it would hardly be necessary for a person who today works for eight or nine hours to work for more than three or four. If people thought in a sensible way about economics they would need to occupy themselves far, far less in the way they occupy themselves now. And then that which corresponds to the destroyed herring eggs would fall into that time. Now people waste so much time in work that will anyhow be destroyed. To begin with, these are stop-gap measures in a quite incorrect economic process, which is done in order to eliminate work that would have troublesome consequences.

REMARK: When one speaks of biological thinking, then one has a certain limited object of perception about which one thinks. In economic thinking one has to indicate through the thinking what one is thinking about.

RUDOLF STEINER: In biology you also have the "limited object of perception," but in a relative way. In earthly objects, for example, that you look at microscopically, or in which you look at the details as arising out of a great combination, you also do not have such a limitation. You can say you have a comprehensively visible object in a drop of blood, but as soon as you look at it microscopically you see more—five to six hundred red blood cells are there in one cubic millimeter, and they are all active. That is certainly visible to the eye in the microscope, but it looks very similar to what one sees when one looks at a limited economic process. Assume you are standing in front of a stall at the annual fair and see how the stall-keeper stands there; how his goods lie there; here are the customers; he hands over their purchases; they put down their money.... When you do all that now—I imagine you can manage to be such a giant—and you contemplate all that at once as something quite compact and belonging together, then there are no real distinctions there. In a limited area I can see economics in an equally relative way. If I consider the stall owner and everything else that goes with him, then that is only relatively different, let us say, than the English selling opium in China; and I consider everything that is connected with that. I cannot understand why no one has any objection to this.

QUESTION: I do not know where economics begins and where it ends.

RUDOLF STEINER: One also does not know where what is biological begins. It is something else to work the comparison to death. I mean only: as regards that which makes it possible to understand the nature of living things, the same kind of understanding makes it surely possible to understand economics. Only one thing is necessary. In looking at an object of nature, the object comes toward us, whereas in economics the subject must come a little way toward the object. In economics one has to have what I yesterday called inspiration. Biologists, if need be, can have really very little inspiration and can work only with the methods. But to think in economic ways one will need some inspiration.

QUESTION: It seems to me that the economic process came about without the thinking first having been economic. Whether the economy proceeds in a healthy or unhealthy way is of no consequence. From here on out I should be able to speak of an object in economics corresponding to that in natural science.

RUDOLF STEINER: Mr. G. is correct. The difference consists in that it is necessary in economics to start out from a certain subjective understanding of what is happening out there in the world. But in economics this subjective element again becomes easier for one than it is in biology. As a human being one stands (since one is not a June bug when one is studying it), of course always stands outside, and must do so; whereas one stands outside to a much lesser degree when considering something in the sphere of economics.

One can always summon so much humanity that one can have a good understanding of the worker as well as of the business person. That is a common human concern, and that takes the place of what is outer perception in biology. To that extent Mr. G. is correct. On the other hand I believe that Goethe, for example, gave such a good definition of the shadow side of trade because he got very far in the way he considered biology. So in Goethe one sometimes finds remarkably pertinent views on economics. This is a bit connected with his morphological-biological way of looking at things. Nature just plays the role in biology of someone who gives one a push if one does not oneself have the *spiritus*. In economics one must really come up with the *spiritus* oneself.

OBJECTION: There are theoreticians who say that there is no economic theory, because economics does not exist. Spann[†] in fact states that.

RUDOLF STEINER: He is much admired and in Vienna he rates as a special luminary among intelligent people. I have occupied myself too little with him to have much of an opinion about him, but what these intelligent people say about him has not been very enlightening to me. But it would only be a clever dialectic to say that there is no such thing as economics. There are also people, of course, who say there is no life, but only a mechanism.

We should now engage in special considerations. Someone should try to show more concretely where economic valuation and devaluation processes are necessary.

Third Seminar

DORNACH, AUGUST 2, 1922

COMMENT: Again the idea of acknowledgment is brought into the discussion and is again characterized by Rudolf Steiner as inappropriate for the science of economics.

RUDOLF STEINER: The idea of acknowledgment leads into the philosophy of economics, not really into the science of economics itself. Besides that, it must be our striving to find such points of view of the science of economics so that—because they are always changing themselves—they can be carried into all areas of economic life. You will hardly reach all the elements of economics with the idea of acknowledgment without very greatly expanding this concept; this you can always do with concepts.

I will say for example: What form would the idea that was developed yesterday take, if we had to deal with the situation that a previously completely unknown Rembrandt was found somewhere in an attic? And what if it was a matter of appraising this Rembrandt's economic value, concerning which we are certainly able to speak? I don't mean how could we actually do this, but how does it relate to the idea of acknowledgment.

COMMENT: The one advocating the idea of acknowledgment says it derives from the "political element," such as from unearned market profits.

RUDOLF STEINER: When we have the possibility to bring about the reality of threefolding, then the concept of the "political element" as you have developed it, will fall away. Because the political element is essentially contained in the rights sphere, it would then completely fall out of the economic sphere and therefore one could not come to the point of bringing in an "acknowledgment" through some kind of political conduct.

But the question remains, What then is the "political element"? It is really an entirely secondary concept that has been forcibly derived. For from the purely economic point of view there is no reason to be political. In the example that you brought up about the business person who is counting on earning two hundred thousand marks while he pays his workers only eighty thousand, and who then takes in five hundred thousand because the business situation has improved. In a case like that there is no necessity to bring in politics. Let us assume the following. With the greater earnings he acquired (provided the workers can make out alright with their eighty thousand marks and are content with that), the business person can quite openly stand before them all and say: I counted on earning 200,000 marks, but I got 300,000 more instead. It was on this assumption, that 200,000 would be earned, that we founded this business; now we have earned 300,000 more. For many reasons I find it more proper for the whole of the economic organism within which we stand to found a school with this 300,000 marks, rather than distribute it to you. Do you agree to that? There you have a format where the economic process has remained the same, but you have no need whatever to reckon with any sort of political factor.

The political element is secondary in the history of the world. That is simply due to the fact that the primitive, perhaps highly unsympathetic, but entirely honest power relationships gradually took on the form of war between people. One cannot, however, say that war is the continuation of politics only with other means, but politics is modern war carried on at the intellectual level. For this war depends on deceiving the opponent, on bringing about situations that deceive one's opponent. Every flanking movement, all kinds of things that are not a direct or open attack, depend on deceiving the opponent.

And a general will earn the more credit, the more he succeeds in outwitting the enemy. Transferred to the intellectual level, that is politics. In politics you find exactly the same categories.

When one speaks of politics, one would like to say, it should be striven for to overcome politics in everything—even in politics.

For basically we have real politics only when all of what plays out in the political field does so in a rightful way. But then we would really have just a constitutional state.

QUESTION: about the example of the tailor.

RUDOLF STEINER: The error arises only because the earnings from a single suit of clothes are extremely small and therefore it would also take a very long time before this little gain in the tailor's monetary balance is so evident that he would actually look upon it as a deficit. This situation comes about because through the division of labor products are in fact made cheaper. If one works for a community influenced by the division of labor, then one's own products appear to be cheaper than when one is working by oneself. That is just what the actual cheapening effect of labor division consists of. If one does not use it at a certain stage then one's self-made articles become more expensive. Now of course the gain from a single suit that the tailor makes for himself would not make much difference, whereas it would be noticeable if all tailors did it.

With further division of labor no one would ever make anything by himself—possibly only on a farm. If a tailor now actually makes a suit for himself and he wants to set up a correct balance sheet, then he would simply have to put his own suit in this balance sheet at a higher price than that of the market. Thus he must enter his expenses higher than the market price. It does not matter very much in deciding an individual case whether or not he now actually buys the suit.

It is a self-evident presumption, of course, that one is not buying the clothes from other tailors, but from dealers. The price of a suit from a dealer is cheaper—otherwise the division of production and sales would make no sense—than the price would be if the tailors concerned were to work without dealers. So the tailor has to set the price somewhat higher if he is working without a dealer, because the dealer brings things to the market more cheaply than the tailor himself could turn them over. At best one could make the objection, which under some circumstances might be justified, that the lower price of the merchandise handled by the dealer is due to the fact that the tailor must include the cost of the trip if he has to get his material from the dealer. Then he would discover that by working through a dealer these trips also become cheaper. Through a simple comparison of the tailor's and the dealer's prices you could of course never find out whether the suit is more or less expensive.

QUESTION: The price of the one suit is supposed to exert a downward trend on the price of the others. Why would the other suits become more expensive?

RUDOLF STEINER: It exerts a downward trend on the price through the fact that the tailor takes out the one suit from all the suits that the dealers are handling, so that for this suit he takes away the possibility of their making a profit; therefore they must demand a greater profit for the other suits. The greater profit demanded by the dealers causes them to raise the price, but for the tailor that means a lowering of the price.

QUESTION: The question is now whether this lowering of the price makes less of a difference than going the dealer route raises the price.

RUDOLF STEINER: You will not find that anywhere. Try once to solve this problem. That is a task that can be directly stated thus: To what extent does using a dealer have a cheapening effect compared with selling by oneself? Put directly like this, it would be important as an topic for a dissertation. You would see that if fifty tailors charge for their travel to sell their goods, it would actually cost more than if dealers made the trips.

OBJECTION: About the suit that the tailor keeps for himself, you say that if it goes through the dealer, then it becomes cheaper. Now with this suit the whole expense of the dealer making the trip is saved.

RUDOLF STEINER: This would be the case if using the dealer did not make it cheaper; but since it does so, then it does not make any difference that he keeps the suit at home.

COMMENT: Let us say the cost of making it is one hundred marks. Through bargaining the price is raised to a hundred and twenty marks. The dealer reduces it to a hundred and ten. But if the tailor does not put his own suit up for sale, then he also saves the ten marks.

RUDOLF STEINER: But in this case you must consider the total balance resulting from both dealers and tailors as an actual economic reality. You would have to investigate how this one item affects the total balance. You cannot find it merely by comparing the individual entries. One would have to see it in the whole picture. Then you would see that because the economic division of labor means that work becomes more fruitful, I would harm myself and others if I return from a complete economic division of labor to a former method. The mistake comes about because it is difficult to maintain the terribly small dividend. But I need only to set up the following progression. If you conceived of the tailors all making their own clothes and setting up an association, then that which would have to be entered differently in the balance as a joint item would be quite significant.

COMMENT: In the ready-made clothes industry that becomes even clearer.

RUDOLF STEINER: Quite certainly that is so. Of course then what the underlying causes are should be looked into. It would be a very small item if it concerns the division of labor only between the producers and the dealers. On the other hand the item becomes very considerable if there is a further division of labor, if then the tailor now no longer makes complete suits but only parts of them. Then if he wants to make his own suit it will be much more expensive than if he bought it somewhere else. I did say that it was just a radical example, as my purpose was to illustrate a principle. But what became clear with further division of labor was also true at its very beginning.

QUESTION: Why could this not be relevant to agriculture?

RUDOLF STEINER: I did not say that. It is becoming ever rarer for people to produce for themselves with the exception of agriculture, where it is obvious the farmer will take care of himself. In agriculture, where there are in any case many revisions of the general economic process, it does not make so much difference whether the farmer eats from his own crop of cabbage or buys it. If, however, a real economic relationship were to exist between agriculture and other areas in the sense of threefolding, then it would also come into consideration for agriculture. However the situation today is such that all kinds of underground rearrangements are taking place through which the relationship of the prices between industry and agriculture is completely undermined. That will be dealt with in the next days.

But if one were to investigate the total balance of an economic area in such a way as to balance out agriculture against industry, then it would become apparent that under present conditions a substantial part of agriculture flows into industry simply in underground ways. But if under the associative principle exactly just as many, or at least, nearly as many, workers worked in one of the branches as far as prices allow, then we would have a quite different division between land and urban areas. People underestimate what it would mean if the associative principle were adopted, therefore it is not very easy to answer the question why "Der Kommende Tag" is not an association.[†]

It is not an association simply because it is not strong enough to have a particular influence on the economic process. For that one first needs an association of a certain size. What else can "Der Kommende Tag" accomplish today between entrepreneurs and workers, other than what also will happen anyway? That accomplishment would be possible only in one situation— once I also said that in a company meeting—namely if all the employees of "Der Kommende Tag" were to decide to quit the unions. Then one would have the beginning of a movement that would also gradually get this business going from the other side, namely from the side of the workers. But so long as they participate in strikes in the same way as all the other workers, it is quite impossible to speak with them in an ideal way.

Through the associative way, a large number of factories would soon relocate from the cities to the country, and similar things would happen as a necessary consequence of working in the associative way. It is not for nothing that there are villages and village economies. In a primitive economic system the village kind is the only form of economics. Then we have the markets. In economics these designations are much more correct than one would think. As long as the market is there with the villages around it, it represents something less harmful economically, even if it operates under the law of supply and demand, than if it were part of an urban economy—unless there are scoundrels around, which is a personal matter. The urban economy radically changes the whole relationship between producers and consumers. Then we no longer have villages that regulate their market themselves, but we have opened the door to all kinds of possibilities that exist when the relationship between consumers and producers is no longer a clear one, when it becomes mixed up. And that is the case when people live together in cities.

In the course of longer periods of time (not, however, exceptionally long) it would turn out that in the cities the administrative officers, the central schools, and so on, would essentially be together in the spiritual-cultural and political life, whereas both the economic and political life would be decentralized together. Also their association would be spatially separate, but not so that there would now be three quite separate parts; rather so that the cities would essentially represent a spiritual-cultural life that is interwoven with a more centralized, a greater, horizontal administration. And smaller administrations like business enterprises would find themselves more decentralized. This would presume that the transport facilities would become much more efficient than they are now. These have not improved so much only because transportation was just not necessary for production when the manufacturers were sitting together in the cities. The relationship between producers and consumers cannot be comprehended in any other way than by forming an association. But then the relationships that came about when they were mixed up, are changed. For the associative system is something that is not only supposed to organize, but something that manages. The associative principle would show that the health of the threefold organism depends at the same time on the health of each single part; it is on that that the working together of the three parts depends.

It is not so easy to speak about threefolding, because there are so many points of view about it. If today one describes to a man what will come about there, he says, prove it to me! Indeed, nobody can theoretically prove to me that he will be hungry tomorrow. However, from experience we know that he will be hungry tomorrow. And so with a correct economic thinking, a correct economic foreknowledge will come about. You must look upon it as something real, what is here meant by correct economic thinking, that one begins to develop a kind of thinking that itself is also really productive. Otherwise I could ask you, What economic value does the theory of economy have? One that is merely reflective has a quite different economic value; it is basically one of consumption, rather than one that is really thought through. The latter is fundamentally one of production.

QUESTION: Tailors reduce the price of their product when they take care of themselves by division of labor. Does that really also hold good for a button or some other partial product?

RUDOLF STEINER: As a boy I lived in a village where there was a shoemaker; his name was Binder. He refused to have any contact with his customers that he did not initiate himself. He delivered every pair of boots, which he made himself, for my father and mother. Now what does a whole pair of boots consist of? In this case the boots consisted of pipings (they had such long ones); the upper piece; the arch; the sole; and the journey of the shoemaker that he had to make to get to us. That belongs to it. It makes no difference at all whether you now speak of the piping, the sole, or his journey. The division of labor first came about when one took away the piece that consisted of his walk. This is the most radical part, especially with the tailor, because there you do not so easily see everything that belongs to it. When I had pulled on my boots I knew I was making the walk that the shoemaker made!

QUESTION: Do I also reduce the price with a button that I myself make?

RUDOLF STEINER: In that case you will possibly lose the most, because then you do not need it at all!

INTERJECTION: I would like to assume that I do need it.

RUDOLF STEINER: Then the question arises what you need the product for. When you so alter it—it can be a small or a great alteration—so that it has a real value, then perhaps you will not lose anything.

REMARK: I need it to be consumed, therefore, to be used up.

RUDOLF STEINER: In agriculture there are other corrections to be made. If the division of labor were carried out, then it would also work there. But you will hardly find it possible, when you hold back what has been produced with division of labor, to make it valuable in such a way so that it brings about a reduction in cost.

A loaf of bread is still very close to agriculture. But just with this loaf of bread we had a really disastrous experience. With the best of intentions—it was before the war—we asked one of the members of our Society to produce a healthy and otherwise good bread. This bread was then supplied only to our members and not given to others. This bread became so expensive that it simply became impossible.

COMMENT: That was really a quality bread.

RUDOLF STEINER: If the price difference was due only to what was justified by the quality, then one could have put it right. But the price difference was considerably larger, caused only because in the general production a more extensive division of labor was used than in that of our member. In his operation the work was not divided among as many people as in that of the others, so that his production was considerably more expensive.

QUESTION: What about fashionable clothes?

RUDOLF STEINER: But there we are now in the realm of aesthetics, not of economics. I did not want to go into the question of whether it would not perhaps be a good thing if the division of labor were avoided in certain areas. I am even against carrying out the division of labor in every area; not for economic reasons, but for reasons of good taste. I even find it gruesome when the division of labor is carried out to the *nth* degree in human clothing, for example. But there we must say: Of course we must advance an independent spiritual-cultural life, which will naturally cost us something at first. It would make some things more expensive, but it would balance out, even though certain products that are not included in the division of labor become more expensive.

But please do not misinterpret this to mean that I want to be a fanatic.

QUESTION: What is the situation when there are significantly more dealers than is economically justified?

RUDOLF STEINER: What I have said presupposes that there are just so many dealers as are economically justified. We are not dealing here with a linear progression, but with a maximum-minimum direction. With a certain number of dealers we have the most favorable influence of having a system of dealers. Less than or more than that is unfavorable.

QUESTION: Can the number be determined?

RUDOLF STEINER: If the business is run at all sensibly, then the number of dealers is determined in the same way as that of the producers. Of course today sensible business management does not exist anywhere. One does not consider what an enormous amount of work is done unnecessarily. Just think about the printing of books. If all this unnecessary work were saved, then you would everywhere find an approach to normal numbers. The saving of unnecessary work already results in the decrease of the normal number of people working in a business. Today the fact is that the dealer system actually costs more than the workers themselves, at least in Germany.

For every article a certain number of dealers are needed. But finally you must also consider that sometimes even the dealer system is disguised. It is replaced by the greatest variety of other things. Just think how much the dealers can be replaced by having great market-places. In that way an entirely different economic category is created.

Fourth Seminar

QUESTION: Can one still speak of value when something has achieved its purpose? What is the situation when something new enters into the economic process? Does the demolition of a house represent devaluation through human labor? Does this devaluation make any kind of sense or not? Can one speak only of devaluation resulting from human labor when no new values are created?

RUDOLF STEINER: Express your opinion about this! Subjects will arise, for example, bituminous coal and lignite. A man could have the idea that simply as a substance bituminous coal is a more valuable object than lignite. But then he would have to defend his thesis. Another would be the rather daring thesis that as a rule mechanical work does not increase the price. To this our esteemed listeners may have one or another objection. Then the question of value distribution and devaluation is not exhausted by bringing up exceptions, such as submarines, but it would be a matter of just referring to economically necessary devaluations caused by labor in the continuous life of the economy.

Various interpolated questions.

RUDOLF STEINER: It is a question of whether—entirely in the sense of economics—one can or cannot speak of valuation and devaluation through work. If machines become devalued that would be economic consumption. It is not a question whether the aim of some work is devaluation but whether devaluations are necessary in the economic process that can be accomplished only by work.

X: The devaluation of values through work is done for the purpose of subsequently putting higher values into place (intermediate values).

RUDOLF STEINER: One can cite this as an example, but it is not entirely free from objections. A much simpler example is a quite ordinary one. If you work to wind thread onto a bobbin, then you have thereby created a product. It is produced by performing work, namely the winding of the thread. If I continue the work, then I must unwind it again. There both pieces of work are actually necessary. In intermediate work it is necessary that work performed during a process has to be undone again.

QUESTION: Would the same apply to the storage of products else-where?

RUDOLF STEINER: At least it would apply when you move a train to another place. There you must take away the initial value in order to give the second one the correct value. If you have a train here and you want to place it there, then you have caused a devaluation through the change in position. And such things are to be found everywhere. They would be devaluations that become necessary, and work is necessary to bring them about.

Except that usually one does not notice them. But they are present everywhere. You only have to consider the one who shovels the coal into a locomotive: the fireman has to shovel it away again. If you want to hold fast only to the concepts then you can say that that is a continuous process. But that would not be enough. Since here the continuous process cannot be performed directly, you would have to calculate what it would cost if I had provided the coal everywhere, compared to what it would cost if I always carry out a partial process and then have to destroy it again.

QUESTION: The packaging industry would also be an example?

RUDOLF STEINER: Yes, of course, a very striking example, one where you cannot really apply the concept of utilization and also not that of being used up through wear and tear, as with the sharpening of razors. There an article of value is used up, and that is a necessary kind of commercial work. The wear and tear only consists of something being made blunt. But in order to depreciate it completely, work is necessary.

QUESTION: To collect, sell, recast and reuse old iron—can the recasting also be called a revaluation?

RUDOLF STEINER: That is equivalent to the revaluation of refuse. You could not call that a devaluation.

REMARK: But the one process is completed!

RUDOLF STEINER: Yes, and then I discover that I can again make valuable use of what lies there like a product of nature. The criterion must be there that human work is needed to bring about a devaluation.

The melting down of iron is not really a process of demolition. Certainly there might be some doubt about it. One can interpret something in different ways. It could also be understood as a product of devaluation.

QUESTION: Devaluation through war—turning out grenades that are simply exploded?

RUDOLF STEINER: For the one who is not victorious, that is a devaluation.

QUESTION: Can one in any way consider war equipment as creating value in the economic sense?

RUDOLF STEINER: That can affect economics only in its results. The war industry does not create value so long as it only produces reserve stock. In that case it actually is a destructive work, but one cannot really say a necessary one.

COMMENT: What is used beyond the normal requirements, warfare implements, and so forth, after the war results in a deficit, for example?

RUDOLF STEINER: It is interesting that the abnormal usage which occurs there has a kind of relationship with the usage of someone having private means in an economic community. This usage is accepted. If one wanted to completely justify it—today it would be fought against—of course there is a certain justification for everything. The usage of the person of private means can be justified when the basic production is greater than can normally be consumed by the rest of the people. Under certain circumstances the usage of the person of private means is good in order to bring about an economic balance. And from this point of view there is a economic justification for the armed forces. The justification lies in that people say these things are there and can be produced. If there were no economic balance, then many people would be out of work if the armed forces did not consume without really being productive. For they actually produce nothing.

QUESTION: Can military economics be considered like the cauterizing of wheat, or something similar?

RUDOLF STEINER: This idea is found in the school of Rodbertus.[†] Defense is counted as a productive factor. There it is a matter of whether one regards an economy with certain presuppositions, or without them, or with other ones. Therefore if one were to think that defense with armed forces was unnecessary, then they could be dispensed with. But a fire engine cannot be dispensed with because it meets a necessary need, just like breakfast. Whoever considers the armed forces to be absolutely necessary must look upon them as performing a necessary task. But then we have the beginning of a discussion about the question of consumption. One knows people who consider the strangest things as absolutely necessary. There the concepts of usage enter into the valuation, and they are variable.

QUESTION: Mechanical work, water power from turbines, for example, saves human labor. Is the valuation made as if the mechanical work was performed by human labor?

RUDOLF STEINER: Think of a set of scales that has arms of unequal length, so that if I hang a heavy weight on one arm, then I must adjust the weight on the other one. So purely by its position a very small weight can balance a very large one. It is the same with the economic distribution of such things that you have called "mechanical work performance." The work to be performed becomes only relatively smaller, as with the set of scales. But you will always find a certain given quantum of actually performed work, also when it is mechanical. You cannot just get nature to do it. When you only want to lay a stone on something so that it does some work, you at least have to go to get it. You always have to put in a small amount of human labor. But these things do not belong to economics at all, where the situation functionally determines the relationship of work done with its achievement.

QUESTION: But mechanical work *per se* surely does not make products more costly?

RUDOLF STEINER: If you consider work in its full context, then you have to work out a quota everywhere.

QUESTION: How does devaluating work enter into the economic process?

RUDOLF STEINER: When you have a continuous economic process in which you have to cut costs—let us assume you have such a large shaving salon that you have to hire a special worker to sharpen the razors—then of course you must enter the labor of this worker differently on the balance sheet than that of those workers doing the shaving. Looked at from the outside it is of course also labor, but in the economic process it is entered differently, namely as a negative item.

QUESTION: What then happens with work that devalues? That is really a gift because there are no proceeds.

RUDOLF STEINER: Except that the prior indications are different. It is the same everywhere. If you have a creation of value that you designate as positive (+) in the continuous economic process, then you must designate a devaluation as negative (-) while you put in zero when nothing happens.

COMMENT: When a new machine replaces a process, then the product becomes cheaper, simply because work is saved. Whether it is value creating or devaluing work makes no difference.

RUDOLF STEINER: Yes, the situation is such that you can in effect always achieve the same thing. For that reason it still always remains an element in creating value and in devaluation. It is a matter of course, when you extract a number from it, that a positive one will result if a machine is to be used at all.... The question to be asked is literally this: whether it is necessary to expend work for putting an end to something, that is, for the devaluation of values that had already been realized in the economic process.

Question not recorded.

RUDOLF STEINER: In order to dispel any unclear concepts it will be necessary to carefully consider that cup of tea, the drinking of which is supposed to be economic work.

OBJECTION: I cannot allow that to be considered as work. The criterion for work is lacking.

FURTHER REMARK: When one takes in nourishment, for example, then one surely creates the values in oneself that enable one to do more work, just as when one makes machines that are meant to create values.

RUDOLF STEINER: But it is not possible to include what happens in the human being in the economy. That would lead to the discovery of Marxist theory.

However the gentleman must have been thinking of something else. You must somehow have in mind that drinking a cup of tea could provide economic value, and therefore is work in the economic sense.

COMMENT: If a man who works with his head is supported by economic values, then the preliminary result will be that he can eat and be intellectually fresh and alert. This result will at first remain within his personality, but that is not all. The results will irradiate the economic process, they will be what is emanating from him.

RUDOLF STEINER: But they cannot be incorporated in the economic process just like that, unless something is added. You cannot regard drinking a cup of tea as productive. The cup of tea would be considered as an economic question only if you wanted to produce something, if besides your usual nourishment you were to drink a cup of tea, and consequently were able to work more than you could without the cup of tea. Then the question would be whether one could conceive this to be an economic achievement.

COMMENT: Because I consume tea, it can be harvested in the colonies. I am really devaluing when I make it possible once more for new economic values to be generated.

RUDOLF STEINER: If you want to determine economic values in a positive sense, then you are on a different level when you bring up the question of the extent consumption is necessary in order to carry on the economic process. That is a question that really has nothing to do with economics as such.

COMMENT: I want to put the devaluation that consists in having drunk a cup of tea so that one can do work again on the same level as the example of the doctor and the shoemaker. The one who picks the tea performs work and I drink the tea. The tea picker helps to make it again possible for me to do work.

RUDOLF STEINER: If the question is put like that, then because of the tea picking our economic value comes from the nature-product tea. That is the creation of an economic value. But with the drinking of the tea, will an economic value arise or disappear in the same way?

X: It will disappear, will be devalued.

Y: I would say the value is changed.

RUDOLF STEINER: You cannot really accomplish this change; then you would have to designate every consumption, every expenditure merely as turn-over.

COMMENT: A turn-over of energy.

Take the process of drinking tea! You drink it up. Then you have allowed this value that was created there to disappear from the economic process. That is unquestionable.

RUDOLF STEINER: Then we leave the realm of economics and enter that of natural science. There you are dealing with a nature process that no longer belongs to economics.

Then as far as I am concerned you might even be strengthened by the tea—I will presume that—and perform an economic task. This as such is not yet of value, but becomes so when you apply it to a nature-product. And now once again a creation of economic value begins in the moment when you approach the nature-product. The question does not arise with the creation of value, whether you have now become stronger or not, but the creation of value begins only after you have been strengthened. Therefore, what occurs in you because of drinking the tea is not what you bring into the economic process, even if you become an athlete as a result of the tea-drinking.

This nature process must be excluded just like the value of soil and ground. Of course you can include it; then it is analogous to the inclusion of earthworms in the economic processes without using human labor to do it. When the earthworms go through the field they make it fertile. You cannot include that in the economic process. Just try to follow this in what happens further. You will then see that if one were to regard it as creating value when you become stronger through consumption, then one would enter into a economic system where work by itself is already creating value. This it does only in connection with nature or the human spirit.

It is not possible to achieve something in economics when you take processes inherent in the human being or in nature into the economy.

QUESTION: How then would one look upon donations?

RUDOLF STEINER: I may speak of a donation as a devaluation, because I cannot yet speak of economics so long as I see only human capacities for which I can use the donation. When I give a stipend I first allow this value to disappear in the economic process, until it reappears again.

COMMENT: One can almost see how the donation would continue to work.

RUDOLF STEINER: What continues to work depends on such factors that absolutely defy any attempt to determine them. Otherwise you would have to include diligence in economics, for example. But diligence would be a fictitious value in economics; not merely fictitious, but even impossible. If I had a workshop, let us say, from a moral point of view I would rebuke my workers when they were lazy; from a economics point of view I would only rebuke them when they did not produce anything for me. From that point of view I am concerned only about what they produce; morally I am concerned about whether they are diligent or lazy.

QUESTION: Can one speak of work only where there is division of labor in the economy?

RUDOLF STEINER: One can speak of work, in the economic sense, only when there is a beginning of reciprocity for one another in the work.

QUESTION: Could one speak of work in a primitive economy?

RUDOLF STEINER: One can do so, but only when one takes into account that the father does a particular job, that he consumes along with his wife, sons, and daughters, that his daughters again perform other work, and so on, and therefore they are working for each other.

QUESTION: Then how does one really arrive at a concept of work?

RUDOLF STEINER: It is very easy to arrive at a concept of work in relation to economics. You arrive at it when you have a product of nature before you that has been changed through human activity for the purpose of being consumed.

QUESTION: Whether or not it is consumed, is that of any consequence?

RUDOLF STEINER: It must at least be made capable of being consumed, because then it has value.

QUESTION: Must one then also always look upon the nature-product or object when value is created through the intellectual organization of work, or must one determine whether there is an object on which the organized work has been performed?

RUDOLF STEINER: You cannot look at an object here, because in the particular case you are concerned with there may possibly not be any fixed object. The intellect can deal merely with the arrangement and organization of the work. Then in some circumstances one is not dealing with any object.

QUESTION: Then that does not fall within the concept of work?

RUDOLF STEINER: That is a secondary concept. Work is that human activity that is performed in order to make a nature-product consumable. In the context of economics that is work. This you must now regard as the ultimate concept. Now the intellect can come along and organize the work. But in the course of things that which you now want to grasp as a coherent economic process can simply separate itself from the nature-product. It can consist in the mere organization, the mere arrangement of the work.

QUESTION: But if the devaluation through work is added?

RUDOLF STEINER: Devaluation is only negative for value. You do not go back with respect to making things consumable. You only go back with respect to the distribution of value.

COMMENT: With respect to making things consumable one is surely going back from a higher process to a lower one.

RUDOLF STEINER: First you wind up the spool. That requires work; there you have created value. And now you unwind the spool; there you destroy the value. But if you consider this situation you will find that a consumable product has been created up to the point of its destruction, and afterwards the final aim of the work is again a consumable product. As far as the work is concerned it is a matter of making something given by nature consumable. If you have under-consumption then you need so and so many procedures in order to let them be consumed by other procedures. In this process of consumption, where devaluation has to take place, a necessary work is performed.

COMMENT: Needless work just has to be designated as work, because its product has been brought to the point of being able to be consumed.

RUDOLF STEINER: If you want to have the concept of economic work then you must define it like that, but this concept is not yet a value. Only the work is defined. Economics is not concerned at all with bringing about economic work, but it is concerned with creating values.

X: One who is teaching also performs work.

RUDOLF STEINER: That is a question that is actually not so easily answered.

X: I mean free intellectual/cultural activity.

RUDOLF STEINER: That belongs in the realm of devaluation, but not devaluation through work.

X: But the person is producing for the future. For this purpose the individual is performing work.

RUDOLF STEINER: There we get the possibility to pursue the concept of work ever further. Of course one must designate education as a economic value in the highest degree, but it is a question, when one begins to imagine the concept of work in the economic process, whether one can then still retain anything of this concept if one calls education work. Of course work is already done in that those who teach speak, walk around and wear themselves out. Some kind of work is performed. But that is not what flows into the economic process. Their organizing activity, which is not even related to what they do as work, is what flows into that. Consequently the work of education is such a different one. A fidget can do a lot of work with fidgeting. Another can also do a lot of work by thrashing. But the one who gives instruction with a certain quiet rhythm will also do work. But this is not what enters into the economic process, rather it is that individual's free intellectual activity.

COMMENT: Also in doing their work some make a great effort but achieve very little, and others make very little effort and achieve a great deal.

RUDOLF STEINER: We also already have work that is relatively liberating. On the one hand we have work that is actually tied to the object. This becomes ever freer from the object. In free intellectual activity it is entirely detached from the object. And what such a person works is irrelevant. The work of teachers is not that for the economic process, which continues to be possible for them in the economic process. Their authority, their education, everything else is economically possible, only not what they do as work.

QUESTION: Why is the free intellectual activity losing its value?

RUDOLF STEINER: It is devaluating in the sense that what is created in the form of values on the one hand is taken away by it again. The Romans had a very subtle instinctive economy (it was one appropriate for a different folk character) in that they spoke not only of bread, but of bread and games. And they included both bread and games in what from their standpoint should be part of the social organism. They reasoned that, just as when I make a loaf of bread it has to disappear again (which it really must), so must the work available for bread production actually disappear again in the social process through what is expended as work in order to do the games. It is a mutual devouring, as everywhere where there is an organism there is a reciprocal building up and demolishing. So also here. You can therefore actually see how the intellectual activity performed on the one side does not continue the process, but brings it back. Therefore I have always described it as a circular process: nature-labor-capital. Nature, labor, and capital returns to itself again, and the whole process is completed when it has returned to nature once again.

QUESTION: Can one also include private economic work in the concept of economics?

RUDOLF STEINER: One must do so! In private business most certainly.

OBJECTION: What I mean is that I cannot include private work in the concept of economics.

RUDOLF STEINER: That arises from the fact that here there is a lack of clarity in the word. This lack of clarity is because one already calls economics a collection of private businesses. One needs to have a superior concept.

QUESTION: Is work only the activity directed towards a particular object in order to make it consumable?

RUDOLF STEINER: That is so. In economics one has the task, I would say, not merely to make abstract philosophical definitions. It is possibly something that one can well do as a philosophical way to pass the time or as a training. But in economics it is not a matter to develop correct concepts, but concepts that can be applied. Especially such people as the economist Lorenz von Stein[†] have developed wonderfully penetrating concepts; but a great number of them are of interest only to philosophers of economics. They have no application to economics.

Fifth Seminar

X: Brings up for discussion the problem of the rate of exchange and its fluctuations. He surmises that certain personalities are behind them.

RUDOLF STEINER: That happens, that is part of the cause. It is very hard to say that anything is the main cause, because that has changed a lot at various times, but the most various causes are at work in the level of the exchange rate. The main cause for the more recent losses in the exchange rate is the discrepancy that has become possible between the gold and paper currency in our own land.

Basically it is the case that gold currency in the countries with a poor exchange rate no longer plays a decisive role, whereas in the countries with a good currency the reserves are still there, which of course determines that such countries that have a gold currency are in a very different credit situation than the others. The question of the exchange rate is primarily a question of credit. Of course, when something happens like the impairment of credit in a trading area, then one can again make use of such a reason in order to proceed further. One can drive the credit down again via the stock exchange. And added to this there are rather senseless ventures in our country. It is entirely out of the question that currently there is no reason for the German mark to have fallen to the extent and in the way that it has; but that here the speculation of our own country also contributed significantly, our country that is making sales abroad and thereby even giving away what it still has. All this then eventually brings the exchange rate into a steep decline.

Then things will happen as in Austria. What also contributed to all this in Russia is hard to say. In Austria and Germany the thing started with the decrease in the gold reserves, the reduced availability of credit, and the speculation in our country. In Germany there is speculation in exports; just now in Austria there is speculation so that foreign supplies are withheld, making them more expensive, with the result that the krone loses value because of the francs, dollars, and so on, which they have in their own country. This could never have happened if the currencies with a high exchange rate had not already begun to rise. This can continue to go on even in our own country and develop into a boundless situation. But the start of this calamity was the enormous extent to which German gold was collected during the war and taken away by the government, which saw to it that it was sent out of the country. The German people have no gold whatsoever; that is the important thing. Today one can compare the gold reserves of the Reichs bank with all the gold owned by the German people before the war.

Of course, other events contributed to this as well, but they are quite difficult to identify. It only takes for a particular currency to be withheld in a country for it to affect the exchange rate once again. Depending on what the exchange rate is abroad, one can initiate an acceleration or a delay; and after that, the exchange rate sinks and falls in the country having a weak currency. In this way, certain personalities can have an easy time of damaging another country. How much is that country's own fault is hard to determine. It must be a considerable sum that played a part in the speculation of certain people.

QUESTION: Some say the fault for the currency distress lies in the change in the balance of payments of the poor countries to the other countries. In Germany this worsening was primarily because payments were made abroad without any proceeds coming back. That creates an account balance in favor of the Entente. That is what is relevant.

RUDOLF STEINER: That could never have led to such a devaluation of the currency as exists in Germany and Austria. The opinion that the discrepancy between the gold standard and paper money is only the outer side is incorrect for the reason that the fact remains that before the war the paper currency was backed by gold. That is a real economic fact. And now we realize that, as long as the paper money is essentially backed with gold, inflation will, as a rule, not take place. That is how that is connected. When the gold is gone, then we have inflation. And with that senseless inflation, which was possible only because it was not felt necessary to still depend on the gold currency, you could of course make the money as cheap as possible. So, because thanks to England's might we have the gold standard, we have one of the primary causes that really mostly lies in the increasing price of gold, and that then undermines the credit. And then, when this affects the credit money, the balance of payments begins to play a role. This situation must only first get under way.

The cause of the currency devaluation already existed before the war. You will remember that during the war it was always said that Germany would be ruined because of its financial straits. This did not happen during the war. But when the war was over and the frontiers were somewhat open economically, what was developing during the war became possible. That was what brought the avalanche into motion. Then all sorts of causes worked together. One should rely on the balance of payments only when its numbers have been made definite. So long as they are only balance numbers one cannot rely on the balance of payments. It must first mean something, not just a difference.

X: Gold just keeps wandering abroad and acts to devalue the money so long as the gold standard exists.

RUDOLF STEINER: The way our economic condition is today—that the gold standard is the underlying element—there is no doubt that countries which have no gold are entirely dependent for the valuation of their products on the countries having gold reserves, and on that then depends the value of the money. One can understand the situation quite well from the tremendous upheavals in the world, but the effects are so enormous that one is tempted to look for "quite hidden causes." But just this devaluation of the currency is not so hidden as one always likes to say; it is rather because of the fact that curiously enough people have come to the point of not being able in any way to judge what is going on.

I often said after the war was over that whoever looks at the situation properly finds that since 1914 we have lived through about as many centuries (with regard to the changes that have taken place), as the number of years we have lived through during this time. And really it seems like an anachronism that certain things have remained the same. One has the feeling that after five to six hundred years the language would normally have changed; it is like an anachronism that today people still speak essentially as they did in 1914. But this has not made a very strong impression on them.

When one looks back into history one usually then surveys longer time periods. Just try for example to study the fluctuations of grain prices in England in the fifteenth and sixteenth centuries; then you will also see that with changes which took place in a much less tumultuous way, there were fluctuations of the price of grain up to twenty times the usual price. From that you can understand how the things that happened in life since 1914 must really be evaluated. People do not believe this, because they have no sense for the qualitative aspects of life. So people noticed only later on what happened (because money is a dishonest companion) when the money was destroyed. For people have an instinct for evaluating only what is in their wallet. Only when the situation becomes evident (people think only in terms of money), do they notice it in the collapse of the currency. But as one now looks at life qualitatively (take Russia, I ask you, take the whole complex of Russian life permeated throughout with the sentiment of "the little father Czar" right up until Lenin), what must you interpose there in the way of forms metamorphosing themselves? Basically even the Russian currency devaluation is only a kind of barometer for whatever else has happened. Therefore the situation is not so incomprehensible. The effect is very terrible and will become even more so. But it is understandable simply from the course of the other events.

QUESTION: Have we in effect a world economy already today?

RUDOLF STEINER: One cannot formulate the thought in quite that way. You first have to consider the state of affairs before the world war. This was to a great degree already leading events into a functioning world economy. You need only to consider the international traffic in checks to have a measure of the great extent which the world economy had already reached.

People's thinking did not keep up with the coming about of the world economy. They still used the definitions of the national economy. It would never have been possible, had one's thinking kept up with the facts, for humanity to have all the annoyances of all kinds of custom barriers that arose already before the war. This was all in line with the world upheaval of Versailles. One did not want to update one's thinking; one wanted to alter the facts. If a problem arose, a customs barrier would be erected somewhere along the frontier. But it is nevertheless the case that we had already reached a high level of world economy despite the customs barriers. When there is a high level of world economy then the price you pay when you go from Dornach to Basel on the train is dependent on conditions in America. Everything now has bit by bit greatly affected the prices of the world economy. That has therefore already happened. Many things in their actual money value simply were what they were largely due to what had developed out of the world economy. Because of the war, barriers were suddenly created which led to business practices that were not in accord with what had developed before.

And after people still had not begun to catch up with their thinking, it was tried in Versailles to correct matters in the old style. The whole dismemberment of Austria is no good for the price of anything, for example the price of taking an Austrian steamboat, the price of coal, for anything at all. This then first created the chaos, this frantic attempt that was made to cope with the facts, with the old thinking, while the world economy was already there to a great extent. With a limited kind of thinking one might say that national economies would come about once again. But that is not the case. That which very greatly contributes to the currency fluctuations proves that the world economy is here, because in Austria there are all kinds of assets from all over the world and so with them one can influence the world economy. Those are things that surely prove that today it won't do to simply ignore the world economy.

QUESTION: If America makes loans to Russia in order to improve its condition (by building railroads, and so on), then the result will be that the money is put into Russia and that the Americans simply have title to the properties without ever getting their money back.

RUDOLF STEINER: If America decided on this money transfer, in whatever form it is made, then that would be a donation. The great loans that took place must result in a donation. But America will not decide to help Europe (that is currently already quite openly advocated in America) until Europe offers to guarantee that it will not engage in any further warlike, that is to say commercial, entanglements. The only reason America does not help (because America would gain thereby, since its own economy would become healthier) consists in the fact that Europe looks as if anything put into it is lost. People in America are afraid of making any loans. They will not be made unless in time more personal credit becomes available. How easy it would be to help Europe can be seen from the fact that when it was believed that Rathenau and Wirth[†] were competent people (which they were not), at that moment good prospects had opened up. But when, especially also in the Entente as well as in the defeated countries, new people came into the leading positions who had nothing to do with what was before the war, when all the people disappeared from public life who still represented the names of yesterday, in that moment Europe would be helped: then it would have personal credit. The situation is such that real credit is no longer available, that personal credit must bring about real credit once again. This could bring about a gradual improvement. If the krone and mark were to increase in value somewhat, then there would be quite a different mood, then there would again be all kinds of reasons that would only then arise to bring about further improvement. But the level of morality has sunk down so far.

OBJECTION: If America makes loans to Russia in order to improve its condition (by building railroads and so on), then the result will be that the money is put into Russia and that the Americans simply have title to the properties without ever getting their money back.

RUDOLF STEINER: The solution of this question is that not everyone was wrong, but that everyone was right, because they all came up with partial causes related to their own experience.

This proves to them the necessity of community in life. In the economic life it is not at all possible for one person to make a comprehensive judgment. Therefore the people were mostly correct. But it seems to me it was Edison[†] who was most correct in that he pointed to the underlying causes, although morally related ones. He is capable of thinking along economic lines, and he said that the main thing is on what principles people are hired who are taken into a business. The experienced businessman puts questions to those to be hired that have nothing to do with the running of the business. They will catch on to that alright so long as they are otherwise competent. Therefore as a businessman I will ask them questions that show me, for example, if they still know or have forgotten what they learned at school. If the one I am questioning tells me absolute nonsense, then my question is answered, and I consider that he is not sufficiently capable of learning. Edison asked a whole range of such questions when he wanted to employ someone. When one takes hold of this in such a practical way it will make a difference whether I hire a man who is sitting at his desk and cannot tell the difference between wheat and rye, or someone who *can* tell the difference. And this is something people do not believe today. People believe one could be quite a competent bookkeeper without knowing what a sunflower is.

That is said with a grain of salt. But what Edison here suggested seemed to me to be very much to the point. It is economical; it is shown here how far the mind takes hold of the work.

QUESTION: What is required by the present economic necessities from those who believe they have to found a new doctrine of economics?

RUDOLF STEINER: I am mainly trying to give you partial answers to this question every day. Because what is important is that one really understands this transition from the partial national economies to the world economy that has been going on for about fifty years, and that one no longer continues to work with the old national economic categories, but that one understands that today certain things have to be done that were not there before and that can only be accomplished with one's thinking.

Consider now the former national economies, then you see that they are simply adjacent to one another. Even earlier the situation was that they were quite separate from each other. That economic situation existed at a time when lands could still simply be conquered. It does not depend on the distances involved. You can think about France when it was still uncultivated, and the Franks who were passing through discovered the empty lands. That leads to quite different economic conditions than when one comes into a comparatively closed region with a greater culture. The Visigoths had a different destiny because they invaded a region that was more advanced economically. And the greatest example of separated national economies that then react on one another is the relationship between England and its colonies, especially India. There separate national economies were combined into a common area through conquest, also through peaceful conquest. That is the first situation. The second is when the territories are adjacent and have independent national economies. And the third is where a closed area is created because nothing can be adjacent to it in a economic sense—because total wastelands are not to be considered in this connection. Now we just need to be aware that we are in a tremendous time of transition, and that the most vital thing is the worldwide promotion of the world economy to which we must adjust ourselves. This new understanding of everything in economics is what everything depends on.

There is a very interesting example of how people are little able to change their understanding in Spengler's book *The Decline of the West*, which also has a chapter on economics. He really provides some excellent glimpses, but has no notion how things actually are. His concepts are nowhere in accord with reality. It is especially bad in the second volume with regard to economics, because Spengler had a relatively good understanding of how business was conducted in certain economic areas a long time ago. On the one hand, he understands the naturalistic agrarian economy extremely well; on the other hand, he also does not lack understanding of modern economic life. Here he distinguishes (and this is Spengler's coyness!) the Faustian from the Homeric. Now it is of enormous significance that such a clever man as Spengler cannot understand that something that has been overcome apparently still affects what comes later, so everything he designates as ancient economics is still there as a field in our midst.

Especially where we have to do with what I have called purchase money, only the kind that Spengler attributes to antiquity finds its way in, except that its form has changed somewhat. Whereas according to him there was only material money formerly, he believes that today we have only functional money, while our money today must go in a direction so that the relationship between material and functional money is understood. He plays around with such superficiality formed concepts and still does not, however, arrive at concepts that are in accord with reality. Hence the brilliance of Spengler's concepts. In this marvelous, yet confusing way, he mixes up the concepts, which is really a danger for those who are not immune to this confusion. Our task is to keep up with these situations with our thinking.

We have these three things together: quite ordinary capital, doing business alongside one another, and the original naturalistic economy, all of which are hidden from us because we use money for everything. There is this conflict between the nominalists and those who advocate the use of metal (metalists) instead of paper money. The former are of the opinion that money is only a sign, so the material of which it is made has no value, only the number that is printed on it; while the metalists say that the value of the material is the essential part of it. People quarrel about something like that, whereas the situation is as follows. In the area where we are mainly dealing with agriculture and what is connected with it, the metalists are correct concerning the function of money; while in industry and in spiritual-cultural life the nominalists are correct, because there money plays the part that they attach to it. And then we have the confused playing around of both sides. Such things we have to deal with! People fight about things that are much too simple, while we have a life that is complicated.

COMMENT: But therefore our course is not really a course on national economics but a course on world economic theory.

RUDOLF STEINER: Well, the names remain. You see, there was even a time when morality was considered part of economic business. In the first and second Christian centuries, morality belonged with economics.

QUESTION: I cannot bring myself to understand the reciprocal movement of nature-product to work to capital, and so forth. Surely the means of production have already undergone a transformation.

RUDOLF STEINER: The reversal does not relate to the making of the means of production, but to their bringing production about. The transformation has significance only at the moment when the means of production cease to be a commodity. It remains a commodity up to the moment when it can be converted to start producing. When it starts to produce then the flow of economic events changes for the means of production. From that moment on it is raised out of the relationship it had when it was a commodity. In the "Threefold Social Order" I have indicated that it begins there to become homogeneous with nature because it can no longer have a price. It stands within the economic processes exactly like nature itself. It is moving itself back to nature once more.

QUESTION: Does that appear on the balance sheet?

RUDOLF STEINER: You mean this loss of value? It appears on the balance sheet only in abnormal cases. It appears only when someone, let us say, starts a business, brings about several means of production, then is ruined, and a man with greater skill takes over the business and he succeeds. Then when you compare these two balances, the one when the business failed and the one when it succeeded, you will discover such a partial appearance of devaluation. Because of the failure, the second one—simply because of the failure process—was able to buy all of the means of production more cheaply than he could ever have done. In that way he got part of it as a gift, so that then this could be expressed on the balance sheet. If you were now to follow the consequence of this procedure further along in the balance sheet, then you would find in it a partly cost-free transfer of the business. Today it could be proved with current accounting practices.

COMMENT: Of course these are exceptions. Today the abnormal is the norm.

RUDOLF STEINER: But this would eventually lead to a monstrous situation, because the means of production are transferred directly to income, whereas the basic rent is produced only when capital is invested.

Question not recorded.

RUDOLF STEINER: You must not forget: when you put capital into an enterprise, then that is something very different than when you do not have capital in it. A very different motive is at work when you have it in there, than when you do not, while not having it is basically only a kind of hallucination. Such hallucinations do happen. You may ask, where actually is the capital money, let us say the loan capital, which is not invested in enterprises? It is there only as production and as ground rent; only there does it exist. And if any man wanted some money for himself then he would have to take it completely out of the economic process for a time, thereby causing a tension, and then give it away again at a different value. He would lose out there because the money would be progressively devalued, since otherwise it is unthinkable for the process to occur in a radical way, and that changes the relationships.

If one were to take hold of the economy in a healthy way, then the right relationships would come about. Today it is rather quaint, for example, the way the problem of wages is often handled. Higher wages are demanded, resulting in higher production costs. Then again the wages are insufficient. Again higher wages are demanded, and so it goes on—who knows where. As a result people throw sand in their own eyes. While we may continue to use the expression "wages," which is inaccurate, in an associative economy wages will be created that are possible. No false wages will ever be created.

QUESTION: Why do wages have to be created at all?

RUDOLF STEINER: Try now to look into this. Here and there workers receive an average of two francs per day. Now you can say that is a very low wage. How can this become a very high wage without amounting to more than two francs?

COMMENT: By products becoming cheaper.

RUDOLF STEINER: Only then will you get the final values. Then you will see that it will all come out the way I have said it. You cannot always put the cart before the horse. One has to put the question like this. We let the worker have the two francs—but under what circumstances will two francs be twice or three times as great a wage as today? One must actually proceed from the dynamic relationship; whereas one always proceeds from the static ones, and then wants what is at rest to bring about movement. But the fact remains that putting five francs in my pocket is nothing by itself, but only something in relation to the whole economy.

Sixth Seminar

Question concerning the depreciation of money: Will it gradually depreciate? Also as purchase money?

RUDOLF STEINER: As purchase money it has the same value until the end. This question is more a technical one concerning its circulation, a question of *how*. The gradual depreciation of money is not easy to imagine. It would require an extraordinarily bureaucratic system.

I would emphasize that I do not want to proceed in a programmatic way, that I want only to acknowledge what *is*—because I recognize that we cannot establish a paradise on earth with economic methods. That would not be possible, but we must try to create the best possible situation. Now one has to ask oneself why we have less than the best possible situation today. It comes about because the various factors of the economy cannot achieve their true value in one place or another, because today it is quite possible that spiritual/cultural workers are by no means paid in the way that is necessary for the whole economy. They are paid either too much or too little; both things do occur. But if they are paid too little they immediately cause prices to change in an unhealthy way because of their low pay. And it is the same if they are paid too much. This needs to be corrected, and it is only a question (without regard to what Wilhelm Förster would say) of what factors would restore commercial balance in the economic life. Thus trade will arise in which there are mutually tolerable prices not only for goods but also for the cultural as well as the necessary spiritual-intellectual life.

From this it directly follows that money must get old. It is just a matter of how this can be technically carried out. You would be able to bring about a gradual depreciation of money in no other way than by attaching coupons to the paper money that have to be torn off at specific times by a public official. This would result in a very complicated bureaucracy. But it is really never a question of carrying out the depreciation with such external means, but that this valuation is brought about by itself through the actual course of events. This will happen when you more or less simply give money of all kinds a characteristic of change—I mean insofar as it has an end point. Of course this cannot be calculated abstractly, but assuming there is a particular moment, it can to begin with only be approximately determined. Then one needs to make corrections until the situation eventually comes to a possible end point.

Then it would be a matter of again finding out for the world economy what was fundamentally already there as a widespread local economy. Because this is the way the Jubilee in the Old Testament was celebrated, which is something very similar to the aging of money: the remission of all debts. With the radical remission of all debts, all harmful loans and investments also disappear. You will recall the length of time between Jubilee years, they occurred every fifty years. This Jubilee year, in contrast to what would be necessary today for the world economy, was determined *a priori* simply by fixing the patriar-chal age. For the moment, I do not recall if it is so stated in the Bible, but in any case it was originally the custom to thus fix the human life span. It was correctly calculated that if one takes the whole course of a human life then everything is contained there: what in youth is there as gift capital, then is there as loan capital, and business capital, that is, commercial or industrial capital. It was assumed that one had a right to consume in youth what one later earns during one's mature years, and then one earns somewhat less towards the end of life. At some time this was looked upon as a kind of borrowing.

Now you see, this was a priori; this would not take place in the world economy in this way. The time periods would be considerably prolonged. But it is also quite clear that when the gradual devaluation of the money begins, this will occur by itself through circulation, because the year it was issued would be printed on the banknote. In actual economic circulation such money will not have a lower purchase value but a lower value for any organizational use. The older it gets, the lower is its use value, so that through the decrease in its use value it can gradually become gift money, and can then be re-issued as young, that is, "new" money again. That must be done only by the association. For products that are as close as possible to nature-products, the work then has its highest value, although the worker is not paid any more than anyone else according to the price formula; but in the economic activity it has the highest value. Only one part goes to the one who is working; the rest goes entirely into the economic process. The possibility to enrich one's own self has thus been taken away from the individual.

QUESTION: How can money be used in different ways if it has the same purchasing power when it is young and when it is old?

RUDOLF STEINER: If you start a business with young money, then because it is young you can invest it in this business over a long time; whereas with old money you could not run it in the same way over a long period.

Question was not recorded.

RUDOLF STEINER: You mean that once I have acquired my means of production, I then have them instead of the money, and someone else has the money that I spent. The money that has now been spent on the production must of course remain there. Under certain circumstances this money can be transformed (it would not be, insofar as it could be spent by the owner), but what is in the production is a question of circulation. This would not involve a great bureaucracy, because the associations would see to it that within similarly based enterprises nothing is used except money of the same age.

Therefore the money merges with the means of production. This does not contradict the other law, where the means of production as such lose their former value as commodities. These two provisions coincide here. This is so also today, except that it is concealed. The money that was lent for production does not come back; it stays in production. It is retained only because the means of production can be sold again. But if one imagines the means of production as something that one does not sell, then the money stays in there at the same age. One must think realistically. Then the question would never arise, how does one manage to make the money in there stay the same age? But one will say this must happen; this step must simply be taken! This is an outer technical question.

Of course you might say there is a certain possibility that such things are circumvented by speculation. But speculation would surely be much less likely to occur in this type of community than in one in which money has an indefinitely long life. In reality, money becomes worn out anyway. Otherwise that Pomeranian peasant could be right who asks himself, "How large is the Prussian national debt? I will invest a little capital at compound interest for a certain number of years, that would cover the debt." This could never happen, because all those who would gradually become obliged to come up with this sum (which would require the appropriate security) would be ruined. Somehow the guarantors would disappear, and after hundreds of years Prussia would not see a penny of the money.

You see there that it does wear out, the actual money. It is only a matter of dealing with these things sensibly; these things really happen and then create harm because they are not handled sensibly. Therefore I consider only what is real, not something that agitates about wanting to be. Because the facts are there! It is a matter of having to ask oneself how one cures the world economy.

QUESTION: What is the relationship between money and the state?

RUDOLF STEINER: According to what I described yesterday, a national bank, a state bank, would be impossible. A banking institute would come about between those who have received gift money and those who through their work, namely, cultivation of the soil, once more create new goods that are in their early stages. This rejuvenation would pass directly over from the state to the economy. And that represents what is necessary for the future. Through the fact that it passes into the economy, this measure to rejuvenate it would combine with other economic measures, but not with the state's rules. And thereby relationships to value would also come about which are quite different from the ones that exist under the present fiscal system. We would then have something that already exists. Things are really hidden only because they do not occur in the right place. We would have converted a fiscal system into an economic one. The possibility for the treasury to function economically would be less than that of an economic association.

QUESTION: What would be the basis of a different currency?

RUDOLF STEINER: It would be brought about by making everything that is paper money and money substitutes very much alike.

The great variations of today were created only by arbitrary rules and provisions. So the state bank notes and all other kinds of money substitutes would become much more alike. There would be a uniform currency, and it would not really matter what it was made of, because at the end of its process it receives a purely nominal character, and in being brought back it receives the metallic character that it would have to start with.

The currency would be something constantly in flux but adapted to the particular nature of the economic process.

QUESTION: At one time did you not praise the usable means of production as a basis for the currency?

RUDOLF STEINER: Let us ask, within such a period of time in which this change to a particular money takes place, what provides the validity for it? It is given by what is there as usable means of production. Assuming there is very little there in the form of usable means of production, then things would have to be converted quickly. Money would pile up everywhere and purchase money would return through the means of production, and so on. But if there are many usable means of production, the cycle would be different, and therefore the money would have an increased value. In this sense, money derives from means of production.

QUESTION: Would something solid like gold have to be used for the material?

RUDOLF STEINER: As far as I can see the actual substance of the money is of no consequence, so that you could just as well put the year's date on paper, which would then determine the value. I cannot see the necessity of introducing a currency such as gold. It would be necessary only in the situation where specialized economies were being created. But to the extent that the world economy is actually a reality—it becomes ever more so to the extent that economics emancipates itself—it is possible to make the money out of any substance whatsoever. What does money then become when what I am saying is realized? Nothing but bookkeeping, which is done throughout the whole economic region. Because if you wanted to introduce a gigantic bookkeeping system—which is quite unnecessary—you could quite well register all this going back and forth of money in a single appropriate location. Then the entries would always appear in the appropriate place. What actually happens is nothing else than that the entry is torn out of its particular place and the one concerned is given a ticket so that the bookkeeping wanders around. Money is bookkeeping in a fluctuating sense. So I cannot see that it needs to have anything but a decorative value, whether it is made of one thing or another.

OBJECTION: Gold would provide a certain standard.

RUDOLF STEINER: That cannot be the case, and if it is, then the bookkeeping would show it. The essential thing is that all money transactions are a matter of bookkeeping. Instead of transferring an entry from the credit to the debit column you just pay over the money.

OBJECTION: It should not be gold, because then the devaluation could be avoided, so that in the end the gold would be kept back.

RUDOLF STEINER: Assuming there is a buyer for the gold. There would have to be one; that is to say, the purchase would have to be advantageous. One would then also have to make an unnecessary calculation, which would not be of any help. If for example one were to make a piece of jewelry out of the gold, one could use it for cheating.

One needs to consider these things only with regard to the economy itself. If you consider them together, you will be able to evaluate these matters, which today are really based on partial observation and inadequate guesswork in dealing with the theory of economics. Here one always finds inadequate methods and faulty observation.

QUESTION: Which kind of capital arose first in the economy, trading capital or industrial capital?

RUDOLF STEINER: Historically, of course the business capital, and indeed trade itself is essentially the very first commercial activity that must come about. Even today in primitive villages you find relatively little business capital. The village craftspeople do not earn any more than the farmers. The merchants on the other hand are able to set money aside, and therefore are in a position to make loans. And so it goes on, because no capital is created unless it is negotiable. Business capital arises only as a third stage; this is so connected with local customs that no rational grounds for it can be found at all.

QUESTION: Must Switzerland go in the direction of national or world economics? Is there not a tendency in many countries to go back to national economics?

RUDOLF STEINER: You mean that Switzerland went over into the world economy too soon, and it turned out that it was not a good move for it? One cannot say that, because Switzerland was not able to test the rightness of the world economic system for its own economy in a natural way. For what you call the "good will" of its neighbors was brought about in an unnatural way by the war. Had it been able to continue to develop as it did until 1914 this would not have been to her disadvantage, but instead she would have continued her development. Of course the same damage would have occurred, which at that time gradually revealed itself and which indicated that one should have peacefully taken up associative economics. But the way matters stand now, one has to say, depends very little on Switzerland. Today, however, we are dealing with the tendency toward a world economy, but with continual disturbance from the political intentions of the economic areas that are striving towards nationalism.

What harms the world economy today are the political intentions. Politics has begun to drive everything back to national economics once again. We cannot use Switzerland as an example here, because it is politically too powerless. Now and then Switzerland is allowed to have its say when we know it will say what we want it to say—and Switzerland also does say what we want it to.

So Switzerland cannot be a valid example, but America can; America, which is decisively heading towards a national economic structure and is impeding the formation of a world economy. It could also possibly be very difficult to overcome this American tendency towards a national economic structure. On the other hand, in such a country that is organized as England is today—which has basically only a pseudo-national economy, but in reality a world economy—in such a country a tendency to a world economy would be able to develop. Because here you have England, over there India, South Africa, Australia, and so forth. What is connected as a national economy basically extends over the whole world. In that way England does not have the economy of the whole world, but it has the types and requirements of economy necessary in the whole world, which it must synthetically combine into what the spirit of world economy must become in a qualitative way. That is what quite essentially must lead to a world economy in the further course of economic development. And in time the politics of North America will have to adjust to this; because the economy will simply make its very powerful demands to the hard-headed people, and they will have to accommodate themselves to the world economy. England could not move forward at all if it now also continued to work in a merely national economic fashion. So you must therefore discover the real antagonism between England and America. Switzerland is not relevant at all.

QUESTION: I cannot imagine how the precious stone in the Crown of England could be said to derive its value from human work and not because of its rarity.

RUDOLF STEINER: It is because economic value is created by the employment of human work or human intelligence/Spirit. Only through that are economic values created, and also through the division of labor. If you now have to explain the value of this precious stone in England's crown, you must say that if it is possible to pick out from the continuous economic process, values that are appropriated by an individual, then the value that was created there can, in fact, also be taken back by the one concerned. So that if in our present circumstances a man wants to keep back a million, he can do so. He can pile up the million. Then for all I care he can put the million in his socks. He can replace this "putting the money in his socks" with a different action, by artfully ascribing to some rare product the same value as his own money, and so letting the money go back into circulation. Then (because purely conventionally and merely by his decree he assigned such a value to this object) with his intellectual capacity he has assigned this particular value to it simply because he happened to take a liking to it. What happened here took place simply under the influence of perhaps not of spiritual-cultural actions, but according to spiritual-cultural rules. The concept of rarity dissolves itself into the economic concept of Spirit or mind.

Objections are brought up that are raised against the threefold social order: It is impossible to separate the three spheres. The task of threefolding could be not so much to build up, as rather in a negative way to bring about separation where there exist harmful influences of the three spheres upon each other, and thereby letting the work take its course. One cannot have any conception especially concerning the boundaries of the three spheres. The economic life would thereby be limited to what is called technology.

RUDOLF STEINER: The thinking of people who make this objection is not sufficiently developed. This is generally the main defect of our teaching institutes of today: that they develop thinking much too little. People can only develop concepts that they can nicely lay next to each other. But the same thing already exists in the threefold organism of the human being. Consider the optic nerve. It belongs to the nerve-sense system but of course it could not survive if it were not nourished during sleep by the metabolic system, if nourishment processes were not present in it, if it did not constantly get inhaled air through the spinal cord, and if a circulation process did not also take place there. This shows that in the human organism things really belong only for the most part to either the nerve-sense, the metabolic, or the rhythmic system.

The same is true in the social organism. It is necessary that the other two systems play into the economic organism. But along with all this, it is still true that the nerve-sense system basically tends towards the head, and that the nourishment and respiration of the head is provided in another way. This working together will take place in the true sense just because these three ways are created. It has always annoyed me when people speak of a division into three parts. The question is how must the three members, which are there anyway, relate to each other in a natural way so that they can act upon one another appropriately? The spiritual-cultural organism will be essentially based on freedom. But of course the economic life must also work into the spiritual-cultural organism, otherwise the professors would have nothing to eat. But that will really work in properly when it takes place from a different source, so that it becomes necessary to develop an economic organism with a different aim—also a spiritual-cultural organism with a different aim, and then one having to do with the law. Only those make objections here who regard this threefolding as a partition. It is well known that this has frequently happened. I found one interpreter who gave lectures on the three parliaments of the social organism. Whoever thinks of it that way _magines something impossible, because there can be a parliament only of the nation, not of the free spiritual-cultural life. There can only be the single individuality who creates a network of self-evident authority. In the economic realm there can only be the associations. In the parliament all the different functions will flow together, and the right rules will be established between the individual members of the social organism.

QUESTION: In the tenth lecture the striving for gain was compared with mass in the physical sense. Can one extend the analogy so that one can let work be a function between trade and the striving for gain?

RUDOLF STEINER: According to the energy formula in physics $e = \frac{1}{2} mv^2$. The energy of the economy would be formulated in a similar way. The possible gains would be multiplied by a function of the rapidity of trade: $e = g \times f$ (trade). Striving for gain must be multiplied by the rapidity of circulation; then one will get the number for the work. This is valid for an individual product. If you get a certain profit from it, and you multiply it by the rapidity of the turn-over, then you will have the quantity of the work. This amount of work becomes zero if you need to multiply the gain by zero; that is to say, when you sell directly: $0 = g \times 0$.

QUESTION: Does the value of the precious stone in the crown of England correspond to the tension between it and the need for rarity?

RUDOLF STEINER: The matter can be explained like that only by a different path, because the tension that arises through consumption is always the tension between the work done on a product of nature and the value that the work receives through the spiritual-cultural order. In this case, for instance, in the case of the stone in the crown of England, one must to begin with not speak of it in a one-sided way. I ask you, what is it then actually worth? It is actually only something of value in a quite particular sense. Indeed, in the sense of a particular spiritually permeated economic ordering through public opinion, that is through Spirit. One cannot at all speak of it in a way that it has really this "value" in itself, but only in a way that this value is attached to it by people's opinion. If one now bought it for what the seller demands, would one put him in the position to do as much work as he can for whatever he gets for it? Then, as if by an avalanche, a whole work organization would be created as a result. Just as is the case in physics, where you have to take into account nothing apart from the mutual relationships involved when you allow an avalanche to be formed from a small snowball—then you need not change the formula—so do you not need to change the formula concerning economics because special conditions arise, among which, viewed purely externally, facts are created such as the following: that a very rare product is equivalent to a tremendous amount of work. That is so only because of its relationship to the economy.

EDITORIAL AND REFERENCE NOTES

Editorial Notes

Rudolf Steiner held this study course in Dornach in the summer of 1922 at the request of the students of "national economy." This was a few weeks after the Congress in Vienna on the theme—also contained in the German collected works with the same title: *Westliche und östliche Weltgegensätzlichkeiten* (GA 83).

In connection with several of the lectures extensive conversations took place, in which the problems presented were expanded and deepened. These discussions were then published in the volume *Nationalökonomisches Seminar* (GA 341).

Rudolf Steiner reserved his presentations only for a small group of students who were familiar with Anthroposophy. He wanted only to give them a stimulus for their further studies, as he could no longer realize his intention to give at a later time a more encompassing presentation on the national economy for practitioners of economics.

Documents for the Texts:
Georg Klenk of Munich was the stenographer for the course. The printed text was based on his transposition of his shorthand into longhand or readable writing. These texts contained inaccuracies, which the German editors attempted in various ways to correct in the various editions. This edition is, with the exception of a few corrections, based on the fourth edition published by Walter Birkigt and Emil Leinhau, both of whom participated in this course. This holds true essentially also for the Reference Notes.

The expanded table of contents was taken from Folkert Wilken's and Wolfram Groddeck's publication of the second edition of the *National Economy Seminar* (GA 341).

About the Blackboard Drawings:
The original blackboard drawings and notes by Rudolf Steiner for this course have been preserved, as he put them on black paper that was stretched across the blackboard. Reproductions are available in *Rudolf Steiner Wandtafelzeichnungen zum Vortragswerk. Band XXIV* (Rudolf Steiner Verlag 2001). Plate 4a was inadvertently omitted from this volume, but it is included in the supplemental volume to the Blackboard Drawings.

Reference Notes

Page 1, "political economy"
The term "political economy" (Volkswirtschaft), which first appeared in the seventeenth century in France, gained popularity in the late eighteenth and early nineteenth centuries, when it grew out of moral philosophy to become the term, used for instance by Adam Smith, to describe production, buying, and selling in relationship to law, custom, and government, as well as national income and wealth. By the late nineteenth century, it was generally replaced by the simple term "economics."

Page 3, "Schmoller, Roscher"
Gustav von Schmoller (1838–1917). Economist. He was the leader of the "jungen Schule der deutschen Volkswirtschaftslehre," [The "younger" (historical) school of economic theory]. During his academic career, he held appointments as a professor at the universities of Halle (1864-72), Strasburg (1872-82), and Berlin (1882-1913). After 1899, he represented the University of Berlin in the Prussian House of Lords. As an economist, he opposed what he saw as the axiomatic-deductive approach of classical economics. Schmoller's approach was inductive, demanding careful, comparative evolutionary and process-based study both in time and space of economic performance and phenomena. He stressed the cultural specificity of economics and the importance of values. Above all, he was concerned with the challenges posed by rapid industrialization and urbanization. He was also an advocate of the assertion of German naval power and imperial expansion. Recently, his work has been reevaluated and found to be still relevant.

Wilhelm Georg Friedrich Roscher (1817–1894). Economist. He was the founder of the "älteren (historischen) Schule der deutschen Volkswirtschaftslehre" [the "older" (historical) school of German economic theory. He tried to establish the laws of economic development by using the historical method from the investigation of histories legal, political, cultural, and other aspects. He also developed a cyclical theory in which nations and their economies pass through youth, adulthood and senile decay.

Page 4, "Beaconsfield ... Richter ... Lasker ... Brentano"
Benjamin Disraeli, Earl of Beaconsfield (1804–1881), was a British Prime Minister, parliamentarian, Conservative statesman, and literary figure, who became famous writing Romantic-realistic social novels. He served in government for four decades, twice as Prime Minister. As member of the Lower House of the House of Commons, he represented the ideas of the Tories concerning democracy and was an opponent of Peel regarding the duty to be paid for protection. As Prime Minister he later became one of the most important statesmen of British Imperialism. Among other things, he attained for England the majority of the shares for the Suez Canal and he brought it about that Queen Victoria became Empress of India.

Eugen Richter (1838–1906). Politician and journalist. Leader of the liberal German Progress Party (later the German Freeminded Party). He was an opponent of Bismark and his economic and social politics, and a strong advocate for free trade and a market economy. He also actively opposed Socialism and Anti-Semitism.

Eduard Lasker (1829–1884). German politician and jurist. His great work was his participation in the judicial reform that occurred during 1867-1877. More than any other individual, he was responsible for the codification of the law. Until 1881 he was the leader of the left wing of the National Liberals. He was against Bismark's political protection duty.

Lujo Brentano (1844–1931) was the nephew of Clemens Brentano and Bettina von Arnim, and the brother of the philosopher Franz Brentano. He was an economist and professor at the universities of Breslau, Strasburg, Vienna, Leipzig and, most important, Munich. Reform-minded, an "academic socialist," and a founder of the Verein fur Sozialpolitic [Union for Social Politics], his main influence was through his idea of a "social market economy."

Page 10, "Rothschild"
The Rothschild family, known as the House of Rothschild, or more simply as the Rothschilds, is a European banking dynasty of German-Jewish origin that established European banking and finance houses starting in the late 18th century. During the 1800s, when it was at its height, the family is believed to have possessed by far the largest private fortune in the world, as well as by far the largest fortune in modern world history.

Page 13, "Adam Smith"
Adam Smith (1723–1790). British philosopher and economist. He has been called the founder of the "classical national (political) economy." He was the first to bring a well-rounded presentation of the individualistic and the liberal economic theories. His main work: *An Inquiry into the Nature and Causes of the Wealth of Nations*, 1776, four volumes.

Page 17, "nature"
Where Steiner uses the term "nature," as an economic category, in classical economics this is usually referred to as "land."

Page 22, "Karl Marx"
Karl Marx (1818–1883). See *Das Kapital* [The capital], volume 1, chapter 5: "Arbeitsprozeß und Verwertungsprozeß" [Work process and commercialization or use process].

Page 26, "rents"
Rent is meant here in the strict economic sense of the value that emerges from land. Confusingly, however, rent has two different meanings for economists.

"Contract rent" designates the income from hiring out land or other durable goods. "Economic rent" is used to define one aspect of the price of goods and services. Generally, it designates the difference between the raw costs of everything needed to produce the goods or service and the price. It is a measure of market power. Economic rent is determined for each of the factors of production used to produce the goods or service. Usually economic rent is due to some exclusivity. For example, for labor, it could be due to celebrity or skill (e.g., higher pay for skilled workers, in a region where there is a scarcity of such skilled workers; or a sports star who is paid $50,000 per week when he would perform for $10,000); for goods, it may be due to the power of a patent; for real estate, it may be due to a favorable location. By contrast, if there is no exclusivity and there is perfect competition, there are no economic rents, as competition drives prices down to their floor. Economic rent was developed by the economist David Ricardo (1722-1823). He defined rent as "the difference between the produce obtained by the employment of two equal quantities of capital and labor."

Page 30, "It was in an essay I wrote at the beginning of the century"
See Rudolf Steiner's essay "Geisteswissenschaft und die soziale Frage" [Spiritual Science and the Social Question] in *Luzifer-Gnosis 1903-1908* (GA 34). In 1941, when this essay appeared for the first time in book form, the term "Theosophy" that was used earlier was replaced by "Spiritual Science." Currently published as *Anthroposophy and the Social Question*.

Page 36, "in the essay I published long ago"
See note above.

Page 64, "what I called 'real associations' in my book *Towards Social Renewal*"
(CW 23). See especially the Forward and Introduction in that book.

Page 71, "Leibniz"
Gottfried Wilhelm Leibniz (1646–1716) was a German mathematician and philosopher. He occupies a prominent place both in the history of mathematics and the history of philosophy. He developed infinitesimal calculus independently of Isaac Newton, and Leibniz's mathematical notation has been widely used ever since it was published. His visionary Law of Continuity and Transcendental Law of Homogeneity only found mathematical implementation in the 20th century. He became one of the most prolific inventors in the field of mechanical calculators. He also refined the binary number system, which is at the foundation of virtually all digital computers. Along with René Descartes and Baruch Spinoza, he was one of the three great 17th century advocates of rationalism. Leibniz made major contributions to physics and technology, and anticipated notions that surfaced much later in philosophy, probability theory, biology, medicine, geology, psychology, linguistics, and information science.

Page 94, "we shall have to observe the interaction between supply and price"
In the first edition (presumably from 1922) it says: "…, that with him we now have to look at the interplay of the demand and the price in money." In Roman Boos' edition of 1933, after a thorough examination of the existing documents, the sentence was changed to the following: …, that with him we have to look at the interplay of demand and price in the money." With a further examination yet another change was made for the fourth edition in 1965 by the editor and course participants at that time, Walter Birkigt and Emil Leinhas. In the current edition this passage reads: "…, that with him we now have to look at the interplay between supply and price." Birkigt and Leinhas pointed out that, with "the producer's equation, which was the question and which was written on the blackboard as $n = f(a\,p)$, … there is no interplay between demand and price. Only the independent variables a (supply) and p (price) can enter into an interplay. An encroachment into another equation is mathematically impossible. In the economics an encroachment of the producer or manufacturer into the realm of the consumer would be quackery or a violation because only the consumer can know what he or she needs. For this reason the change was made from speaking of demand and price in the money to supply and price."

Page 95, "inasmuch as here (in the consumer's case) the supply is a supply of money, while in the producer's case it is a supply of commodities In the case of the merchant we deal with something that lies midway between "money" and "commodity"[price]"
In the early documents mentioned above, it reads here: "with the producer or manufacturer it is a demand for commodities." This volume also uses the change made by Birkigt and Leinhas in their edition of 1965. The phrase of the earlier publisher ("demand for commodities") does not fit with the sense of the complete sentence, nor does it correspond to the economic facts. The sentence quoted later only makes sense and the facts become visible only when it reads: "with the producer or manufacturer it is supply of commodities." This shows itself clearly when one compares the sentence to a note that Rudolf Steiner entered into a diary three days after the lecture. The sentence and the note deal with the same problem and show themselves to be, in all details, in complete agreement. The corrected sentence reads as follows:

> "We have always to make these equations *qua*litatively different, in that with the consumer the supply or offering is in money; and with the producer the supply or offering is in commodities. With the merchant or trader we have to do with something that is somewhere between money and commodities."

The note from August 3, 1922, summarizes briefly the qualitatively different supplies or offerings.

The producer offers commodities.

The consumer offers money.

The merchant offers money-commodities.

Rudolf Steiner starts from supply or offering (a). However, one could also start from the demand (n).

With the merchant from the demand (n) to commodities (w) and money (g) ($n\,{}^w_g$)
With the consumer from the demand to commodities ($^n\,w$)
With the producer or manufacturer from the demand for money ($^n\,g$)

The merchant asks for commodities and offers money; and asks, however, also for money and offers commodities. Thus there must also be two equations each for the consumer and for the producer. The merchant equation always included both. (Birkigt/Leinhas)

The arrangement of the equations on the blackboard does not necessarily correspond with the order in which Rudolf Steiner wrote them on the board. According to the content of the lecture, he apparently wrote first the formula $x = f\,(a\ n\ p)$, then the merchant equation, then the producer's equation, and finally consumer equation.

In addition to the equations that Rudolf Steiner wrote on the board during the course, there is a second presentation in the notebook entries of August 3, 1922. It reads:

$$p = f(a\ n)\ \text{merchant}$$
$$a = f(p\ n)\ \text{producer}$$
$$n = f(a\ p)\ \text{consumer}$$

If we place the equation from the blackboard and those in the notebook beside each other, we get the following picture:

	On the Blackboard	In the Notebook
Merchant	$p = f(a\frac{g}{w}, n\frac{g}{w})$	$p = f(a\frac{g}{w}, n\frac{g}{w})$
Producer	$n_g = f(a_w, p)$	$a_w = f(n_g, p)$
Consumer	$a_g = f(n_w, p)$	$n_w = f(a_g, p)$

In the course Rudolf Steiner gave only the one set of equations—those on the blackboard. The editors did not wish to withhold the equations from the notebook, because they complete the picture of the complicated price-building process. (Birkigt and Leinhas)

Page 104, "Unruh"
Hans Viktor von Unruh. (1806–1886) was a Prussian Public Official and Politician.

Page 109, "Siemens ... Gwinner"
Georg von Siemens (1839–1901). German banker and liberal politician. He was the nephew of the inventors and industrialists Werner, William, and Carl von Siemens. His father, a high judicial officer, provided most of the funds of the later Siemens A G. Georg von Siemens was on the board of directors of the Deutsche Bank from 1870 to 1900. One of his top priorities was the financing of international railway projects, including the Northern Pacific and Baghdad Railways. From 1874 until his death, Siemens was voted several times to both the Prussian House of Representatives and the German Reichstag. Until 1880, he represented the National Liberal Party, then the Secession; from 1884 to 1893 the German Freeminded party, and for the last years the Free-minded Union.

Arthur von Gwinner (1856–1931). Banker. From 1880, member of the board of management of the Deutsche Bank, later the successor of Georg von Siemens.

Page 113, "Clausewitz"
Carl Philipp Gottfried von Clausewitz (1780–1831[2]) was a Prussian soldier and military theorist who stressed the moral (in modern terms, "psychological") and political aspects of war. His most notable work, *Vom Kriege* [On war], was unfinished at his death. He is known for many aphorisms, of which the most famous is "War is the continuation of *Politik* by other means" ("Politik" being variously translated as "policy" or "politics," terms with very different implications), a description that has won wide acceptance.

Page 116, "Hilferding"
Rudolf Hilferding (1877–1941). Austrian-born Marxist economist, leading socialist theorist, physician, politician, and chief theoretician for the Social Democratic Party (SPD) during the Weimar Republic. He participated in the November Revolution in Germany and was Finance Minister in 1923 and from

1928 to 1929. In 1933 he fled into exile, living in Zürich and then Paris, where he died in custody of the Gestapo in 1941. Hilferding, was a propounder for the "economic" reading of Karl Marx, identifying himself with the Austro-Maxian group. He was the first to put forward the theory of organized capitalism and was the main defender to the challenge to Marx by Austrian School economist, Eugen von Böhm-Bawerk. He edited leading publications such as *Vorwärts, Die Freiheit, Die Gesellschaft*. His most famous work was *Das Finanzkapital* (Finance capital), one of the most influential and original contributions to Marxist economics.

Page 128, "Think of the people like Professor Förster and his kind"
A take-off on the Catholic moral-pedagogue, Friedrich Wilhelm Foerster (1869–1966).

Page 131, "kingdom of the Merovingians."
Region in Gaul and Germany founded by Clovis, under the rule of the Frankish kings from 500–752 AD.

Page 132, "we see how private economies gradually passed over into national economies"
The German "Volkswirtschaft" here translated "national economy" is also the ordinary word for "political economy." The fact (indicated in the lecture) that the *science* of "political economy" owes its form to its origin in the period of national economies is emphasized by the German word in a way that is not possible in English, though one is reminded of it by the title of Adam Smith's book *The Wealth of Nations*. See also note for page 1.

Page 132, "which again at a certain time—at the beginning of the modern period—tended to become state economies."
See lecture 1, page 1.

Page 133, "Ricardo or Adam Smith"
David Ricardo (1772–1823), English political economist. Besides Adam Smith the most significant theorist of the classical school of English economic theory. On the basis of the economic freedom he developed a theory of value and, above all, his own theory of the basic pension. His main work was *Principles of Political Economy and Taxation*, 1817.

For "Adam Smith," see note for page 13.

Page 133, "Mercantilism ... was based on the advantages arising from such exchange between national economies"
Mercantilism is the economic doctrine that government control of foreign trade is of paramount importance for ensuring the military security of the state. Mercantilism was the dominant school of thought in Europe through-

out the late Renaissance and early modern period (from the 15th to the late 18th century). Mercantilism encouraged the many intra-European wars of the period and arguably fueled European expansion and imperialism — both in Europe and throughout the rest of the world — until the 19th century or early 20th century. High tariffs, especially on manufactured goods, are an almost universal feature of mercantilist policy. Other policies have included: building a network of overseas colonies; forbidding colonies to trade with other nations; monopolizing markets with staple ports; banning the export of gold and silver, even for payments; forbidding trade to be carried in foreign ships; export subsidies; promoting manufacturing with research or direct subsidies; limiting wages; maximizing the use of domestic resources; and restricting domestic consumption with non-tariff barriers to trade. Jean-Baptiste Colbert's work in 17th-century France exemplified classical mercantilism. In the English-speaking world its ideas were criticized by Adam Smith with the publication of *The Wealth of Nations* in 1776 and later David Ricardo with his explanation of comparative advantage. Mercantilism was rejected by Britain and France by the mid-19th century.

Page 134, "Hume"
David Hume (1711–1776). English philosopher and historian. He had a strong influence on the French Enlightenment and the positivism, as well as on psychologism of the nineteenth century.

Page 140, "Physiocrats"
The Physiocrats were a group of economists who believed that the wealth of nations was derived solely from the value of "land agriculture" or "land development." Their theories originated in France and were most popular during the second half of the 18th century. Physiocracy is perhaps the first well-developed theory of economics. It immediately preceded the first modern school, classical economics, which began with the publication of Adam Smith's *The Wealth of Nations* in 1776. The most significant contribution of the Physiocrats was their emphasis on productive work as the source of national wealth in contrast to earlier schools, in particular mercantilism, which often focused on the ruler's wealth, accumulation of gold, or the balance of trade. At the time the Physiocrats were formulating their ideas, economies were almost entirely agrarian. That is presumably why the theory considered only agricultural labor to be valuable. Physiocrats viewed the production of goods and services as consumption of the agricultural surplus, since the main source of power was from human or animal muscle and all energy was derived from the surplus from agricultural production.

The perceptiveness of the Physiocrats' recognition of the key significance of land was reinforced in the following half-century, when fossil fuels had been harnessed through the use of steam power. Productivity increased manyfold. Railways, and steam-powered water supply and sanitation systems made possible cities of several millions, with land values many times greater than agricultural land.

Page 142, "Charles the Bald"
Charles the Bald (823–877), Holy Roman Emperor (875–877, as Charles II) and King of West Francia (840–877, as Charles II, with the borders of his land defined by the Treaty of Verdun, 843.

Page 142, "Scotus Erigena"
Johannes Scotus Erigena (c. 815– c. 877) was an Irish theologian, Neoplatonist philosopher, and poet. He is regarded as Europe's greatest philosopher of the early Middle Ages.

Page 145, "Lycurgus"
Greek (c. 820–730 BC ?) legendary lawgiver of Sparta. Symbolic founder of the Spartan State.

Page 147, "Spengler"
Oswald Manuel Arnold Gottfried Spengler (1880–1936) was a German historian and philosopher. He is best known for his book *The Decline of the West* (*Der Untergang des Abendlandes*), published in 1918 and 1922, where he proposed that the lifespan of civilizations is limited, and ultimately they decay. See volume 2, chapter 5: "Money."

Page 149, "it becomes working capital."
The literal translation of *Unternehmergeld* would be "enterpriser money."

Page 167, "I said yesterday to a few of those present"
See the fifth seminar discussion of August 4, 1922.

Page 186, "Ricardo"
See previous note to page 133.

Page 186, "Let us take the 'ironclad wage law' of Lassalle."
Ferdinand Johann Gottlieb Lassalle (1825–1864) was a German-Jewish jurist, philosopher, and socialist political activist. Lassalle is best remembered as an initiator of international-style socialism in Germany.

Page 189, "Oppenheimer"
Franz Oppenheimer (1864–1943) was a German-Jewish sociologist and political economist who published also in the area of the fundamental sociology of the state. In the 1920s *Der Staat* was a widely read and heatedly discussed book. It was translated into English, French, Hungarian, Serbian, Japanese, Hebrew, Yiddish and Russian, and has inspired many different thinkers.

Page 212, "Spann"
Othmar Spann (1878–1950) was a conservative Austrian philosopher, sociologist, and economist whose radical anti-liberal and anti-Socialist views, based on

early 19th-century Romantic ideas expressed by Adam Müller, et al. and popularized in his books and lecture courses, helped antagonize political factions in Austria during the interwar years.

Page 228, "Rodbertus"
Johann Karl Rodbertus (1805–1875), also known as Karl Rodbertus-Jagetzow, was a German economist and socialist of the scientific or conservative school from Greifswald. He defended the labor theory of value as well as the view, as an inference from that, that interest or profit is theft. He believed that capitalist economies tend toward overproduction.

Page 238, "Lorenz von Stein"
(1815–1890). Lorenz von Stein was a German economist, sociologist, and public administration scholar from Eckernförde. As an advisor to Meiji period Japan, his conservative political views influenced the wording of the Constitution of the Empire of Japan.

Page 244, "Rathenau and Wirth"
Walter Rathenau (1867–1922) was a German industrialist, politician, writer, and statesman who served as Foreign Minister of Germany during the Weimar Republic. His German Jewish heritage and his wealth were both factors in establishing his deeply divisive reputation in German politics at a time of anti-Semitism. He became a leading industrialist in the late German Empire and early Weimar Republic periods. A strong German nationalist, Rathenau was a leading proponent of a policy of assimilation for German Jews. As a powerful, affluent and highly visible German Jewish politician, Rathenau was hated by Germany's extreme right, despite himself being a German nationalist, culminating in his 1922 assassination.

Karl Joseph Wirth, known as Joseph Wirth, (1879–1956) was a German politician of the Catholic Center Party who served as Chancellor of Germany from 1921 to 1922.

Page 245, "Edison"
Thomas Alva Edison (1847–1931) was an American inventor and businessman. Dubbed "The Wizard of Menlo Park" by a newspaper reporter, he was one of the first inventors to apply the principles of mass production and large-scale teamwork to the process of invention, and because of that, he is often credited with the creation of the first industrial research laboratory. Edison is the fourth most prolific inventor in history, holding 1,093 US patents in his name, as well as many patents in the United Kingdom, France, and Germany. He is credited with numerous inventions that contributed to mass communication and, in particular, telecommunications. Edison developed a system of electric-power generation and distribution to homes, businesses, and factories – a crucial development in the modern industrialized world.

RUDOLF STEINER'S COLLECTED WORKS

The German Edition of Rudolf Steiner's Collected Works (the Gesamtausgabe [GA] published by Rudolf Steiner Verlag, Dornach, Switzerland) presently runs to over 354 titles, organized either by type of work (written or spoken), chronology, audience (public or other), or subject (education, art, etc.). For ease of comparison, the Collected Works in English [CW] follows the German organization exactly. A complete listing of the CWs follows with literal translations of the German titles. Other than in the case of the books published in his lifetime, titles were rarely given by Rudolf Steiner himself, and were often provided by the editors of the German editions. The titles in English are not necessarily the same as the German; and, indeed, over the past seventy-five years have frequently been different, with the same book sometimes appearing under different titles.

For ease of identification and to avoid confusion, we suggest that readers looking for a title should do so by CW number. Because the work of creating the Collected Works of Rudolf Steiner is an ongoing process, with new titles being published every year, we have not indicated in this listing which books are presently available. To find out what titles in the Collected Works are currently in print, please check our website at www.steinerbooks.org, or write to SteinerBooks 610 Main Street, Great Barrington, MA 01230.

Written Work

CW 1	Goethe: Natural-Scientific Writings, Introduction, with Footnotes and Explanations in the text by Rudolf Steiner
CW 2	Outlines of an Epistemology of the Goethean World View, with Special Consideration of Schiller
CW 3	Truth and Science
CW 4	The Philosophy of Freedom
CW 4a	Documents to "The Philosophy of Freedom"
CW 5	Friedrich Nietzsche, A Fighter against His Own Time
CW 6	Goethe's Worldview
CW 6a	Now in CW 30
CW 7	Mysticism at the Dawn of Modern Spiritual Life and Its Relationship with Modern Worldviews
CW 8	Christianity as Mystical Fact and the Mysteries of Antiquity
CW 9	Theosophy: An Introduction into Supersensible World Knowledge and Human Purpose
CW 10	How Does One Attain Knowledge of Higher Worlds?
CW 11	From the Akasha-Chronicle
CW 12	Levels of Higher Knowledge
CW 13	Occult Science in Outline

CW 14	Four Mystery Dramas
CW 15	The Spiritual Guidance of the Individual and Humanity
CW 16	A Way to Human Self-Knowledge: Eight Meditations
CW 17	The Threshold of the Spiritual World. Aphoristic Comments
CW 18	The Riddles of Philosophy in Their History, Presented as an Outline
CW 19	Contained in CW 24
CW 20	The Riddles of the Human Being: Articulated and Unarticulated in the Thinking, Views and Opinions of a Series of German and Austrian Personalities
CW 21	The Riddles of the Soul
CW 22	Goethe's Spiritual Nature And Its Revelation In "Faust" and through the "Fairy Tale of the Snake and the Lily"
CW 23	The Central Points of the Social Question in the Necessities of Life in the Present and the Future
CW 24	Essays Concerning the Threefold Division of the Social Organism and the Period 1915-1921
CW 25	Cosmology, Religion and Philosophy
CW 26	Anthroposophical Leading Thoughts
CW 27	Fundamentals for Expansion of the Art of Healing according to Spiritual-Scientific Insights
CW 28	The Course of My Life
CW 29	Collected Essays on Dramaturgy, 1889-1900
CW 30	Methodical Foundations of Anthroposophy: Collected Essays on Philosophy, Natural Science, Aesthetics and Psychology, 1884-1901
CW 31	Collected Essays on Culture and Current Events, 1887-1901
CW 32	Collected Essays on Literature, 1884-1902
CW 33	Biographies and Biographical Sketches, 1894-1905
CW 34	Lucifer-Gnosis: Foundational Essays on Anthroposophy and Reports from the Periodicals "Lucifer" and "Lucifer-Gnosis," 1903-1908
CW 35	Philosophy and Anthroposophy: Collected Essays, 1904-1923
CW 36	The Goetheanum-Idea in the Middle of the Cultural Crisis of the Present: Collected Essays from the Periodical "Das Goetheanum," 1921-1925
CW 37	Now in CWs 260a and 251
CW 38	Letters, Vol. 1: 1881-1890
CW 39	Letters, Vol. 2: 1890-1925
CW 40	Truth-Wrought Words
CW 40a	Sayings, Poems and Mantras; Supplementary Volume
CW 42	Now in CWs 264-266
CW 43	Stage Adaptations

Lectures to the Members of the Anthroposophical Society

CW 270   Esoteric Instructions for the First Class of the School for Spiritual Science at the Goetheanum 1924, 4 Volumes

CW 271   Art and Knowledge of Art. Foundations of a New Aesthetic

CW 272   Spiritual-Scientific Commentary on Goethe's "Faust" in Two Volumes. Vol. 1: Faust, the Striving Human Being

CW 273   Spiritual-Scientific Commentary on Goethe's "Faust" in Two Volumes. Vol. 2: The Faust-Problem

CW 274   Addresses for the Christmas Plays from the Old Folk Traditions

CW 275   Art in the Light of Mystery-Wisdom

CW 276   The Artistic in Its Mission in the World. The Genius of Language. The World of Self-Revealing Radiant Appearances – Anthroposophy and Art. Anthroposophy and Poetry

CW 277   Eurythmy. The Revelation of the Speaking Soul

CW 277a   The Origin and Development of Eurythmy

CW 278   Eurythmy as Visible Song

CW 279   Eurythmy as Visible Speech

CW 280   The Method and Nature of Speech Formation

CW 281   The Art of Recitation and Declamation

CW 282   Speech Formation and Dramatic Art

CW 283   The Nature of Things Musical and the Experience of Tone in the Human Being

CW 284/285   Images of Occult Seals and Pillars. The Munich Congress of Whitsun 1907 and Its Consequences

CW 286   Paths to a New Style of Architecture. "And the Building Becomes Human"

CW 287   The Building at Dornach as a Symbol of Historical Becoming and an Artistic Transformation Impulse

CW 288   Style-Forms in the Living Organic

CW 289   The Building-Idea of the Goetheanum: Lectures with Slides from the Years 1920-1921

CW 290   The Building-Idea of the Goetheanum: Lectures with Slides from the Years 1920-1921

CW 291   The Nature of Colors

CW 291a   Knowledge of Colors. Supplementary Volume to "The Nature of Colors"

CW 292   Art History as Image of Inner Spiritual Impulses

CW 293   General Knowledge of the Human Being as the Foundation of Pedagogy

CW 294   The Art of Education, Methodology and Didactics

CW 295   The Art of Education: Seminar Discussions and Lectures on Lesson Planning

CW 296   The Question of Education as a Social Question

CW 297   The Idea and Practice of the Waldorf School

SIGNIFICANT EVENTS
IN THE LIFE OF RUDOLF STEINER

1829: June 23: birth of Johann Steiner (1829-1910)—Rudolf Steiner's father—in Geras, Lower Austria.

1834: May 8: birth of Franciska Blie (1834-1918)—Rudolf Steiner's mother—in Horn, Lower Austria. "My father and mother were both children of the glorious Lower Austrian forest district north of the Danube."

1860: May 16: marriage of Johann Steiner and Franciska Blie.

1861: February 25: birth of *Rudolf Joseph Lorenz Steiner* in Kraljevec, Croatia, near the border with Hungary, where Johann Steiner works as a telegrapher for the South Austria Railroad. Rudolf Steiner is baptized two days later, February 27, the date usually given as his birthday.

1862: Summer: the family moves to Mödling, Lower Austria.

1863: The family moves to Pottschach, Lower Austria, near the Styrian border, where Johann Steiner becomes stationmaster. "The view stretched to the mountains...majestic peaks in the distance and the sweet charm of nature in the immediate surroundings."

1864: November 15: birth of Rudolf Steiner's sister, Leopoldine (d. November 1, 1927). She will become a seamstress and live with her parents for the rest of her life.

1866: July 28: birth of Rudolf Steiner's deaf-mute brother, Gustav (d. May 1, 1941).

1867: Rudolf Steiner enters the village school. Following a disagreement between his father and the schoolmaster, whose wife falsely accused the boy of causing a commotion, Rudolf Steiner is taken out of school and taught at home.

1868: A critical experience. Unknown to the family, an aunt dies in a distant town. Sitting in the station waiting room, Rudolf Steiner sees her "form," which speaks to him, asking for help. "Beginning with this experience, a new soul life began in the boy, one in which not only the outer trees and mountains spoke to him, but also the worlds that lay behind them. From this moment on, the boy began to live with the spirits of nature...."

1869: The family moves to the peaceful, rural village of Neudorfl, near Wiener-Neustadt in present-day Austria. Rudolf Steiner attends the village school. Because of the "unorthodoxy" of his writing and spelling, he has to do "extra lessons."

1870: Through a book lent to him by his tutor, he discovers geometry: "To grasp something purely in the spirit brought me inner happiness. I know that I first learned happiness through geometry." The same tutor allows him to draw, while other students still struggle with their reading and writing. "An artistic element" thus enters his education.

1871: Though his parents are not religious, Rudolf Steiner becomes a "church child," a favorite of the priest, who was "an exceptional character." "Up to the age of ten or eleven, among those I came to know, he was far and away the most significant." Among other things, he introduces Steiner to Copernican, heliocentric cosmology. As an altar boy, Rudolf Steiner serves at Masses, funerals, and Corpus Christi processions. At year's end, after an incident in which he escapes a thrashing, his father forbids him to go to church.

1872: Rudolf Steiner transfers to grammar school in Wiener-Neustadt, a five-mile walk from home, which must be done in all weathers.

1873-75: Through his teachers and on his own, Rudolf Steiner has many wonderful experiences with science and mathematics. Outside school, he teaches himself analytic geometry, trigonometry, differential equations, and calculus.

1876: Rudolf Steiner begins tutoring other students. He learns bookbinding from his father. He also teaches himself stenography.

1877: Rudolf Steiner discovers Kant's *Critique of Pure Reason*, which he reads and rereads. He also discovers and reads von Rotteck's *World History*.

1878: He studies extensively in contemporary psychology and philosophy.

1879: Rudolf Steiner graduates from high school with honors. His father is transferred to Inzersdorf, near Vienna. He uses his first visit to Vienna "to purchase a great number of philosophy books"—Kant, Fichte, Schelling, and Hegel, as well as numerous histories of philosophy. His aim: to find a path from the "I" to nature.

October 1879-1883: Rudolf Steiner attends the Technical College in Vienna—to study mathematics, chemistry, physics, mineralogy, botany, zoology, biology, geology, and mechanics—with a scholarship. He also attends lectures in history and literature, while avidly reading philosophy on his own. His two favorite professors are Karl Julius Schröer (German language and literature) and Edmund Reitlinger (physics). He also audits lectures by Robert Zimmerman on aesthetics and Franz Brentano on philosophy. During this year he begins his friendship with Moritz Zitter (1861-1921), who will help support him financially when he is in Berlin.

1880: Rudolf Steiner attends lectures on Schiller and Goethe by Karl Julius Schröer, who becomes his mentor. Also "through a remarkable combination of circumstances," he meets Felix Koguzki, a "herb gatherer" and healer, who could "see deeply into the secrets of nature." Rudolf Steiner will meet and study with this "emissary of the Master" throughout his time in Vienna.

1881: January: "... I didn't sleep a wink. I was busy with philosophical problems until about 12:30 a.m. Then, finally, I threw myself down on my couch. All my striving during the previous year had been to research whether the following statement by Schelling was true or not: *Within everyone dwells a secret, marvelous capacity to draw back from the stream of time—out of the self clothed in all that comes to us from outside—into our innermost being and there, in the immutable form of the Eternal, to look into ourselves.* I believe, and I am still quite certain of it, that I discovered this capacity in myself; I had long had an inkling of it. Now the whole of idealist philosophy stood before me in modified form. What's a sleepless night compared to that!"

Rudolf Steiner begins communicating with leading thinkers of the day, who send him books in return, which he reads eagerly.

July: "I am not one of those who dives into the day like an animal in human form. I pursue a quite specific goal, an idealistic aim—knowledge of the truth! This cannot be done offhandedly. It requires the greatest striving in the world, free of all egotism, and equally of all resignation."

August: Steiner puts down on paper for the first time thoughts for a "Philosophy of Freedom." "The striving for the absolute: this human yearning is freedom." He also seeks to outline a "peasant philosophy," describing what the worldview of a "peasant"—one who lives close to the earth and the old ways—really is.

1881-1882: Felix Koguzki, the herb gatherer, reveals himself to be the envoy of another, higher initiatory personality, who instructs Rudolf Steiner to penetrate Fichte's philosophy and to master modern scientific thinking as a preparation for right entry into the spirit. This "Master" also teaches him the double (evolutionary and involutionary) nature of time.

1882: Through the offices of Karl Julius Schröer, Rudolf Steiner is asked by Joseph Kurschner to edit Goethe's scientific works for the *Deutschen National-Literatur* edition. He writes "A Possible Critique of Atomistic Concepts" and sends it to Friedrich Theodore Vischer.

1883: Rudolf Steiner completes his college studies and begins work on the Goethe project.

1884: First volume of Goethe's *Scientific Writings* (CW 1) appears (March). He lectures on Goethe and Lessing, and Goethe's approach to science. In July, he enters the household of Ladislaus and Pauline Specht as tutor to the four Specht boys. He will live there until 1890. At this time, he meets Josef Breuer (1842-1925), the coauthor with Sigmund Freud of *Studies in Hysteria*, who is the Specht family doctor.

1885: While continuing to edit Goethe's writings, Rudolf Steiner reads deeply in contemporary philosophy (Edouard von Hartmann, Johannes Volkelt, and Richard Wahle, among others).

1886: May: Rudolf Steiner sends Kurschner the manuscript of *Outlines of Goethe's Theory of Knowledge* (CW 2), which appears in October, and which he sends out widely. He also meets the poet Marie Eugenie Delle Grazie and writes "Nature and Our Ideals" for her. He attends her salon, where he meets many priests, theologians, and philosophers, who will become his friends. Meanwhile, the director of the Goethe Archive in Weimar requests his collaboration with the *Sophien* edition of Goethe's works, particularly the writings on color.

1887:   At the beginning of the year, Rudolf Steiner is very sick. As the year progresses and his health improves, he becomes increasingly "a man of letters," lecturing, writing essays, and taking part in Austrian cultural life. In August-September, the second volume of Goethe's *Scientific Writings* appears.

1888:   January-July: Rudolf Steiner assumes editorship of the "German Weekly" (*Deutsche Wochenschrift*). He begins lecturing more intensively, giving, for example, a lecture titled "Goethe as Father of a New Aesthetics." He meets and becomes soul friends with Friedrich Eckstein (1861-1939), a vegetarian, philosopher of symbolism, alchemist, and musician, who will introduce him to various spiritual currents (including Theosophy) and with whom he will meditate and interpret esoteric and alchemical texts.

1889:   Rudolf Steiner first reads Nietzsche (*Beyond Good and Evil*). He encounters Theosophy again and learns of Madame Blavatsky in the Theosophical circle around Marie Lang (1858-1934). Here he also meets well-known figures of Austrian life, as well as esoteric figures like the occultist Franz Hartman and Karl Leinigen-Billigen (translator of C.G. Harrison's *The Transcendental Universe*.) During this period, Steiner first reads A.P. Sinnett's *Esoteric Buddhism* and Mabel Collins's *Light on the Path*. He also begins traveling, visiting Budapest, Weimar, and Berlin (where he meets philosopher Edouard von Hartmann).

1890:   Rudolf Steiner finishes volume 3 of Goethe's scientific writings. He begins his doctoral dissertation, which will become *Truth and Science* (CW 3). He also meets the poet and feminist Rosa Mayreder (1858-1938), with whom he can exchange his most intimate thoughts. In September, Rudolf Steiner moves to Weimar to work in the Goethe-Schiller Archive.

1891:   Volume 3 of the Kurschner edition of Goethe appears. Meanwhile, Rudolf Steiner edits Goethe's studies in mineralogy and scientific writings for the *Sophien* edition. He meets Ludwig Laistner of the Cotta Publishing Company, who asks for a book on the basic question of metaphysics. From this will result, ultimately, *The Philosophy of Freedom* (CW 4), which will be published not by Cotta but by Emil Felber. In October, Rudolf Steiner takes the oral exam for a doctorate in philosophy, mathematics, and mechanics at Rostock University, receiving his doctorate on the twenty-sixth. In November, he gives his first lecture on Goethe's "Fairy Tale" in Vienna.

1892:   Rudolf Steiner continues work at the Goethe-Schiller Archive and on his *Philosophy of Freedom. Truth and Science*, his doctoral dissertation, is published. Steiner undertakes to write introductions to books on Schopenhauer and Jean Paul for Cotta. At year's end, he finds lodging with Anna Eunike, née Schulz (1853-1911), a widow with four daughters and a son. He also develops a friendship with Otto Erich Hartleben (1864-1905) with whom he shares literary interests.

1893: Rudolf Steiner begins his habit of producing many reviews and articles. In March, he gives a lecture titled "Hypnotism, with Reference to Spiritism." In September, volume 4 of the Kurschner edition is completed. In November, *The Philosophy of Freedom* appears. This year, too, he meets John Henry Mackay (1864-1933), the anarchist, and Max Stirner, a scholar and biographer.

1894: Rudolf Steiner meets Elisabeth Förster Nietzsche, the philosopher's sister, and begins to read Nietzsche in earnest, beginning with the as yet unpublished *Antichrist*. He also meets Ernst Haeckel (1834-1919). In the fall, he begins to write *Nietzsche, A Fighter against His Time* (CW 5).

1895: May, *Nietzsche, A Fighter against His Time* appears.

1896: January 22: Rudolf Steiner sees Friedrich Nietzsche for the first and only time. Moves between the Nietzsche and the Goethe-Schiller Archives, where he completes his work before year's end. He falls out with Elisabeth Förster Nietzsche, thus ending his association with the Nietzsche Archive.

1897: Rudolf Steiner finishes the manuscript of *Goethe's Worldview* (CW 6). He moves to Berlin with Anna Eunike and begins editorship of the *Magazin fur Literatur*. From now on, Steiner will write countless reviews, literary and philosophical articles, and so on. He begins lecturing at the "Free Literary Society." In September, he attends the Zionist Congress in Basel. He sides with Dreyfus in the Dreyfus affair.

1898: Rudolf Steiner is very active as an editor in the political, artistic, and theatrical life of Berlin. He becomes friendly with John Henry Mackay and poet Ludwig Jacobowski (1868-1900). He joins Jacobowski's circle of writers, artists, and scientists—"The Coming Ones" (*Die Kommenden*)—and contributes lectures to the group until 1903. He also lectures at the "League for College Pedagogy." He writes an article for Goethe's sesquicentennial, "Goethe's Secret Revelation," on the "Fairy Tale of the Green Snake and the Beautiful Lily."

1898-99: "This was a trying time for my soul as I looked at Christianity.... I was able to progress only by contemplating, by means of spiritual perception, the evolution of Christianity .... Conscious knowledge of real Christianity began to dawn in me around the turn of the century. This seed continued to develop. My soul trial occurred shortly before the beginning of the twentieth century. It was decisive for my soul's development that I stood spiritually before the Mystery of Golgotha in a deep and solemn celebration of knowledge."

1899: Rudolf Steiner begins teaching and giving lectures and lecture cycles at the Workers' College, founded by Wilhelm Liebknecht (1826-1900). He will continue to do so until 1904. Writes: *Literature and Spiritual Life in the Nineteenth Century; Individualism in Philosophy; Haeckel and His Opponents; Poetry in the Present;* and begins what will become (fifteen years later) *The Riddles of Philosophy* (CW 18). He also meets many artists and writers, including Käthe Kollwitz, Stefan

Zweig, and Rainer Maria Rilke. On October 31, he marries Anna Eunike.

1900: "I thought that the turn of the century must bring humanity a new light. It seemed to me that the separation of human thinking and willing from the spirit had peaked. A turn or reversal of direction in human evolution seemed to me a necessity." Rudolf Steiner finishes *World and Life Views in the Nineteenth Century* (the second part of what will become *The Riddles of Philosophy*) and dedicates it to Ernst Haeckel. It is published in March. He continues lecturing at *Die Kommenden*, whose leadership he assumes after the death of Jacobowski. Also, he gives the Gutenberg Jubilee lecture before 7,000 typesetters and printers. In September, Rudolf Steiner is invited by Count and Countess Brockdorff to lecture in the Theosophical Library. His first lecture is on Nietzsche. His second lecture is titled "Goethe's Secret Revelation." October 6, he begins a lecture cycle on the mystics that will become *Mystics after Modernism* (CW 7). November-December: "Marie von Sivers appears in the audience...." Also in November, Steiner gives his first lecture at the Giordano Bruno Bund (where he will continue to lecture until May, 1905). He speaks on Bruno and modern Rome, focusing on the importance of the philosophy of Thomas Aquinas as monism.

1901: In continual financial straits, Rudolf Steiner's early friends Moritz Zitter and Rosa Mayreder help support him. In October, he begins the lecture cycle *Christianity as Mystical Fact* (CW 8) at the Theosophical Library. In November, he gives his first "Theosophical lecture" on Goethe's "Fairy Tale" in Hamburg at the invitation of Wilhelm Hubbe-Schleiden. He also attends a gathering to celebrate the founding of the Theosophical Society at Count and Countess Brockdorff's. He gives a lecture cycle, "From Buddha to Christ," for the circle of the *Kommenden*. November 17, Marie von Sivers asks Rudolf Steiner if Theosophy needs a Western-Christian spiritual movement (to complement Theosophy's Eastern emphasis). "The question was posed. Now, following spiritual laws, I could begin to give an answer...." In December, Rudolf Steiner writes his first article for a Theosophical publication. At year's end, the Brockdorffs and possibly Wilhelm Hubbe-Schleiden ask Rudolf Steiner to join the Theosophical Society and undertake the leadership of the German section. Rudolf Steiner agrees, on the condition that Marie von Sivers (then in Italy) work with him.

1902: Beginning in January, Rudolf Steiner attends the opening of the Workers' School in Spandau with Rosa Luxemburg (1870-1919). January 17, Rudolf Steiner joins the Theosophical Society. In April, he is asked to become general secretary of the German Section of the Theosophical Society, and works on preparations for its founding. In July, he visits London for a Theosophical congress. He meets Bertram

Keightly, G.R.S. Mead, A.P. Sinnett, and Annie Besant, among others. In September, *Christianity as Mystical Fact* appears. In October, Rudolf Steiner gives his first public lecture on Theosophy ("Monism and Theosophy") to about three hundred people at the Giordano Bruno Bund. On October 19-21, the German Section of the Theosophical Society has its first meeting; Rudolf Steiner is the general secretary, and Annie Besant attends. Steiner lectures on practical karma studies. On October 23, Annie Besant inducts Rudolf Steiner into the Esoteric School of the Theosophical Society. On October 25, Steiner begins a weekly series of lectures: "The Field of Theosophy." During this year, Rudolf Steiner also first meets Ita Wegman (1876-1943), who will become his close collaborator in his final years.

1903: Rudolf Steiner holds about 300 lectures and seminars. In May, the first issue of the periodical *Luzifer* appears. In June, Rudolf Steiner visits London for the first meeting of the Federation of the European Sections of the Theosophical Society, where he meets Colonel Olcott. He begins to write *Theosophy* (CW 9).

1904: Rudolf Steiner continues lecturing at the Workers' College and elsewhere (about 90 lectures), while lecturing intensively all over Germany among Theosophists (about a 140 lectures). In February, he meets Carl Unger (1878-1929), who will become a member of the board of the Anthroposophical Society (1913). In March, he meets Michael Bauer (1871-1929), a Christian mystic, who will also be on the board. In May, *Theosophy* appears, with the dedication: "To the spirit of Giordano Bruno." Rudolf Steiner and Marie von Sivers visit London for meetings with Annie Besant. June: Rudolf Steiner and Marie von Sivers attend the meeting of the Federation of European Sections of the Theosophical Society in Amsterdam. In July, Steiner begins the articles in *Luzifer-Gnosis* that will become *How to Know Higher Worlds* (CW 10) and *Cosmic Memory* (CW 11). In September, Annie Besant visits Germany. In December, Steiner lectures on Freemasonry. He mentions the High Grade Masonry derived from John Yarker and represented by Theodore Reuss and Karl Kellner as a blank slate "into which a good image could be placed."

1905: This year, Steiner ends his non-Theosophical lecturing activity. Supported by Marie von Sivers, his Theosophical lecturing—both in public and in the Theosophical Society—increases significantly: "The German Theosophical Movement is of exceptional importance." Steiner recommends reading, among others, Fichte, Jacob Boehme, and Angelus Silesius. He begins to introduce Christian themes into Theosophy. He also begins to work with doctors (Felix Peipers and Ludwig Noll). In July, he is in London for the Federation of European Sections, where he attends a lecture by Annie Besant: "I have seldom seen Mrs. Besant speak in so inward and heartfelt a manner...." "Through Mrs. Besant I have found the way to H.P. Blavatsky."

September to October, he gives a course of thirty-one lectures for a small group of esoteric students. In October, the annual meeting of the German Section of the Theosophical Society, which still remains very small, takes place. Rudolf Steiner reports membership has risen from 121 to 377 members. In November, seeking to establish esoteric "continuity," Rudolf Steiner and Marie von Sivers participate in a "Memphis-Misraim" Masonic ceremony. They pay forty-five marks for membership. "Yesterday, you saw how little remains of former esoteric institutions." "We are dealing only with a 'framework'... for the present, nothing lies behind it. The occult powers have completely withdrawn."

1906: Expansion of Theosophical work. Rudolf Steiner gives about 245 lectures, only 44 of which take place in Berlin. Cycles are given in Paris, Leipzig, Stuttgart, and Munich. Esoteric work also intensifies. Rudolf Steiner begins writing *An Outline of Esoteric Science* (CW 13). In January, Rudolf Steiner receives permission (a patent) from the Great Orient of the Scottish A & A Thirty-Three Degree Rite of the Order of the Ancient Freemasons of the Memphis-Misraim Rite to direct a chapter under the name "Mystica Aeterna." This will become the "Cognitive-Ritual Section" (also called "Misraim Service") of the Esoteric School. (See: *Freemasonry and Ritual Work: The Misraim Service* (CW 265). During this time, Steiner also meets Albert Schweitzer. In May, he is in Paris, where he visits Edouard Schuré. Many Russians attend his lectures (including Konstantin Balmont, Dimitri Mereszkovski, Zinaida Hippius, and Maximilian Woloshin). He attends the General Meeting of the European Federation of the Theosophical Society, at which Col. Olcott is present for the last time. He spends the year's end in Venice and Rome, where he writes and works on his translation of H.P. Blavatsky's *Key to Theosophy*.

1907: Further expansion of the German Theosophical Movement according to the Rosicrucian directive to "introduce spirit into the world"—in education, in social questions, in art, and in science. In February, Col. Olcott dies in Adyar. Before he dies, Olcott indicates that "the Masters" wish Annie Besant to succeed him: much politicking ensues. Rudolf Steiner supports Besant's candidacy. April-May: preparations for the Congress of the Federation of European Sections of the Theosophical Society—the great, watershed Whitsun "Munich Congress," attended by Annie Besant and others. Steiner decides to separate Eastern and Western (Christian-Rosicrucian) esoteric schools. He takes his esoteric school out of the Theosophical Society (Besant and Rudolf Steiner are "in harmony" on this). Steiner makes his first lecture tours to Austria and Hungary. That summer, he is in Italy. In September, he visits Edouard Schuré, who will write the introduction to the French edition of *Christianity as Mystical Fact* in Barr, Alsace. Rudolf Steiner writes the autobiographical statement known as the "Barr Document." In *Luzifer–Gnosis*, "The Education of the Child" appears.

1908: The movement grows (membership: 1,150). Lecturing expands. Steiner makes his first extended lecture tour to Holland and Scandinavia, as well as visits to Naples and Sicily. Themes: St. John's Gospel, the Apocalypse, Egypt, science, philosophy, and logic. *Luzifer-Gnosis* ceases publication. In Berlin, Marie von Sivers (with Johanna Mücke (1864-1949) forms the *Philosophisch-Theosophisch* (after 1915 *Philosophisch-Anthroposophisch*) *Verlag* to publish Steiner's work. Steiner gives lecture cycles titled *The Gospel of St. John* (CW 103) and *The Apocalypse* (104).

1909: *An Outline of Esoteric Science* appears. Lecturing and travel continues. Rudolf Steiner's spiritual research expands to include the polarity of Lucifer and Ahriman; the work of great individualities in history; the Maitreya Buddha and the Bodhisattvas; spiritual economy (CW 109); the work of the spiritual hierarchies in heaven and on earth (CW 110). He also deepens and intensifies his research into the Gospels, giving lectures on the Gospel of St. Luke (CW 114) with the first mention of two Jesus children. Meets and becomes friends with Christian Morgenstern (1871-1914). In April, he lays the foundation stone for the Malsch model—the building that will lead to the first Goetheanum. In May, the International Congress of the Federation of European Sections of the Theosophical Society takes place in Budapest. Rudolf Steiner receives the Subba Row medal for *How to Know Higher Worlds*. During this time, Charles W. Leadbeater discovers Jiddu Krishnamurti (1895-1986) and proclaims him the future "world teacher," the bearer of the Maitreya Buddha and the "reappearing Christ." In October, Steiner delivers seminal lectures on "anthroposophy," which he will try, unsuccessfully, to rework over the next years into the unfinished work, *Anthroposophy (A Fragment)* (CW 45).

1910: New themes: *The Reappearance of Christ in the Etheric* (CW 118); *The Fifth Gospel; The Mission of Folk Souls* (CW 121); *Occult History* (CW 126); the evolving development of etheric cognitive capacities. Rudolf Steiner continues his Gospel research with *The Gospel of St. Matthew* (CW 123). In January, his father dies. In April, he takes a month-long trip to Italy, including Rome, Monte Cassino, and Sicily. He also visits Scandinavia again. July-August, he writes the first mystery drama, *The Portal of Initiation* (CW 14). In November, he gives "psychosophy" lectures. In December, he submits "On the Psychological Foundations and Epistemological Framework of Theosophy" to the International Philosophical Congress in Bologna.

1911: The crisis in the Theosophical Society deepens. In January, "The Order of the Rising Sun," which will soon become "The Order of the Star in the East," is founded for the coming world teacher, Krishnamurti. At the same time, Marie von Sivers, Rudolf Steiner's coworker, falls ill. Fewer lectures are given, but important new ground is broken. In Prague, in March, Steiner meets Franz Kafka (1883-1924) and Hugo Bergmann (1883-1975). In April, he delivers his paper to the

Philosophical Congress. He writes the second mystery drama, *The Soul's Probation* (CW 14). Also, while Marie von Sivers is convalescing, Rudolf Steiner begins work on *Calendar 1912/1913*, which will contain the "Calendar of the Soul" meditations. On March 19, Anna (Eunike) Steiner dies. In September, Rudolf Steiner visits Einsiedeln, birthplace of Paracelsus. In December, Friedrich Rittelmeyer, future founder of the Christian Community, meets Rudolf Steiner. The *Johannes-Bauverein*, the "building committee," which would lead to the first Goetheanum (first planned for Munich), is also founded, and a preliminary committee for the founding of an independent association is created that, in the following year, will become the Anthroposophical Society. Important lecture cycles include *Occult Physiology* (CW 128); *Wonders of the World* (CW 129); *From Jesus to Christ* (CW 131). Other themes: esoteric Christianity; Christian Rosenkreutz; the spiritual guidance of humanity; the sense world and the world of the spirit.

1912: Despite the ongoing, now increasing crisis in the Theosophical Society, much is accomplished: *Calendar 1912/1913* is published; eurythmy is created; both the third mystery drama, *The Guardian of the Threshold* (CW 14) and *A Way of Self-Knowledge* (CW 16) are written. New (or renewed) themes included life between death and rebirth and karma and reincarnation. Other lecture cycles: *Spiritual Beings in the Heavenly Bodies and in the Kingdoms of Nature* (CW 136); *The Human Being in the Light of Occultism, Theosophy, and Philosophy* (CW 137); *The Gospel of St. Mark* (CW 139); and *The Bhagavad Gita and the Epistles of Paul* (CW 142). On May 8, Rudolf Steiner celebrates White Lotus Day, H.P. Blavatsky's death day, which he had faithfully observed for the past decade, for the last time. In August, Rudolf Steiner suggests the "independent association" be called the "Anthroposophical Society." In September, the first eurythmy course takes place. In October, Rudolf Steiner declines recognition of a Theosophical Society lodge dedicated to the Star of the East and decides to expel all Theosophical Society members belonging to the order. Also, with Marie von Sivers, he first visits Dornach, near Basel, Switzerland, and they stand on the hill where the Goetheanum will be built. In November, a Theosophical Society lodge is opened by direct mandate from Adyar (Annie Besant). In December, a meeting of the German section occurs at which it is decided that belonging to the Order of the Star of the East is incompatible with membership in the Theosophical Society. December 28: informal founding of the Anthroposophical Society in Berlin.

1913: Expulsion of the German section from the Theosophical Society. February 2-3: Foundation meeting of the Anthroposophical Society. Board members include: Marie von Sivers, Michael Bauer, and Carl Unger. September 20: Laying of the foundation stone for the *Johannes Bau* (Goetheanum) in Dornach. Building begins immediately. The third mystery drama, *The Soul's Awakening* (CW 14), is completed.

Also: *The Threshold of the Spiritual World* (CW 147). Lecture cycles include: *The Bhagavad Gita and the Epistles of Paul* and *The Esoteric Meaning of the Bhagavad Gita* (CW 146), which the Russian philosopher Nikolai Berdyaev attends; *The Mysteries of the East and of Christianity* (CW 144); *The Effects of Esoteric Development* (CW 145); and *The Fifth Gospel* (CW 148). In May, Rudolf Steiner is in London and Paris, where anthroposophical work continues.

1914: Building continues on the *Johannes Bau* (Goetheanum) in Dornach, with artists and coworkers from seventeen nations. The general assembly of the Anthroposophical Society takes place. In May, Rudolf Steiner visits Paris, as well as Chartres Cathedral. June 28: assassination in Sarajevo ("Now the catastrophe has happened!"). August 1: War is declared. Rudolf Steiner returns to Germany from Dornach—he will travel back and forth. He writes the last chapter of *The Riddles of Philosophy*. Lecture cycles include: *Human and Cosmic Thought* (CW 151); *Inner Being of Humanity between Death and a New Birth* (CW 153); *Occult Reading and Occult Hearing* (CW 156). December 24: marriage of Rudolf Steiner and Marie von Sivers.

1915: Building continues. Life after death becomes a major theme, also art. Writes: *Thoughts during a Time of War* (CW 24). Lectures include: *The Secret of Death* (CW 159); *The Uniting of Humanity through the Christ Impulse* (CW 165).

1916: Rudolf Steiner begins work with Edith Maryon (1872-1924) on the sculpture "The Representative of Humanity" ("The Group"—Christ, Lucifer, and Ahriman). He also works with the alchemist Alexander von Bernus on the quarterly *Das Reich*. He writes *The Riddle of Humanity* (CW 20). Lectures include: *Necessity and Freedom in World History and Human Action* (CW 166); *Past and Present in the Human Spirit* (CW 167); *The Karma of Vocation* (CW 172); *The Karma of Untruthfulness* (CW 173).

1917: Russian Revolution. The U.S. enters the war. Building continues. Rudolf Steiner delineates the idea of the "threefold nature of the human being" (in a public lecture March 15) and the "threefold nature of the social organism" (hammered out in May-June with the help of Otto von Lerchenfeld and Ludwig Polzer-Hoditz in the form of two documents titled *Memoranda*, which were distributed in high places). August-September: Rudolf Steiner writes *The Riddles of the Soul* (CW 20). Also: commentary on "The Chemical Wedding of Christian Rosenkreutz" for Alexander Bernus (*Das Reich*). Lectures include: *The Karma of Materialism* (CW 176); *The Spiritual Background of the Outer World: The Fall of the Spirits of Darkness* (CW 177).

1918: March 18: peace treaty of Brest-Litovsk—"Now everything will truly enter chaos! What is needed is cultural renewal." June: Rudolf Steiner visits Karlstein (Grail) Castle outside Prague. Lecture cycle: *From Symptom to Reality in Modern History* (CW 185). In mid-November,

Emil Molt, of the Waldorf-Astoria Cigarette Company, has the idea of founding a school for his workers' children.

1919: Focus on the threefold social organism: tireless travel, countless lectures, meetings, and publications. At the same time, a new public stage of Anthroposophy emerges as cultural renewal begins. The coming years will see initiatives in pedagogy, medicine, pharmacology, and agriculture. January 27: threefold meeting: " We must first of all, with the money we have, found free schools that can bring people what they need." February: first public eurythmy performance in Zurich. Also: "Appeal to the German People" (CW 24), circulated March 6 as a newspaper insert. In April, *Towards Social Renewal* (CW 23) appears—"perhaps the most widely read of all books on politics appearing since the war." Rudolf Steiner is asked to undertake the "direction and leadership" of the school founded by the Waldorf-Astoria Company. Rudolf Steiner begins to talk about the "renewal" of education. May 30: a building is selected and purchased for the future Waldorf School. August-September, Rudolf Steiner gives a lecture course for Waldorf teachers, *The Foundations of Human Experience (Study of Man)* (CW 293). September 7: Opening of the first Waldorf School. December (into January): first science course, the *Light Course* (CW 320).

1920: The Waldorf School flourishes. New threefold initiatives. Founding of limited companies *Der Kommende Tag* and *Futurum A.G.* to infuse spiritual values into the economic realm. Rudolf Steiner also focuses on the sciences. Lectures: *Introducing Anthroposophical Medicine* (CW 312); *The Warmth Course* (CW 321); *The Boundaries of Natural Science* (CW 322); *The Redemption of Thinking* (CW 74). February: Johannes Werner Klein—later a cofounder of the Christian Community—asks Rudolf Steiner about the possibility of a "religious renewal," a "Johannine church." In March, Rudolf Steiner gives the first course for doctors and medical students. In April, a divinity student asks Rudolf Steiner a second time about the possibility of religious renewal. September 27-October 16: anthroposophical "university course." December: lectures titled *The Search for the New Isis* (CW 202).

1921: Rudolf Steiner continues his intensive work on cultural renewal, including the uphill battle for the threefold social order. "University" arts, scientific, theological, and medical courses include: *The Astronomy Course* (CW 323); *Observation, Mathematics, and Scientific Experiment* (CW 324); the *Second Medical Course* (CW 313); *Color.* In June and September-October, Rudolf Steiner also gives the first two "priests' courses" (CW 342 and 343). The "youth movement" gains momentum. Magazines are founded: *Die Drei* (January), and—under the editorship of Albert Steffen (1884-1963)—the weekly, *Das Goetheanum* (August). In February-March, Rudolf Steiner takes his first trip outside Germany since the war (Holland). On April 7, Steiner receives a letter regarding "religious renewal," and May 22-23, he agrees to address the question in a practical way. In June, the Klinical-Therapeutic Institute opens in Arlesheim under the direction of Dr. Ita Wegman. In August, the Chemical-Pharmaceutical Laboratory opens in Arlesheim (Oskar Schmiedel and Ita Wegman are directors). The Clinical Therapeutic Institute is inaugurated in Stuttgart (Dr. Ludwig Noll is director); also the Research Laboratory in Dornach (Ehrenfried Pfeiffer and Gunther Wachsmuth are directors). In November-December, Rudolf Steiner visits Norway.

1922: The first half of the year involves very active public lecturing (thousands attend); in the second half, Rudolf Steiner begins to withdraw and turn toward the Society—"The Society is asleep." It is "too weak" to do what is asked of it. The businesses—*Der Kommende Tag* and *Futura A.G.*—fail. In January, with the help of an agent, Steiner undertakes a twelve-city German lecture tour, accompanied by eurythmy performances. In two weeks he speaks to more than 2,000 people. In April, he gives a "university course" in The Hague. He also visits England. In June, he is in Vienna for the East-West Congress. In August-September, he is back in England for the Oxford Conference on Education. Returning to Dornach, he gives the lectures *Philosophy, Cosmology, and Religion* (CW 215), and gives the third priests' course (CW 344). On September 16, The Christian Community is founded. In October-November, Steiner is in Holland and England. He also speaks to the youth: *The Youth Course* (CW 217). In December, Steiner gives lectures titled *The Origins of Natural Science* (CW 326), and *Humanity and the World of Stars: The Spiritual Communion of Humanity* (CW 219). December 31: Fire at the Goetheanum, which is destroyed.

1923: Despite the fire, Rudolf Steiner continues his work unabated. A very hard year. Internal dispersion, dissension, and apathy abound. There is conflict—between old and new visions—within the society. A wake-up call is needed, and Rudolf Steiner responds with renewed lecturing vitality. His focus: the spiritual context of human life; initiation science; the course of the year; and community building. As a foundation for an artistic school, he creates a series of pastel sketches. Lecture cycles: *The Anthroposophical Movement; Initiation Science* (CW 227) (in England at the Penmaenmawr Summer School); *The Four Seasons and the Archangels* (CW 229); *Harmony of the Creative Word* (CW 230); *The Supersensible Human* (CW 231), given in Holland for the founding of the Dutch society. On November 10, in response to the failed Hitler-Ludendorf putsch in Munich, Steiner closes his Berlin residence and moves the *Philosophisch-Anthroposophisch Verlag* (Press) to Dornach. On December 9, Steiner begins the serialization of his *Autobiography: The Course of My Life* (CW 28) in *Das Goetheanum*. It will continue to appear weekly, without a break, until his death. Late December-early January: Rudolf Steiner refounds the Anthroposophical Society (about 12,000 members internationally) and takes over its leadership. The new board members are: Marie Steiner, Ita Wegman, Albert Steffen, Elizabeth Vreede, and Guenther Wachsmuth. (See *The Christmas Meeting for the Founding of the General Anthroposophical Society* (CW 260). Accompanying lectures: *Mystery Knowledge and Mystery Centers* (CW 232); *World History in the Light of Anthroposophy* (CW 233). December 25: the Foundation Stone is laid (in the hearts of members) in the form of the "Foundation Stone Meditation."

1924: January 1: having founded the Anthroposophical Society and taken over its leadership, Rudolf Steiner has the task of "reforming" it. The process begins with a weekly newssheet ("What's Happening in the Anthroposophical Society") in which Rudolf Steiner's "Letters to Members" and "Anthroposophical Leading Thoughts" appear (CW 26). The next step is the creation of a new esoteric class, the "first class" of the "University of Spiritual Science" (which was to have been followed, had Rudolf Steiner lived longer, by two more advanced classes). Then comes a new language for Anthroposophy—practical, phenomenological, and direct; and Rudolf Steiner creates the model for the second Goetheanum. He begins the series of extensive "karma" lectures (CW 235-40); and finally, responding to needs, he creates two new initiatives: biodynamic agriculture and curative education. After the middle of the year, rumors begin to circulate regarding Steiner's health. Lectures: January-February, *Anthroposophy* (CW 234); February: *Tone Eurythmy* (CW 278); June: *The Agriculture Course* (CW 327); June-July: Speech [?] Eurythmy (CW 279); *Curative Education* (CW 317); August: (England, "Second International Summer School"), *Initiation Consciousness: True and False Paths in Spiritual Investigation* (CW 243); September: *Pastoral Medicine* (CW 318). On September 26, for the first time, Rudolf Steiner cancels a lecture. On September 28, he gives his last lecture. On September 29, he withdraws to his studio in the carpenter's shop; now he is definitively ill. Cared for by Ita Wegman, he continues working, however, and writing the weekly installments of his *Autobiography* and *Letters to the Members/Leading Thoughts* (CW 26).

1925: Rudolf Steiner, while continuing to work, continues to weaken. He finishes *Extending Practical Medicine* (CW 27) with Ita Wegman. On March 30, around ten in the morning, Rudolf Steiner dies.

INDEX